Speaking of Women

Speaking of Women

INTERPRETING PAUL

Andrew Perriman

APOLLOS

APOLLOS (an imprint of Inter-Varsity Press),
38 De Montfort Street, Leicester LE1 7GP, England

First published 1998

British Library Cataloguing in Publication Data
A catalogue record for this book is available from the British Library.

ISBN 0-85111–458–X

Set in Bembo
Typeset in Great Britain by Parker Typesetting Service, Leicester
Printed in Great Britain by Creative Print and Design Group

For Nancy, Belinda and Abigail

Contents

Introduction

A wise woman I know once remarked that there are two types of people in the world: those who divide people into two groups, and those who don't. Whether we like it or not, the church is fractured in many different directions. But the division of opinion over the proper relation between the man and the woman and the role of women in Christian ministry is proving at the moment to be one of the deepest and most damaging fault-lines.

On one side, there are those who believe that the church should remain faithful to the historical tradition of biblical patriarchy, teaching the subordination of the woman to the man both in marriage and in the church. Sometimes this is labelled the 'complementarian' position: the differences between men and women, including the assignment of final authority to the man, express a divinely ordained complementarity. On the other side, there are the 'egalitarians', who argue either that the church is not bound by Scripture to place women under the authority of men and accordingly to restrict their ministry, or that the church is simply not bound by Scripture.

To those not already embroiled in the conflict between the complementarians and the egalitarians this may sound like one of the more obscure episodes from *Gulliver's Travels*. But despite the partisan and intemperate character of much of the debate, the issues at stake are of considerable importance for Christians who wish to take the Bible seriously. The controversy cuts to the heart of who and what we are as men and women before God – our aspirations, our sense of calling, our sense of self-worth. It impinges upon serious moral issues. For example, has the promotion of female equality and the ordination of women to positions of authority within the church contributed to the breakdown of the traditional family, the high level of sexual immorality in the church, and the promotion of homosexual relationships? It raises the dreadful spectre of cultural accommodation, of a feckless, adulterous church in lustful pursuit of the spirit of the age. And it threatens to undermine the church's confidence in Scripture. If by the casuistical arguments of exegetes the stitching of biblical patriarchy can be unpicked, what about the rest of the garment? These are real and deeply felt concerns.

What then are the basic issues? Let us suppose, first, that a Christian couple choose to live as equals, accepting shared responsibility for leadership within the family. Perhaps this is hardly a conscious choice; it is simply the way in which they have come to relate to one another. Are they contravening apostolic teaching? Is there something intrinsic to the created nature of man and woman that makes one irrevocably subordinate to the other? What does the figure of the man as 'head' of the woman mean? That he has a God-given authority over her? Or, as many have argued, that he is her 'source'? What significance does Paul attach to the creation of the woman after, and 'for the sake of', the man? Is the instruction to the wife to submit herself to her husband permanantly valid, or should it now be regarded as an anachronism, a culturally conditioned requirement that history has since rendered irrelevant?

Can the appointment of a woman to a position of authority within the church, such as that of pastor or elder or priest, ever be judged to be in accordance with the Word of God? Although Paul clearly encouraged the ministry of women, perhaps even at the apostolic level, does he not also impose significant restrictions on the type of role that a woman may play in the church? We may no longer require women to cover their heads or keep absolute silence in church, but are these regulations not indicative of a general subordination of the ministry of women to the authority of men in the church? There appear to have been no women elders in the New Testament church. Why should we presume to do things differently today?

Can a woman legitimately teach Christian doctrine to men, or is she to be judged somehow unfit for this critical ministry? Do women suffer from an innate flaw, ultimately attributable to God's intentions in creation, that disqualifies them from teaching, regardless of whatever educational or charismatic aptitude they may possess? Or should we recognize that Paul's approach was essentially pragmatic and dictated by the perceived condition of women in the ancient world and by the particular activities of women in the churches?

In other words, is the patriarchal colouring of Scripture, and of Paul's letters in particular, permanent or can it be washed out?

These are characteristically *evangelical* questions. They presuppose the conviction that Scripture is trustworthy and in some sense normative for the church of Jesus Christ. There are other important questions that might be asked concerning the nature of the ordained priesthood and the role of tradition and authority in the church, but these matters lie beyond the scope of this book. Our interest is almost entirely in understanding Paul. In the first place, what exactly did he teach about the relation between men and women? Secondly, what would he have made of the current controversy? If he were here today and not simply disgusted by all the wrangling, would he count himself a complementarian or an egalitarian?

But to view these as 'evangelical' questions means more than that the answers must be found through faithful interpretation of Scripture. The heart of evangelicalism is not Scripture but Christ. Scripture leads us to Christ and should still lead us to Christ even when we are engaged in controversy. If the debate is reduced to theological feuding, to exegetical pedantry, or to the ransacking of Scripture to feed our prejudices, it becomes *sub-evangelical*. If we lose our sense of the grace and mercy of God, of the sovereignty of Christ over the church, or of the obligation to love one another, then our struggle to understand and articulate the truth will be subverted. This is neither to diminish the significance of Scripture nor to prejudge the issue. But we must be sure that our priorities and our motives for engaging in the controversy are correct.

The aims of this book

The present study has three main aims.

First, there is certainly a need for a new exegetical initiative. The mine of New Testament teaching on the role and status of women has been worked to the point of exhaustion. If any further excavation is to be justified, then we must be reasonably confident that we can open up a new seam. Perhaps the strongest conviction behind this book is that not everything has been said, that not everything has been properly understood, and that there is still some hope of breaking the current stalemate.

At the same time we might presume to arbitrate, if only imperfectly and not always impartially, between the two positions. If consensus is attainable, it will not come about because one side or the other has finally constructed an irrefutable set of proofs. Consensus will come only with time, through a persistent sifting of opinions and a reworking of arguments, through an evaluation of the many practical experiments in egalitarianism that have been undertaken at the level both of the family and of the church, and above all through a commitment on both sides to maintain the unity of the Spirit in the bond of peace.

Secondly, we should take to heart the concerns expressed in the Danvers Statement issued by the Council on Biblical Manhood and Womanhood with regard to 'the increasing prevalence and acceptance of hermeneutical oddities devised to reinterpret plain meanings of Biblical texts' and 'the consequent threat to Biblical authority as the clarity of Scripture is jeopardized and the accessibility of its meaning to ordinary people is withdrawn into the restricted realm of technical ingenuity'.[1]

This, however, begs a number of questions. There are surely many aspects of Scripture that are not immediately transparent to 'ordinary people'. If Peter found Paul's writings hard to understand (2 Pet. 3:16), should we expect to find them any easier? The hermeneutical difficulties cannot simply be dismissed; meaning is not a pure property of the text alone, but arises out of the interaction between the text on the one hand and the presuppositions and circumstances of the reader on the other. The world has changed considerably

---

[1] See J. Piper and W. Grudem (eds.), *Recovering Biblical Manhood and Womanhood* (Wheaton: Crossway, 1991): 469.

in the last two thousand years and we cannot naïvely assume that Paul would address superficially similar situations in exactly the same way. There are often elements in the background of the text that acquire greater significance under different interpretive conditions. But having said that, the pitfalls are real enough. It is very difficult to approach a topic like this with complete objectivity, and ideological bias very easily leads to the construction of spurious arguments. It is incumbent upon every interpreter of Scripture both to pursue exegetical integrity and to subject his or her own presuppositions to critical appraisal.

Thirdly, there is no clear middle ground in this debate: the authority of the man may be mitigated in various ways, the contribution of the woman to family and church may be enthusiastically promoted, but in the end the one either has authority over the other or he does not. In its main conclusions this book comes down frankly on the egalitarian side of the divide: the subordination of the woman is not understood by Paul to be an eternally binding principle. But in the process, and in some of the concomitant findings, I think that we can go a long way towards repairing the rift that divide: the church. Through careful examination of his argumentation and rhetoric, it is possible, I believe, to reformulate Paul's central presuppositions in such a way that important insights articulated on both sides of the debate retain their relevance.

There is a need for some measure of theological disarmament. As positions become increasingly polarized and entrenched, as influential pastors and scholars enlist in opposing ranks, as rhetoric hardens and theological standpoints are more precisely and urgently articulated, so it becomes ever more difficult to listen to one another and, more importantly, to listen to the voice of Scripture. Personally, I am of the opinion, notwithstanding all the arguments of this book, that the unity of the body of Christ is more important than the question of whether or not the woman should be under the authority of the man – not just a superficial unity, but a willingness to live together, worship together, work together and pray together.

1. An argument that stands upon its head

The word that has most usefully and succinctly encapsulated the biblical understanding of the relationship between the man and the woman is 'head'. Paul – and only Paul – says that the man is the 'head' of the woman (1 Cor. 11:3; Eph. 5:23), and for most of the history of New Testament interpretation this has been taken to mean that the man has, and should have, authority over his wife. He may exercise this authority in a more or less Christlike way, but the idea of headship is not so radically reinterpreted by the model of servanthood that the basic hierarchal order is abolished (see esp. Piper 1991: 37–42).

In popular usage the man is often designated the 'head' of the household, though strictly this is an Old Testament rather than a New Testament formulation. This is commonly taken to mean that the man, as head, has a unique responsibility for both the material and the spiritual well-being of the family. The many ills that beset families in the modern world are frequently attributed directly to the failure of the man to fulfil his God-ordained role as head. One often hears it said that while a husband and wife should seek to agree as far as possible, in the final analysis it is the man, as head, who gets to make the decision. This is generally intended as an apologetic argument. In practice it is a somewhat spurious nod to equality, since under such conditions agreement can only mean that the wife agrees with the husband. This ultimate hegemony of the male is even described as carrying a 'burden' (Piper 1991: 40) – yes, in the sense that it is more burdensome to be an adult than a child.

But the notion of male headship extends beyond the sphere of the family. It serves to validate a far-reaching presumption, barely obscured by the modern ideology of feminism and equal-rights legislation, that the natural place of the man is the public world of influence and power, while the natural place of the woman is the private, domestic world of the home. It encompasses also the organization of the church. If the man is head of the household, it is only to be expected that headship or leadership within the household of God should be a male prerogative. This has various implications: any woman who ministers should do so under male authority; a wife should not be put in a position where she exercises any sort of doctrinal or pastoral authority over her husband; and so on.

Our starting-point, therefore, must be this metaphorical description of the man as 'head' – *kephalē*. When one looks at the vast number of studies that

13

have fallen from the tree of knowledge in recent years, it becomes apparent that they have for the most part landed on one side or other of a single interpretive dichotomy. Either the traditional meaning of *kephalē* has been endorsed – one who has authority over another or others – or 'head' has been understood to denote that which is the 'source' of something, the archetype being the 'head' of a river, which is its source. The leading protagonists in the debate have endeavoured to build their case on a comprehensive examination of literary evidence from outside the New Testament. We have little choice but to follow them in this; but in doing so we shall find that the fabric of the metaphor has been stretched and pinned down by some heavy-handed exegesis to cover areas of the semantic field for which it was not originally cut. If we allow it to recover its natural shape, a more reasonable and coherent interpretation emerges, which will provide a sounder basis for an examination of the Pauline passages in the next chapter.[1]

Does *kephalē* signify a position of leadership and authority?

Two scholars in particular – J. A. Fitzmyer and W. Grudem – have argued that in Hellenistic Greek *kephalē* naturally signifies one who holds a position of leadership or authority over others. Their evidence is drawn mostly from the Septuagint (LXX), from the Hellenistic Jewish philosopher Philo (*c.* 30 BC–AD 45), and from the Greek historian and moralist Plutarch (*c.* AD 46–120).[2] Evidence from the Septuagint, of course, is particularly valuable because Paul made extensive use of this translation of the Old Testament.

The Septuagint

For the most part, when *rō'š* ('head') is used in the Hebrew text of the Old Testament to denote the relation of one person to a group (the head of a tribe or house, for example), the translators of the Septuagint avoid using *kephalē*. The preference by far is for words that unambiguously convey the idea of rule or leadership, particularly the word-groups consisting of *archē*, *archōn* and *archēgos* (*e.g.* Nu. 25:15; Dt. 20:9; Jos. 22:14), and of *hēgeomai* and *hēgoumenos* (*e.g.* Dt. 1:15; 1 Sa. 15:17; Mi. 2:13).[3] The word *archōn* ('ruler, commander, chief'), for example, appears at least 100 times as a translation for *rō'š*, whereas Fitzmyer lists only nine instances where *rō'š*, denoting a ruler or chief, is translated by *kephalē*, of which one is a duplication and four make use of the same head–tail metaphor (Fitzmyer 1993: 54). In view of this it is difficult to

---

[1] See also an earlier study, Perriman 1994: 602–622, out of which chapter 1 developed by permission of Oxford University Press.

[2] Fitzmyer 1989: 506–510; and a perfunctory review of the material in Fitzmyer 1993: 52–59; Grudem 1985: 46–59; Grudem 1990.

[3] *Cf.* Bedale 1954: 213. We also find such words as *patriarchēs* (2 Ch. 19:8), *archipatriōtēs* and *archiphylos* (Jos. 21:1). See Schlier 1965: 675 n. 2.

avoid the impression that *kephalē* was considered an inappropriate term to use for the person who was leader or chief of a group of people. This already raises serious doubts about the validity of the argument that Paul and his readers would have understood *kephalē* to signify specifically one who has authority over others.

The exceptions to this translational preference, where *kephalē* is used as a translation for *rō'š* to describe the relation between a person, or group of persons, and others, need to be examined. We shall see that the conclusions reached by Fitzmyer and Grudem concerning the meaning of *kephalē* in the Septuagint are not at all secure.

But first we should recognize the theoretical likelihood that in the process of translation *kephalē* has assimilated something of the metaphorical sense of *rō'š*. There is a natural tendency for the language of the translation to be deformed in order to follow more closely the language of the original text, rather as clothing that is too tight may be stretched out of shape to fit the body. So where *kephalē* is used in the Septuagint in the manner that *rō'š* is used in the Hebrew text to refer to a chief or leader, there is always the possibility – a strong possibility – that the word has been chosen not because in normal usage *kephalē* was understood to have the same metaphorical sense as *rō'š*, but because it is the *literal* equivalent.

Such a departure from the normal metaphorical sense may, of course, have an influence on subsequent usage; tight clothing may become permanently misshapen. But to be confident that this is what has happened in the case of *kephalē* we should need to establish two things. First, is the new sense that *kephalē* has supposedly acquired through association with *rō'š* in a few obscure and dubious texts strong enough and unambiguous enough to have had such an impact on later writings? Secondly, is there good reason to think that in the writings influenced by the Septuagint (for example, the letters of Paul) the meaning of *kephalē* has in fact been affected in this way? (As it is, the first problem faced by those who would interpret Paul on the basis of these texts is that there is no instance in the Septuagint of *kephalē* being used to describe the relationship of a man to a woman.) We shall examine each of the relevant passages in turn.

Judges 10:18; 11:8–9

In the Hebrew text of Judges 10:18; 11:8–9, the word *rō'š* is used to describe the man (Jephthah) who would lead the Israelites to fight against the 'sons of Ammon': 'He shall be head over all the people of Gilead.'[4]

There are three main manuscripts of the Septuagint: *Codex Vaticanus* and

---

[4] Unless otherwise indicated, all translations of ancient texts, including Scripture, in this book are my own.

Codex Sinaiticus (both fourth century AD), and *Codex Alexandrinus* (fifth century AD). In the Alexandrian text of these verses, *rō'š* is translated by *kephalē*, whereas the Vatican text, in conformity with the general pattern, has *archōn* ('ruler'). From this it has been inferred, not unreasonably, that in the view of the translator of the Alexandrian version, *kephalē* carried the same metaphorical meaning as *rō'š* and was essentially synonymous with *archōn*.[5]

It would be wrong, however, to assume that the relationship between the two texts at this point is explicable only in terms of synonymy – particularly in view of what will emerge about the metaphorical sense of *kephalē* from the study of other texts. So we might ask whether the use of *kephalē* in the Alexandrian text of Judges 10:18; 11:8–9 and in both versions of 11:11 is not in fact meant to suggest prominence or precedence rather than the exercise of authority. What the people of Israel needed at that moment was not so much a ruler (someone to have authority over them) as someone to *represent* them before the king of Ammon (11:12) and if necessary to lead them into battle – someone to '*begin* to fight against the sons of Ammon' (10:18; *cf.* 11:8). As 'head', Jephthah would be the one to go first in the fight. If this explains the use of *kephalē* in 10:18, it would also account for the use of the word in the later verses.

The force of this nuance may also be reflected in the fact that in 10:18 and 11:8–9, *kephalē* is followed by the dative ('for all the inhabitants of Gilead'), not *epi* ('over all the inhabitants of Gilead'). The preposition *eis* is found in 11:11, but in this case in both translations *kephalē* is in direct apposition to a word meaning 'ruler' or 'leader': 'they set him over them as head and as leader [*eis kephalēn eis hēgoumenon*]' (Alexandrian); 'the people placed him over them as head and as ruler [*eis kephalēn kai eis archēgon*]' (Vatican). This apposition, moreover, is found in the Hebrew text, and in itself neither accounts for the unexpected use of *kephalē* nor elicits from it the sense of 'one who has authority over'.

As we examine the other passages, we may find that the apparent synonymy suggested by the two translations of the Hebrew texts is illusory, perhaps no more than a scribal idiosyncrasy.[6] The fact remains that whereas the use of *rō'š* in the Hebrew text here is perfectly consistent with its usage throughout the Old Testament, the appearance of *kephalē* in the Alexandrian text at this point is exceptional. If *kephalē* in these verses does not have the sense of 'one who goes first or is most prominent', then it should probably be regarded as a translational anomaly.

---

[5] *Cf.* Grudem 1985: 54; Fitzmyer 1989: 505–506; 1993: 54.
[6] *Cf.* Payne 1986: 123; Cervin 1989: 96. It may account for the exceptional translation that in the Hebrew text of Judges it is only in this story that *rō'š* is used with this metaphorical sense.

3 Kingdoms 8:1

Origen's text of the Septuagint has *pasas kephalas tōn rhabdōn* as a translation of 'all the heads of the tribes' in 3 Kingdoms (= 1 Kings) 8:1, with respect to which Grudem (1990: 29) comments, 'The heads of these tribes are of course the leaders of the tribes.' The Hebrew word translated 'tribe' here is *maṭṭeh*. It is frequently used in the Old Testament in its original sense of 'rod' or 'staff', but it has come to mean 'tribe' by metonymy: the chief of the tribe bore a staff. The connection between the two ideas is graphically illustrated by Numbers 17:2–3 (Nu. 17:17–18, LXX), where Moses takes a 'rod' (*rhabdos* in the Septuagint, *maṭṭeh* in the Hebrew text) from the leader of each house of Israel, with a man's name written on it (*cf.* Ezk. 37:16). *Rhabdos*, however, is used nowhere else in the Septuagint as a translation for *maṭṭeh* when it has the sense of 'tribe'. The word *rhabdos* does not mean 'tribe' (Grudem's translation 'staff of office' takes us no closer), and the association with *maṭṭeh* in that sense can hardly have been strong. On the one hand, therefore, the use of *rhabdos* for *maṭṭeh* points to a predilection for the literal equivalent on the part of the translator that has clearly also influenced the use of *kephalē* here. On the other, the use of *kephalē* probably has as much to do with the normal meaning of *rhabdos* (thus 'heads of the staffs') as with *rō'š* which it translates. The meaning is simply 'that which is at the top'.

Isaiah 7:8

There is nothing in the context of Isaiah 7:8 to indicate that 'head' means 'leader' in the statement 'the head of Aram is Damascus, and the head of Damascus Rasim'. The significance of the verse is not entirely clear, but the point seems rather to be one of representation by virtue of primacy or prominence: Aram is summed up in Damascus, Damascus in Rasim. A similar statement is made about Ephraim in verse 9; but the preceding warning that 'the kingdom of Ephraim shall cease from being a people' suggests that it is not the sovereignty of the head that is at issue but the shocking contrast between the presumptuousness of the head and the fate of the people. Fitzmyer's assumption that *rō'š* in the Hebrew text means 'chief' is in any case not easily sustained, since nowhere else in the Hebrew Bible is a man said to be 'head' of a city, or a city 'head' of a country: *rō'š* always refers to the status of individuals with regard to groups of people – families, tribes, armies, priests, and so on. This gives further ground for doubting that the conventional metaphorical sense of *rō'š* ('leader, chief') is appropriate.

3 Kingdoms 20:12

The statement 'they set up Naboth as head of the people' (1 Ki. 21:12 = 3 Kingdoms 20:12, Alexandrian text) is misleadingly translated by Fitzmyer

(1989: 508) and taken out of context.[7] The reference is to the prominent position that Naboth was made to take during the fast in order that he might be publicly accused; he is placed 'at the head of the people'.[8] The verb used in both Hebrew and Greek means 'they made [him] sit', and clearly refers only to the physical circumstances, not to a position of authority.

Jeremiah 38:7, LXX

The 'remnant of Israel' returning from exile is described as *kephalēn ethnōn* in Jeremiah 38:7, LXX (31:7 in the Hebrew text and English versions): 'For thus says the Lord to Jacob, Rejoice and exult over the head of the nations; make a proclamation and give praise; say, the Lord has delivered his people, the remnant of Israel.' But although there is cause for rejoicing, it is certainly not because Israel finds herself in a position of authority and leadership; the sense must again be something like 'foremost or pre-eminent nation' in that Israel was God's chosen people.[9] The statement in verse 9 ('for I became a father to Israel, and Ephraim is my first-born') may provide the most appropriate gloss on the idea of Israel as 'head of the nations'. It is the special redemption and blessing of God's own people that is proclaimed to the nations and islands (vv. 10–14), not Israel's authority over them.

2 Kingdoms 22:44 and Psalm 17:43, LXX

The expression *kephalēn ethnōn* is also found at 2 Kingdoms (= 2 Samuel) 22:44 (and in the parallel text in Ps. 17:43, LXX [= 18:43]): 'you shall keep me as head of the nations'. The context here – David's song of victory 'in the day in which the Lord rescued him from the hand of all his enemies, and from the hand of Saul' (v. 1 in both texts) – lends a certain plausibility to the idea that in this phrase David is depicted as one who has authority over his enemies, but this interpretation is by no means inevitable. A distinction may still be maintained between the idea of prominence or primacy and that of leadership; nothing in the psalm as it stands in the Septuagint suggests that David expected to exercise authority over the nations. His enemies are scattered or destroyed (vv. 38–42), not subjugated; he is delivered from them (v. 44a), not set to rule over them. 2 Kingdoms 22:48 speaks of the nations being 'chastened' under David (*cf.* Ps. 17:48 [= 18:47]: 'It is God who gives vengeance to me and who subdued the

---

[7] The passage is omitted from Fitzmyer's later article (1993).

[8] The Alexandrian codex has *en kephalē tou laou*, the Vatican *en archē tou laou*. *Cf.* 1 Kingdoms 9:22, which has *etheto autois en prōtois tōn keklēmenōn* for 'gave them a place at the head [*bᵉrō'š*] of those who had been invited'.

[9] *Cf.* Payne 1986: 122 and n. 34. Cervin, though for the most part ill-disposed towards Fitzmyer's analysis, appears to agree with him here (Cervin 1989: 108).

nations under me'), but this should be understood in terms of military defeat, not rulership.[10]

Connotations of authority cannot be ruled out entirely in this passage, but they are not *required* by the context and quite possibly run counter to the meaning of the text. Moreover, if the idea of David as 'head of the nations' is to be read at all in the light of the description of his victory over his enemies, then it must be understood as a figure for violent overthrow. What light would this shed on Paul's description of the husband as head of the wife? I would suggest, rather, that the *pre-eminence* of David as God's anointed king and of Israel as God's chosen people (*cf.* Je. 38:7, LXX) constitutes a more relevant set of associations for the interpretation of *kephalē* here.

Deuteronomy 28:13, 44; Isaiah 9:14–15

Those verses that speak of the 'head' and 'tail' of Israel also prove on closer inspection to be of little value to the traditional argument. In the first place, *kephalē* as a translation of *rō'š* is manifestly required by the metaphorical pairing of 'head' and tail'. Whatever metaphorical sense the word appears to have in the context, therefore, cannot be treated as normative. But it is still not evident in such instances that *kephalē* means 'leader, chief'.[11] In Deuteronomy 28:13, 44, the significance of the metaphor lies in the contrast between two extremes, between prominence and prosperity on the one hand and subjection and humiliation on the other. The spatial aspect of the metaphor is made clear in verse 13: 'and you shall then be above, and you shall not be below'.[12] Verses 43–44 are concerned not with the idea of 'headship over' (H. Schlier's view; 1965: 675), but with a relative distinction between head and tail understood

---

[10] Fitzmyer's appeal to the words that follow ('a people whom I knew not served me') is also misplaced (Fitzmyer 1989: 508). These words do not in the Septuagint (where the reading diverges somewhat from the Hebrew text) constitute an explanation of *kephalēn ethnōn*, as the change from the future tense to the aorist makes clear. Rather, they belong with the subsequent aorist clauses, which appear to describe a situation prior to David's victory: 'Alien children lied [*epseusanto*] to me, at the hearing of the ear they heard me.' The people 'whom I knew not' are the 'alien children' who deceived David. The use of *pseudomai*, moreover, indicates that the subservience of the people was a sham – a state of affairs quite at odds with the present expectation of being kept as 'head of the nations'.

[11] The formula appears in Jubilees 1:16, where nothing suggests that 'head' implies a position of authority. The reference is to Israel's favoured status; juxtaposed is the antithesis between blessing and curse. *Cf.* also *1 Enoch* 103:11.

[12] It is true that verse 12 has 'you shall rule over many nations, and they shall not rule over you', which, curiously, is not in the Hebrew text. But against taking this as interpretative of the head–tail metaphor is the fact that this statement belongs with verse 12 rather than with verse 13. This appears from both (a) the parallelism between verse 12 and verse 13 (*Anoixai soi Kyrios . . . Katastēsai se Kyrios*); and (b) the parallelism between this statement and that which immediately precedes it ('you shall lend to many nations, and you shall not be lent to').

essentially in commercial terms: 'He shall lend to you, and you shall not lend to him.'[13] In Isaiah 9:14–15 the 'head' of Israel is interpreted as the 'elder and those who respect persons' and is designated further as *hē archē*, whereas the 'tail' is the 'prophet teaching unlawful things'; the contrast is also characterized as one between 'great and small'. It seems clear that the 'head' is distinguished from the 'tail' by virtue of its prominence or excellence or social standing, not because it has sovereignty or authority: the tail is not that which is ruled but that which is disreputable. The association with *archē* must be understood in the same way; it refers to those who are foremost in Israel.[14]

Conclusion

There is clearly some scope for confusion in interpreting the meaning of *kephalē* in these passages; it is never easy to delimit the connotations a metaphor may acquire in context. Nevertheless, the evidence suggests quite strongly that the figure was not used in the Septuagint to denote a position of authority. The basic sense, applicable in all the passages considered, appears rather to be that which is first, foremost, prominent, pre-eminent. We shall find this conclusion confirmed as we turn to the non-biblical writers.

Non-biblical writers

Philo

Fitzmyer (1989: 509–510) points to a number of passages in Philo as further grounds for attributing the sense 'leader' or 'ruler' to *kephalē*. On occasion the head is said to be the ruling part of the body or soul. Referring to the dream that the chief baker related to Joseph (Gn. 40:16), Philo writes: ' "Head" we interpret allegorically to mean the ruling part [*hēgemona*] of the soul, the mind on which all things lie . . .' (*De Somnis* 2.207, Loeb). Similarly, in the *Special Laws* he says that 'Nature conferred the sovereignty of the body on the head when she granted it also possession of the citadel as the most suitable position for its kingly rank . . .' (*De Specialibus Legibus* 3.184, Loeb). In the same way, Philo argues, the 'lordship of the senses' has been given to the eyes. These texts, however, also require a more critical appraisal.

In the first place, the method of interpretation used in *De Somnis* 2.207 is explicitly described as 'allegorical'. In view of this, we should be wary of assuming that the idea of 'leading' or 'ruling' introduced by *hēgemona* is a

---

[13] *Cf.* La. 1:5: 'Those afflicting her have become the head, and her enemies have prospered.'

[14] The singular form of *archē* here can hardly mean 'ruler', since it is predicated of a group that is defined by social and moral categories rather than by office; nor, since the reference is to people, does it make any sense to translate it as 'office' or 'authority'. *Kephalē* and *archē* are also set in apposition in Is. 19:15, where again the reference is to the top and bottom of the social scale, this time in Egypt.

natural or obvious extension of the meaning of *kephalē*; there is a degree of artificiality in allegorical interpretation that makes it a very unreliable guide to the normal meaning of a word. If anything, the self-consciousness of the interpretation suggests that the thought of ruling was not an obvious sense of *kephalē*. Allowance should be made generally for the fact that the meaning of *kephalē* in these passages is determined to a large extent by the particular philosophical framework of Philo's thought; connotations arising through association with the *hēgemōn* word group in a context of sophisticated allegorical interpretation are not necessarily appropriate in other contexts.

In *De Specialibus Legibus* 3.184 the point of the analogy is that the head owes its *hēgemonia* to its elevated position: the head is the hill-top citadel (*akra*) to which the mind is conducted on high; the body is set under it like the pedestal beneath a statue (*cf.* Cervin 1989: 109). It is not because 'head' signifies 'that which has authority' that sovereignty has been conferred upon it; it is because it corresponds in situation to the royal citadel set on a hill.

In a footnote, Fitzmyer (1989: 509 n. 1) also mentions, but does not discuss, two other passages. First, in *De Vita Mosis* 2.82 the mind is said to be 'head and ruler of the sense-faculty in us [*tēs en hēmin aisthēseōs kephalē men kai hēgemonikon*]'. But since this belongs to an allegorical interpretation of the pillars of the temple, it seems likely that the use of *kephalē* here has been determined principally by the common use of the word to denote the top of a pillar; the thing perceived (*to aisthēton*), correspondingly, is the 'extremity and, as it were, the base' of the pillar. Nor is there any reason to think that *kephalē* is interpreted by *hēgemonikon*: *kephalē* in this passage conveys the quite separate idea that the mind is the highest and pre-eminent sense-faculty. Secondly, in *De Vita Mosis* 2.290 the story of Moses' death is said to be the head of the whole law. The point, however, is not that this story has authority over the rest of the law, but that it is the 'most wonderful' (*thaumasiōtaton*) part: the head of the law is that which is pre-eminent, outstanding.

Finally, no instance is provided from Philo in which *kephalē* is used metaphorically to denote the authority or sovereignty of one man or of men over others. When it is said of Ptolemy II Philadelphus that he was in some sense the 'head' of the other kings in the Ptolemaic dynasty 'as the head is the leading part [*to hēgemoneuon*] in a living body' (*De Vita Mosis* 2.30), the point is evidently not that he ruled over them – they were dead – but that he was outstanding or pre-eminent among them. This idea is anticipated in the preceding sentence where it is said that 'as the house of the Ptolemies flourished in comparison with the other dynasties, so did Philadelphus among the Ptolemies'. In *De Praemiis et Poenis* 114 an analogy is drawn between the superiority of one man over a city, or of a city over the surrounding region, or of one nation over other nations, and the superiority of the head over the body. The basis of the comparison, however, is not a relationship of authority but the *visibility* of that which is superior. Positioned at the top of the body, the head is 'conspicuous on every side'. The benefit to those around is not that they are governed but that gazing 'continuously upon noble models imprints their likeness in souls which are not entirely hardened and stony' (Loeb).

Plutarch and other writers

Philo's description of the head as the ruling part of the body or soul may be classed with a number of similar passages in which the *literal* head is attributed a ruling function. Plato, for example, says that the 'spherical body . . . which we now name the head . . . is the most divine part and the one that reigns over [*despotoun*] all the parts within us' (*Timaeus* 44D), from which Grudem (1985: 54) has inferred that 'a metaphor that spoke of the leader or ruler of a group of people as its "head" would not have been unintelligible to Plato or his hearers'.

Two considerations, however, raise doubts about the validity of this inference, at least for the study of Pauline language. The first is that these examples presuppose a quite clearly defined and limited context of thought, and one very different from the world of Paul's letters. Connotations that arise in one context are not necessarily transferred with the word into another; a truck may drive across these conceptual boundaries, but often it will dump much of its semantic cargo along the way. The second is that the language of 'ruling' in these passages derives, if only implicitly, from a figurative conception of the human body as a state or similar collective entity – in other words, an inversion of the more usual metaphor. Plato's use of the verb *despozō* unmistakably evokes the rule of a human leader rather than any more literal notion of mental control. In the following clause it is said that the gods assembled together (*synathroisantes*) the whole body, in effect as a group of soldiers or subjects, and handed it over to the head for service.

The same is true of Plutarch's statement in *Table Talk* 6.7 (*Moralia* 692E) that we 'are accustomed to speak affectionately [or euphemistically] of a person as "soul" or "head" from his ruling parts [*apo tōn kyriōtatōn*]'.[15] It is even clearer in the passage from Philo's *Special Laws* that we looked at earlier (*De Specialibus Legibus* 3.184), where the head is said to have been conducted by nature to the summit (*akran*) as the place most suitable for a king. The words *hēgemōn* and *hēgemonia*, used by Philo to denote the head's sovereignty, also belong to the realm of human affairs and are applied to the head only figuratively. While it

---

[15] Grudem also treats Plutarch, *Moralia* 647C, as evidence for the meaning 'authority over', citing the Loeb translation: 'For pure wine, when it attacks the head and severs the body from the control of the mind, distresses a man' (Grudem 1990: 28). But the Greek does not in fact afford an equation of the head with the controlling mind. The words *tas tōn aisthēseōn archas* do not mean 'the control of the mind' but 'the beginnings (or origins) of the senses'.

may be true that the governing function of the head is expressed through the analogy with a human ruler, can we make the reverse inference, that the governing function of a person is expressed through the analogy with the head, particularly when in most cases the vocabulary of ruling is absent? Or can we assume that the same connotation of sovereignty is valid where there is not the clear thought, as there is in all these passages, of the body over which the head rules?

A number of other passages are cited by Grudem and by Fitzmyer in his later article which appear to constitute a recurrent, though minor, motif in Greek writings. Herodotus, for example, records the advice of the Delphic oracle to the Argives: 'protect the head; and the head will safeguard the body' (7.148.3). In Plutarch, *Cicero*, 14.4, Catiline addresses a riddle to Cicero in which he compares the people to a headless body for which he proposes to become the head. In similar manner Plutarch describes the provinces of Gaul as 'a strong body in need of a head' (*Galba* 4.3), and a general as the head of a body whose hands are the lightly armed troops, whose feet are the cavalry, and so on (*Pelopidas* 2.1). Libanius (fourth century AD) appears to employ *kephalē* in a double sense when he says of certain rioters that, having failed to break down the governor's house, they 'heaped upon their heads insults' (*Oration* 20.3, Loeb). According to the footnote in the Loeb edition, *tōn heautōn kephalōn* ('their own heads') refers both to 'their sovereign heads' (*i.e.* the occupants of the governor's house) and to 'their own persons'.

These passages undoubtedly illustrate a certain association of *kephalē* with the figure of a ruler or leader. Yet we still cannot uncritically assume that the same association lies behind the Pauline texts. In the first place, the metaphor of the 'head' in each instance presupposes, at least implicitly, not only the larger metaphor of the *collective* 'body' but also a distinct literary tradition, neither of which is apparent in Paul's description of the man as head of the woman.[16] Secondly, the commonplace association does not necessarily imply a commonplace equivalence of meaning. It has been suggested, for example, that the passages from *Cicero* and *Galba* may reflect the recognized Latin use of *caput* ('head') to mean 'leader' (Cervin 1989: 102–103).[17]

More significantly, the point of the analogy in both these passages is only that a vacant position at the top of the collective body needed to be filled, not that the Roman people or the Gallic provinces needed to have authority exercised over them. The context in *Pelopidas* suggests that the head is that which safeguards the life of the body, in that if the head is cut off, the body dies; in taking undue risks, the general endangers not only himself but all, for

---

[16] Libanius' use of *kephalē* to denote the governor derives from the idiomatic expression 'to heap insults upon someone's head' rather than from the body metaphor.

[17] *Cf. e.g.* Livy, 5.46.5.

'their safety depends on him, and their destruction too'. The same idea may lie behind the passage from Herodotus, though the precise application of the oracle is by no means easy to ascertain.[18] Otherwise, generally speaking, nothing in these texts requires *kephalē* to be taken to mean 'one who has authority over' rather than simply 'one who is foremost or pre-eminent'.[19] In the passage from Libanius, 'their own heads' may *refer* to the governing authorities, but it goes beyond the evidence to conclude that this is the *meaning* of the term. In any case, it is the play on words that dictates the use of *kephalē* here.

Josephus and Hermas

Two final instances are proposed by Fitzmyer as evidence for the view that *kephalē* commonly means 'ruler' or 'leader'. First, the Jewish historian Josephus (AD 37–after 93) describes Jerusalem as the 'front and head [*to prosōpon kai tēn kephalēn*] of the whole nation' (*Jewish War* 4.261, Loeb); but the context and the close association with *prosōpon* indicate that the idea behind *kephalē* is one not of authority but of prominence or pre-eminence. Josephus is speaking of the affront caused by the activities of terrorists in a place which is 'revered by the world and honoured by aliens from the ends of the earth who have heard its fame' (Loeb).[20] With this we might compare an earlier passage in the *Jewish War* (3.54) in which Jerusalem is said to stand out above (*proanischousa*) – not rule – the surrounding area 'as the head does the body'.

Secondly, when Hermas is described as the 'head of the household' (Hermas *Similitudes* 7.3), nothing is found in the context to suggest that the expression denotes his authority rather than simply his *position* sociologically defined. It is something more like a representative function that is at issue; Hermas is the most prominent figure in the household, and if he were to escape punishment, the affliction of his family would be to no avail. It is the participation of the family in the experience of the head, and *vice versa*, that accounts for the state of affairs, not the authority of the head over the family.

---

[18] Grudem (1990: 27) cites the interpretation of 'head' supplied by the Loeb editor: 'those with full citizenship, the nucleus of the population'. This may be correct, but it surely suggests that 'head' stands for 'that which is prominent, foremost, illustrious' rather than 'that which rules'.

[19] Plutarch's fable of the serpent whose tail rebels against the head and takes the lead with disastrous consequences (*Agis* 2.3, discussed in Grudem 1990: 32–33) is interpreted in terms of the head's ability to see and hear, and therefore to lead: the multitude, the tail, can only wander at random. Within the particular interpretative context of the fable the head is the one who is equipped to go first, having eyes and ears: it is not the point of the story that the head has authority over the tail.

[20] Note Appian, *Roman History* 10.4.19, where the town of Metulus is described as *hē tōn Iapodōn . . . kephalē*; this does not mean 'governing city' but 'largest, most prominent town'.

There is also the likelihood, of course, that the phrase is dependent on Pauline usage.[21]

Conclusion

Little evidence has emerged from this examination of passages outside the Septuagint to make me change my view that in common usage the *kephalē* metaphor signified no more than that someone or something was prominent or pre-eminent. Where the association with the person of a ruler is strongest, we also find that *kephalē* most clearly belongs either to a distinct literary or philosophical context or to the larger metaphor of the body. Even then it is arguable that the *meaning* of the figure has less to do with the exercise of authority than with the *position* of the head in relation to the body, or with the significance of the head for the life of the body.

Does *kephalē* mean 'source' or 'origin'?

The first thing to notice as we turn to the alternative metaphorical translation commonly proposed for *kephalē* – 'source' or 'origin' – is that it has virtually no support in the Septuagint.[22] Reference is frequently made to S. Bedale's article on 'The Meaning of *kephalē* in the Pauline Epistles' (1954: 211–215),[23] but the case presented in that study is surprisingly flimsy. Since *rō'š* in the sense of 'chief' or 'ruler' is translated in the Septuagint sometimes by *kephalē* and sometimes by *archē*, Bedale concludes that the two terms 'at least tended to become interchangeable as renderings of *rō'š*'.[24] More concrete support for this claim is supposed to emerge from the apparent equation of *kephalē* and *archē* in Isaiah 9:14–15. But since the head–tail motif is dominant in this context, it seems more likely that *kephalē* has determined the interpretation of *archē* than *vice versa*. In any case, 'source' is no more suitable as a translation of *kephalē* here than is 'ruler'. The prominent people in Israel – the elder and those who respect persons – cannot be considered as the source or origin of the others; they are, as we have said, simply those who are foremost in society.

There appear to be, therefore, two fundamental difficulties with Bedale's

---

[21] Grudem (1985: 56) cites Gregory of Nazianzus (fourth century AD), *Greek Anthology* 8.19, as evidence for the meaning 'ruler' or 'authority over': 'I am the scion of no holy root, but head of a pious wife and three children'. Again Pauline influence may be presupposed, but the idea of 'authority over' is in any case quite irrelevant: the word denotes his *position* within the family, as the contrast with 'scion of no holy root' makes clear.

[22] For the 'source' interpretation see *e.g.* Fiorenza 1983: 229; Evans 1983: 65–66; Fee 1987: 503; Witherington 1988: 84–85; Jervis 1993: 240; Kroeger 1993: 375–376.

[23] The same argument is found in Bedale 1956: 70. See also Scroggs 1972: 298 n. 41; 1974: 534 n. 8; Murphy-O'Connor 1980: 492; Kroeger 1987.

[24] Paradoxically, Schlier (1965: 675) also notes that *kephalē* and *archē* are interchangeable, but takes this as evidence for the interpretation of *kephalē* as 'ruler'.

argument. The first is that the argument from the association of *kephalē* and *archē* with *rō'š* carries little weight. After all, the common use of *rō'š* in the Hebrew text to mean 'chief' or 'ruler' is barely, if at all, reflected in the use of *kephalē* in the Septuagint despite the consistent correspondence at the level of literal usage, as commentators who support the 'source' interpretation would be the first to point out. We have argued already that associations that emerge in the process of translation do not always constitute evidence for semantic determination. The second difficulty is that it is by no means clear that 'beginning' must imply 'source'. There is an important distinction to be made between the idea of precedence or commencement and that of the source from which something is generated.[25] A racing driver in 'poll' position is not the 'source' or the 'source of life' of the other drivers; nor, for that matter, does he have authority over them.

More substantial support for the thesis has purportedly been found in non-biblical texts, but still the arguments of those who favour the 'source' interpretation may be contested, on a number of counts.

1. When Philo, for example, describes Esau as *genarchēs* ('progenitor') of all the parts of the tribe, the 'head as it were of the living creature' (*De Congressu Eruditionis Gratia* 61), he has in mind no more than the patriarch's priority and historical prominence. The significance of Esau within the rather complex allegorical argument in progress here is that he is the foremost embodiment of certain characteristics, not that he is the source of that which is summed up in him. Whereas in the Greek text *genarchēs* is the subject and Esau the predicate (*ho genarchēs estin Esau*), in the Loeb translation the order of predication is reversed ('Esau is the progenitor, the head as it were . . .'), encouraging the idea that the two terms are semantically equivalent. The sentence should be translated, albeit somewhat cumbersomely: 'Head – as of a living creature – of all the parts described here, the progenitor is Esau.' Now it appears that rather than interpreting 'head' in terms of 'progenitor', we must take 'head' as the determinative term; the point is not that *kephalē* means 'source' but that in this context 'progenitor' means 'that which comes first'.[26]

2. Equally unconvincing is the citation from Philo, *De Praemiis et Poenis*

---

[25] Note Delling 1964: 481: in the LXX *archē* 'usually denotes temporal beginning'. Liddell-Scott-Jones offer only one instance of *archē* meaning 'source' (of an action), and even here the attribution is difficult to account for: [*anthrōpos*] *echei archēn allēn eleutheran* (Plotinus 3.3.4).

[26] Grudem's (1990: 51) suggestion that *genarchēs* means 'ruler' in this context cannot be defended: Esau was not ruler over the tribe that descended from him. Grudem points out that the meaning 'ruler of created beings' is given in Liddell-Scott-Jones, but in the two passages cited (*Corp. Herm.* 13.21; *Orph. Hym.* 13.8; *cf.* 82.3) the word constitutes a technical appellation which neither clearly means 'ruler' nor constitutes an appropriate parallel to Philo's usage.

125: 'the zealous one [*ton spoudaion*], whether one man or a people, will be the head of the human race, and all the others like the parts of a body animated [*psychoumena*] by the forces in the head at the top'.[27] Clearly the zealous individual or nation is not meant to be understood as the 'source' of the human race; the most that can be said is that the 'head' is the source of its vitality, but even this is to be understood in a motivational sense with the emphasis on the active influence of the 'head'. This point has been masked by the Loeb translation, which renders *ton spoudaion* doubtfully as 'the virtuous one' (the primary meaning is 'hasty, energetic, earnest') and *psychoumena* as an active verb more appropriate to the body metaphor than to social relations ('draw their life'). Philo does not mean that the human race depends on *ton spoudaion* for its life but that such an individual or nation, by virtue of its prominence and excellence, is able to motivate and inspire others. Again, much confusion has been generated by commentators taking the verse out of context. The analogy sets the head of an animal, which is 'first and most noble' (*prōton kai ariston*), in contrast to the tail, which is good for little more than swatting flies. This contrast in itself is enough to preclude the meaning 'source' for *kephalē*; the inferiority of the tail lies not in the fact that it is not the source but in the ignobility of its function. But it should also be noted that the analogy is prompted by a probable allusion in *De Praemiis et Poenis* 124 ('it was not dragged down tailwards but lifted up to the head', Loeb) to Deuteronomy 28:13, which, as we have seen already, has to do with the contrast between prominence and humiliation.

3. In her article on 'Head' in the *Dictionary of Paul and his Letters*, C. C. Kroeger (1993: 376) refers to two similar passages in Philo where *kephalē* purportedly means 'source'. Neither is convincing. In *On Flight and Finding* it is not the head but the 'dominant faculty in the soul' which is compared to a spring from which all the senses are watered (*De Fuga et Inventione* 182, Loeb). Philo also says that God raised man's head upwards, in contrast to the animals, so that 'his nourishment may be celestial and imperishable, not perishable and earthly' (*Quod Deterius Potiori Insidiari Soleat* 85, Loeb). But this hardly shows that 'head' means 'source'; on the contrary, the point is that the head, being elevated, *receives* nourishment from a heavenly source.

4. In his commentary on 1 Corinthians, C. K. Barrett (1971: 248) claims that Herodotus uses *kephalai* ('heads') for the source of a river: 'The heads of the river Tearos supply the best and finest water of all rivers' (4.91). But we must ask, first, whether 'source' is a direct or a secondary connotation. It does not necessarily mean that *kephalai* signifies 'source'; more probably the word

---

[27] See Schlier 1965: 676; Payne 1986: 124; Fee 1987: 503 n. 45; Cervin 1989: 100–101.

denotes only the highest or furthest point of the river, the 'head waters'.[28] Metaphor is a form of speech that is particularly sensitive to context, and while it is the case that when the reference is to a river, the idea of 'source' may emerge quite naturally as a secondary connotation, there is no reason to suppose that the same connotation is relevant when the metaphor is applied to some quite different subject.[29] Secondly, the verb used, *parechontai* ('give up, offer, grant'), does not require 'source' as its subject – a reference to the furthest point of the river suits just as well. Even more telling, thirdly, is the fact that *kephalē* may also be used for the *mouth* of a river (*e.g.* Callim. Aetia, P. Oxy., XVII, 2080, 48), which is consistent with the idea that the word denotes that which is prominent or extreme, but sits ill with the notion of 'source'.

5. Certain passages from Artemidorus (late second century AD) are sometimes cited in defence of the 'source' hypothesis. In *Oneirocriticum* (*Interpretation of Dreams*) 1.2 there is the story of a man who dreamed he was beheaded: 'In real life, the father of this man, too, died; for just as the head is the source [*aitios*] of life and light for the whole body, he was responsible for the dreamer's life and light.' And in 1.35 it is said that 'the head resembles parents in that it is the cause [*aitian*] of one's living' (3.66 also has the motif).[30] In both cases, however, the basis for the analogical relation is set out in the explicit equation of 'head' with *aitia/aitios*, and one is inclined to infer from this, as with Philo's 'allegorical' interpretation of 'head', that 'source' does not belong to the natural metaphorical sense of *kephalē* but derives from the special application of the figure. Artemidorus has established at the outset (1.2) a rather elaborate system of correspondences between parts of the body and members of the household, according to which, dreams may be interpreted.[31]

The translation of *aitia* as 'source' is also questionable. The meaning is not given in the Liddell-Scott-Jones lexicon; the idea is rather the active one of 'responsible (often culpable) cause' – as parents are responsible for the existence of their children. This active, causative interpretation of *kephalē*

---

[28] The Loeb translation, 'From the sources . . . flow', is misleading. Note also the use of *archas* for *rā'šîm* in Gn. 10, LXX.

[29] Cervin astutely comments that reference is made earlier to the thirty-eight 'sources' (*pēgai*, 4.90) of the river which flow from the same rock, but he wrongly infers from this that the words *kephalai* and *pēgai* are synonymous (Cervin 1989: 89–90).

[30] See Payne 1986: 124–125; Fee 1987: 503 n. 45.

[31] *Cf.* Cervin 1989: 92–93. Grudem's (1990: 52–53) objection to the source interpretation (that if 'head' means 'source', it must also mean 'house', 'monetary capital', 'master of a slave', *etc.*, because it is compared to all of these) is flawed. Artemidorus does not liken the head to a source but to parents *on the grounds that* both are the cause of one's living. Nevertheless, the sheer variety of functions attributed to the head in this work (including authority over the body) makes it impossible to promote any one function to the level of common metaphorical denotation of *kephalē*.

would be quite inappropriate for the Pauline texts. Allowance should also be made for the probability that the form of the analogy has been at least partly determined by factors other than the intrinsic suitability of the 'head' metaphor, such as, first, the circumstances of the story, the need in particular to interpret the dream of beheading in relation to the father's death; and secondly the presence in the background of the general image of the father as head of the family.

6. The use of *kephalē* in the difficult Orphic fragment 21a is probably better understood to mean 'beginning' than 'source': 'Zeus the head, Zeus the middle, and by Zeus all things are perfected.'[32] For if *kephalē* carried the implication that all things derived from Zeus as source, the statement that 'Zeus is the middle' would appear to be redundant; and the proper antithesis to the completion of all things is the act of their creation, not their source. This is perhaps a rather fine argument, but it does bring the interpretation of *kephalē* in line with the general pattern of usage that has emerged in this study, and it is difficult to see what could be said conversely in favour of the 'source' interpretation. That *archē* is found in some versions of the verse in place of *kephalē* would seem to confirm this view, and certainly does not serve as unambiguous evidence that *kephalē* can mean 'source'.

R. S. Cervin (1989: 90–92) has drawn attention to the marginal comment (or scholion) on fragment 21 (which has *archē* for *kephalē*) and has argued that this supports the 'source' interpretation: 'and he is the beginning, as the producing cause [*kai archē men houtos hōs poiētikon aition*]'.[33] The argument is that if *kephalē* can be replaced with *archē*, which is understood to mean 'the producing cause', *kephalē* may have this same nuance. But two thoughts count against this. First, as we have seen, *aitios* denotes active and creative responsibility, not source; Zeus as *archē* is interpreted as a creative (*poiētikon*) power. Secondly, the statement made by the scholiast is not a semantic definition, of the form '*archē* means "producing cause"'. If this were the case, we should have to conclude either that the comment is redundant or that 'productive cause' (*poiētikon aition*) was not at all an obvious interpretation of *archē* and therefore a highly unlikely meaning for *kephalē*. The statement is rather an explanation of why the poem attributes to Zeus the status of *archē*; the one who is the cause of everything is the beginning of everything, but 'beginning' does not *mean* 'cause'.[34]

7. Finally, two closely related passages from the Old Testament

---

[32] Against Barrett 1971: 248; Fee 1987: 503 n. 45. A thorough and somewhat scathing refutation of the interpretation of *kephalē* as 'source' in this text is found in Grudem 1985: 45. Fragment 168 has *tetyktai* (from *teuchō*, 'to make, produce') for *teleitai*.

[33] *Cf.* Fitzmyer 1993: 54.

[34] Kroeger (1993: 376) cites Irenaeus as evidence for the 'source' interpretation on the grounds that *kephalē* is equated with *archē*: *kephalēn men kai archēn tēs idias ousias* (Migne,

Pseudepigrapha need to be considered. In the *Life of Adam and Eve* (Apoc.) 19:3 we find in Eve's account of her trespass the statement, 'Desire is the head of every sin'; one manuscript has 'root and beginning' instead of 'head'.[35] The original text is dated by M. D. Johnson between 100 BC and AD 200, and the Greek translation prior to AD 400 (Charlesworth 1985: 252). The idea here is most probably only that 'desire' comes first. The context makes nothing of the idea that every sin *derives from* desire. Only the temporal aspect is required; desire is the poison sprinkled by Satan on the fruit from which Eve ate, and is thus the beginning of every sin.

In the *Testament of Reuben* 2:2 (second century BC) the seven spirits of deceit established against humankind are said to be 'the head of the deeds of youth'. The best interpretation to be drawn from the context (see 3:2–8) is that 'head' conveys the idea of 'instigation', that is, the spirits exert an active, controlling influence; they are the beginning of the deeds of youth. This is particularly clear in the description of the 'spirit of procreation and intercourse', one of 'seven other spirits' given to man at creation, which 'leads the young person like a blind man into a ditch' (2:9, Johnson's translation). Another consideration, however, presents itself in relation to both passages, namely that a particular metaphorical application of 'head' may lie in the background: the metaphor may have been mediated through a more familiar but suppressed image, such as 'head of a river' or 'head of a group of people (*e.g.* family)'. If this is the case, then it would still be a mistake to assign 'source' to *kephalē* as a standard and transferable metaphorical sense.

Headship and pre-eminence

These analyses have demonstrated that neither the 'authority over' nor the 'source' interpretation of *kephalē* is as well established lexicologically as its proponents would like to think.

Patrologia Graeca 7:496). But here *kephalēn* probably means no more than 'beginning, that which comes first'. In the Latin version *archēn* is translated by *initium*.

[35] It is difficult to say whether 'root and beginning' should be taken as synonymous with 'head' or a correction of a too literal translation. If, as is likely, the Greek text is a translation from a Hebrew original (see Charlesworth 1985: 251), then we must also reckon with the possibility that *rōʾš*, which does not normally mean 'source', was used for the sake of a play on its two denotations, 'head' and a type of poisonous plant, since the 'desire' that the serpent sprinkles on the fruit is described as 'his evil poison'. A similar idea is found in *Apocalypse of Abraham* 24.9: 'And I saw there desire, and in her hand (was) the head of every kind of lawlessness; and her torment and her dispersal destined to destruction' (Charlesworth 1983: 701). Here too 'beginning' is a more appropriate interpretation than 'source'. Philo, on the other hand, says that the 'head of our deeds is their end' (*kephalē de pragmatōn esti to telos autōn*) and that if you cut off their head, they die (*De Sacrificiis* 115). The point is that without a purpose actions die, just as with animals, 'if you take from them the head, all else goes with it' (Loeb).

In the case of the texts invoked in support of the traditional view, it has been shown either that the idea of 'ruler or chief' is quite inappropriate when the passage is properly understood, or that the more natural metaphorical sense of that which is 'prominent, foremost, first, representative' is at least as suitable (*cf.* Mickelsen & Mickelsen 1986: 104). To be 'head' of a group of people simply means *to occupy the position at the top or front.* While the sort of prominence signified by 'head' will in many instances also entail authority and leadership, it is a mistake to include this as part of the common denotation of the term. In other words, the metaphorical use of *kephalē* does not of itself introduce ideas of authority or sovereignty into the text. In very few, if any, of the passages considered does the argument depend on *kephalē* having such a meaning.

Arguably, this is as true for *rō'š* as it is for *kephalē*, despite the tendency of the Septuagint to translate *rō'š* in such contexts by *archōn* and *archēgos*. Bedale (1956: 70) records the comment in the Brown-Driver-Briggs lexicon on the meaning of *rō'š* as 'chief . . . apparently combined with the idea of first in a series', and then applies it to the phrase 'head of the family': 'No doubt the idea of authority is implicit in that phrase: but then a father's or a chieftain's authority in social relationships is largely dependent upon his "priority" in the order of being.' It is possible that the *archōn* and *hēgoumenos* word-groups were used for *rō'š* not so much because they were felt to represent the meaning of the word more accurately than *kephalē* but because there was a strong linguistic or stylistic aversion to using *kephalē* in this sense.

The argument that *kephalē* may mean 'source' is greatly weakened by the lack of support in the Septuagint. It is weakened still further if we recognize that the evidence adduced from extra-biblical sources is less persuasive than some have claimed. The basic problem is that while it is possible to bring forward a few instances where 'source' can quite coherently be substituted for 'head', this does not demonstrate that 'source' should be taken as a standard and familiar sense of *kephalē*.[36] The word may be used to *refer* to that which functions as a source – just as it may refer to someone who functions as ruler or chief – but it may *mean* something other than that. It should be stressed that the trade in metaphors is not a precise or systematic business; meanings emerge, overlap, disappear according to context without necessarily leaving their mark on normal usage. Arbitrary appeal to texts that either belong to a very different religious or philosophical tradition or have reference to some quite different object, whether or not they have been correctly interpreted, does not constitute sound exegetical method. The only safe approach is to determine as

---

[36] It is surely significant, as a general point, that no instances have been brought forward in which *kephalē* has displaced or has been displaced by *pēgē*, the more obvious word for 'source' (see *e.g.* Pr. 13:14).

precisely as possible the conventional metaphorical usage as Paul would have understood it, and then to consider what adjustments need to be made within the context of interpretation.

Admittedly, no interpreter is blameless in this respect. Still, it appears that the scrap of semantic material which is the *kephalē* metaphor has been pulled out of shape in both directions by polemical interest. On the one hand, it is the force of patriarchal tradition and the presumptions of New Testament interpretation that have induced in scholars the fancy that *kephalē* commonly signified a position of leadership or authority.[37] On the other, the 'source' interpretation has been seized upon rather uncritically by interpreters anxious to excise from Pauline thought what has been regarded as the cancer of sexual prejudice.

In the tumult of lexicological battle the simplest, most obvious, most natural, most elegant metaphorical sense – one which in effect underlies both these misinterpretations – has been largely overlooked: that which is most prominent, foremost, uppermost, pre-eminent.[38] In Hellenistic Greek the *kephalē* metaphor appears essentially to be spatial or temporal, not hierarchal or organic. Setting aside the occasional philosophical conceit, the literal head was not popularly viewed as a controlling object: it was that which was at the top of the body and which, by virtue of its prominence, visibility and expressiveness represented the whole person. I would suggest, therefore, that the common metaphorical application of *kephalē* embraces a coherent range of meanings that can be mapped as follows, and that it is within this area that we should expect to find the proper background to Paul's use of the word: (1) the physical top or extremity of an object, such as a mountain or river or pillar (*e.g.* Jdg. 9:25, 36; 3 Kingdoms 7:4, 27; 8:8, LXX; = 1 Ki. 7:16, 41; 8:8);[39] (2) more abstractly, that which is first, extreme, either in temporal or spatial terms; (3) that which is prominent or outstanding; and (4) that which is determinative or representative by virtue of its prominence.

When the word is used to describe personal or social relations, a social order

---

[37] Perhaps the original misunderstanding arose with the shift from Greek to Latin; Tertullian interprets the statement 'the head of a man is Christ' in terms of authority (*Adversus Marcionem* 5.8).

[38] Cervin (1989) moves some way towards this but a failure to distinguish between normative metaphorical meaning and secondary, contextually dependent connotations renders his analysis inconsistent. Schlier (1965: 674) includes as part of the secular usage: 'not merely what is first, or supreme, at the beginning or the end, but also what is "prominent," "outstanding" or "determinative".' In his view the use of *kephalē* to denote the head of a society is first found in the sphere of the Greek Old Testament. Grudem (1990: 37–38), however, objects that 'prominent part' is not attested in the lexicons.

[39] Although *rō'š* is used frequently in the Hebrew text for the 'top' of a mountain, it is usually translated by *koryphē* ('head, top, highest point'); Gn. 8:5 is something of an exception.

is certainly brought into view – inevitably, because family and society were hierarchally organized. But the *kephalē* metaphor only speaks of one aspect of this order: the dimension of visibility, prominence, eminence, social superiority, not the other dimension of authority and subservience, for which other terminology was available. The one who is head may have higher social standing, may be more excellent: the head is the one whose achievements have raised him above others. The metaphor suggests something of the public recognition that goes with these things: the head is conspicuous. In certain contexts the idea of priority emerges: the one who is head is the one who precedes others chronologically or who goes first in some undertaking. Something of the character and destiny of the group may be summed up and represented in the head, or, conversely, the head determines the identity of the group.

In stressing the thought of prominence or pre-eminence, moreover, we remain in sight of the commonest figurative usage of *kephalē* in the Septuagint, by which the head, representative of the whole person by synecdoche, serves as the locus of a wide range of moral and religious experiences. Blessings, mischief, blood, recompense, reproach, and judgment all come upon the head, typically from the hand of God (*e.g.* Gn. 49:26; 1 Ki. 25:39; 2 Ki. 1:16; Ne. 4:4; Ezk. 9:10; Judith 9:9); a vow is made upon the head (Nu. 6:7); transgressions abound over the head (Ezr. 9:6; Ps. 37:4); joy and praise are over the head (Is. 35:10; 51:11; 61:7); shame and dishonour are closely associated with the head (Nu. 5:18; Dt. 21:12; Je. 14:4; Epistle of Jeremiah 31).

In this rather straightforward idea of 'prominence, pre-eminence', there-fore, we have what appears to be an ideologically neutral starting-point for an investigation of those texts in which Paul speaks of the man as 'head' of the woman. The possibility is there, of course, that Paul will add his own slant to the meaning of the figure; but at least we do not bring with us any strong lexical bias. In fact, we will find that Paul hardly diverges from conventional usage.

2. Headship and submission
1 Corinthians 11:3 and Ephesians 5:21–24

If *kephalē* is used in Hellenistic literature generally to signify neither a position of authority over others nor the source of something, but the logically simpler idea of prominence or pre-eminence, what of its use in Paul? The word is used figuratively in 1 Corinthians 11:3 and in various contexts in Ephesians and Colossians to describe Christ's relation to the church and to the cosmos, and also the relation of the man to the woman in marriage. In 1 Corinthians 11:2–16 it is linked to certain restrictions imposed upon women who pray and prophesy in church. In Ephesians and Colossians it is closely associated with the idea of Christ's exaltation, on the one hand, and with that of the submission or subordination of the woman in marriage, on the other.

These passages need to be examined with careful attention to the development of Paul's argument in each case, because this is the best defence we have against the tendency to introduce the interpreter's own presuppositions into the text. The meaning of a word is always a product both of its accepted public sense and of the particular context in which it is employed. As we proceed, therefore, a number of questions need to be kept in mind. Is Paul's use of the figure of headship consistent with what we have found in the previous chapter? Does his argument compel us to think that he understood the figure to mean something more specific than simply 'foremost, prominent, pre-eminent'? What bearing does the use of *kephalē* to designate the status of Christ have on Paul's understanding of the headship of the man? What does it mean, for that matter, to speak of Christ as 'head'? What logical connection does Paul make between the statement that the man is 'head' of the woman and the exhortation that she be subordinated to him?

Headship and glory

> *Thelō de hymas eidenai hoti pantos andros hē kephalē ho Christos estin, kephalē de gynaikos ho anēr, kephalē de tou Christos ho theos.*
>
> I want you to know that the head of every man is Christ, the head of a woman is the man, the head of Christ is God (1 Cor. 11:3).

Authority over the woman?

This emphatic and systematic statement introduces a complex exposition of the relation between men and women and especially of why a woman who prays or prophesies in church should cover her head. It would seem a natural

34

assumption for the reader to make that Paul meant this assertion to stand as a logical and theological premise for the following argument.[1] So his point would be: *given that*, or *because*, the head of the woman is the man, she should cover her head when praying or prophesying. We should then have to look to some prior theological conception of the man as head of the woman – known to Paul but presumably not to the Corinthians – in order to understand exactly what *kephalē* signifies here.

This 'natural' assumption, however, can be questioned. In Hellenistic literature, when *kephalē* is used in such a figurative sense, it almost always describes the relation of an individual to a group. It is very rare to find one person described as the head of one other person in the way that Paul speaks here of the man as head of the woman. The only non-biblical occurrence of such a usage that has emerged from the studies of *kephalē* discussed in the previous chapter is found in the *Oneirocriticum* of Artemidorus (late second century AD): a man's father is compared to his head because the father was the cause of his living.[2] But even here it appears that the metaphor is introduced not because it is the natural term for speaking of the relation between a father and his son but because the head has an actual (symbolic) significance in the story; the son had dreamed of being beheaded, and this is interpreted as a premonition of the death of his father. The special usage, therefore, is localized; it arises out of the particular context.

In 1 Corinthians 11 we have a similar situation. Paul's concern in the passage is first with the head in its literal sense, as that which is either covered or uncovered in worship: then secondly with the head as the object of shame or glory – an idiomatic usage which, as we have seen, is common in the Old Testament.[3] This is the practical moral and religious issue with which he has to deal. What this suggests, however, is that the use of *kephalē* to describe the relation between the man and the woman does not look back to any preconceived notions of male 'headship' or of a hierarchal order of being – for which, in any case, no evidence exists. (The same can be said for the description of Christ as the head of each man and of God as the head of Christ: these are equally novel and *ad hoc* formulations.) Instead, the language in verse 3 appears to have been taken from the parenesis of verses 4–15; the verse, therefore, needs to be interpreted in terms of what follows, not of what has – conceptually – preceded it. When Paul describes the man as head of the woman, he is not so much stating a premise – something already understood – as anticipating the later argument that the woman is the glory of the man and

---

[1] *Cf.* Schreiner 1991a: 131: 'Verses 4–6 are an inference or conclusion drawn from the fundamental proposition in verse 3.'

[2] Artemidorus, *Oneirocriticum* 1.2; 3.66. See discussion of this passage in chapter 1 above.

[3] Shame and dishonour, for example: Nu. 5:18; Dt. 21:12; Je. 14:4; Epistle of Jeremiah 31.

that unseemly behaviour on her part is likely to bring dishonour upon him (verses 4–7).[4] This is a further extension of the figurative use of *kephalē*, but as with the passage from Artemidorus it really makes sense only within the context of the particular discussion.

The use of *kephalē* in this passage, therefore, to describe the relation of the man to the woman is governed by two literary factors. The first is the conventional metaphorical sense of *kephalē* as meaning simply 'most prominent', and on that basis perhaps 'representative'. This agrees much better with the general theme of glory and shame than would an interpretation along the lines either of 'authority over' or of 'source'. It is because the man holds the pre-eminent position in the patriarchal family, because he represents the family in the public sphere, that he is susceptible to dishonour brought upon him by his wife's behaviour. The metaphor of headship naturally defines the visible or social aspect of the relationship; the whole passage has to do with appearance and attire, not with inner relations of subservience or origination. The second factor is the significance of the word *kephalē* for Paul's argument. This is both practical, in that he is speaking about headwear, and symbolic, in view of the common Jewish idiom that associates moral and religious qualities with the head.

The real premise of the argument, however, is not that man is head of the woman but that woman is the glory of man. This is the basis for what Paul has to say, and it is this assertion which is supported by the appeal to the creation story in verses 8–9: woman is from man and was created for the sake of the man. The allusion here is evidently to the creation of woman from the man's side as a 'helper according or corresponding to him' (Gn. 2:22, LXX; *cf.* 2:18). The reason for introducing the thought at this point appears to have been the need to explain the difference between the sexes with respect to 'glory' – that woman is the glory of man while man is the glory of God. That woman was created 'for the sake of the man' may mean no more in this context than that she brings glory to the man.[5] What Paul understood by this for the relation between men and women will be considered further in chapter 4 below.

The passage, therefore, has little or nothing to do with the question of the man's authority over the woman.[6] What damages the headship relationship, whether between man and woman or between Christ and

[4] There is no logical or inferential conjunction ('so', 'therefore', 'for this reason') connecting verses 4ff. with verse 3.

[5] We should not assume that in verse 7 Paul means to deny that the woman is also the glory of God; it may only be that to his mind in the context of worship the social and sexual relationship between the man and the woman overrides her direct relationship to God.

[6] Against, for example, Fitzmyer 1989: 510–511. Reversing an earlier judgment (Witherington 1988: 84–85; 1990: 167–168), Witherington rules out the 'source' interpretation and agrees with Fitzmyer, arguing that 'the context has to do with authority,

man, is not disobedience but dishonour (*cf.* Keener 1992: 33). So the woman praying or prophesying with her head uncovered 'dishonours her head' (v. 5): nothing suggests that the real fault is insubordination. The question of authority is irrelevant to a discussion of the proper manner in which men and women should pray and prophesy. Paul concludes only that a woman should cover herself in worship. Nothing is said about her attitude *towards the man*. The woman is by her created nature the glory of man, that is, she brings honour to the man by virtue of who she is; but Paul does not infer from this that she should honour him as a matter of conscious obedience or submission.

The relationship between Christ and God has no significance for Paul's discussion beyond the analogical function that it has in the parallel assertions of verse 3. But the point is essentially the same: the one to whom Christ brings glory is God (*cf.* 2 Cor. 4:6; Eph. 3:21; Phil. 2:11); that is, 'the head of Christ is God'. It is a mistake to interpret the relationship between Christ and God here in terms of 1 Corinthians 15:28.[7] The subordination of the Son in that passage comes when all his enemies have been defeated, including the final enemy, death – in other words, at the end of time. But it is the *current* relationship between Christ and God that is signified by the word *kephalē* in 1 Corinthians 11:3.

It is also difficult to argue that the covering of the woman in worship is a sign of her husband's – or any man's – authority over her. While there is an enigmatic reference in verse 10 to the 'authority' (*exousia*) that a woman should have over (*epi*) her head, we cannot simply take this to mean that the head-covering is a symbol of her submission to the man's authority. On the one hand, there are grammatical objections to this view. The phrase *exousian echein* nowhere has the passive sense 'to have another's authority over oneself'; it ought to mean that the woman herself has authority, not that someone has authority over her. We shall consider this problem, and the curious phrase 'because of the angels', in chapter 4. On the other hand, we should have to suppose, if we are to be consistent, that the man's obligation *not* to cover his head (v. 7) signifies that he is exempt from divine authority (*cf.* Hooker 1964: 414).[8] What verse 7 makes clear, in fact, is that the wearing of a head-covering by a woman draws its significance from the relation indicated by the

---

authorization, and order in worship' (Witherington 1995: 237–238). Also Hurley 1981: 167; Fung 1987: 186–188.

[7] Against Fung 1987: 186; Schreiner 1991a: 128.

[8] If, as Hurley (1981: 170) thinks, for a man to cover his head would signify that he is under another man's authority, what would happen in the case of slaves who pray or prophesy? As a man, according to Hurley's argument, a male slave should be 'under Christ alone' and therefore should not cover his head; but as a slave he is under the authority of his master, and therefore should cover his head.

expression 'glory of a man'; and, as we have seen, there is no reason to interpret this in terms of obedience or submission.[9] The difference, therefore, is that whereas in the context of worship it is appropriate for the 'image and glory of God' to be seen, the 'glory of man' should be concealed. Hooker (1964: 415) makes the point very clearly:

> In her case . . . her uncovered head will reflect his glory, both because she is his 'glory', and because he is her 'head'. It is for this reason that the judgement in her case is different; her head must be covered, not because she is in the presence of man, but because she is in the presence of God and his angels – and in their presence the glory of man must be hidden.

We should also take account of the significance of veiling generally in the ancient world. Whether the same standards would have applied in public life for the women of Corinth is not clear; nor can we say for certain what significance a married woman appearing with her head exposed would have had (see Keener 1992: 22–31). Some further thought will be given to this matter later. But what evidence there is suggests at least that the wearing of a head-covering was a sign of modesty and chastity in a married woman, rather than of subservience.[10] Also rather illuminating is the connection that Plutarch makes between head-coverings and 'glory' in *Quaestiones Romanae* 266F (Loeb):

> Why do they also sacrifice to the god called 'Honor' with the head uncovered? One might translate Honor as 'renown' [*doxan*, 'glory'] or 'honour'. Is it because renown is a brilliant thing, conspicuous, and widespread, and for the reason that they uncover in the presence of good and honoured men, is it for this same reason that they also worship the god who is named for 'honour'?

The significance of head-coverings both for the Romans and the Greeks is discussed at some length in this passage (266–267); nowhere is it suggested that

[9] The idea that woman brings glory to man is found in Pr. 11:16 and 1 Esdras 4:17. In neither passage is glory linked to obedience to the man. On the contrary, in the latter the point is made in the context of a speech asserting the superior strength of women: 'Who is it then who rules them [*i.e.* kings, men, wine], or who has lordship over them? Is it not the women?' (1 Esdras 4:14). In Pr. 11:16 it is a gracious and righteous wife who brings glory to her husband.

[10] Frame (1991: 228) asserts that 'covering the head connoted subservience to another creature', citing Morris 1985 on 11:4. But Morris provides no evidence for this. Neither does Hurley (1973: 205; 1981: 167). Martin emphasizes the sexual significance of veiling in Graeco-Roman culture (Martin 1995: 235). Unfortunately, the evidence that is brought forward is rather too eclectic and imaginative to give grounds for much confidence in his interpretation.

the covering of the head denotes subordination. The basic theological premise is very different from Paul's, but the repeated association with the theme of honour and glory that we find here is entirely congruent with the terms of his argument in 1 Corinthians 11.

Man as 'source' of the woman?

What of the other view, that man as head is the 'source' of woman or of her life? G. D. Fee (1987: 503) observes that the only other place in the passage where the relationship between men and women is picked up is verses 8–9, where it is said that 'woman is from man'.[11] Does this not indicate that man as head is the source of the woman? Yet this conclusion is contradicted by two important observations. The first is that according to the parallel assertion in verse 12 man is 'through the woman', which must undermine the argument of verse 3 if the question of origin is really at issue. Secondly, verses 8–9 do not stand in the argument as an interpretation of *kephalē*. They provide a theological rationale for the claim in verse 7 that 'woman is the glory of man', and while this statement is very close in meaning to the idea that the man is head of the woman, it certainly cannot be interpreted to mean that he is her source. The primary theme in the passage concerns the shame that attaches to a woman who prays or prophesies with her head uncovered. It is to this theme that verse 3 must relate, not to the subordinate argument about the order of creation in verses 8–9.

In fact, Paul's whole line of reasoning in this section effectively rules out an interpretation of headship in terms of the creational relationship between man and woman. It is not Adam who is dishonoured by the unseemly behaviour of women in Corinth, but their own husbands. Although a creational reality certainly lies behind what Paul has to say here about man and woman, the conception of headship has to do not with historical origins but with the current state of affairs, with the contemporary relation between Christ and man, man and woman, God and Christ – particularly as it is expressed in the context of worship. As Paul makes clear in verses 11–12, the *present* relationship between man and woman 'in the Lord' is characterized by reciprocity and mutual dependence: 'neither woman without man, nor man without woman . . . for as the woman is from the man, so also the man is

[11] *Cf.* Scroggs 1972: 298 n. 41; 1974: 534 and n. 8; Swidler 1979: 329; Murphy-O'Connor 1980: 492–493; Payne 1986: 126; Giles 1986: 46; Witherington 1988: 85; Jervis 1993: 240; Baumert 1996: 187–188. Martin, however, argues to the contrary that verses 8–9 support the patriarchal interpretation of verse 3: to the ancient reader the creation of the woman because of the man 'would clearly imply hierarchy, since only those of lower status are said to exist for the sake of someone else; slaves, for example, exist for the sake of their owners, to "please" (*areskein*) them' (Martin 1995: 232). But the context is sexual rather than hierarchal.

through the woman'. The Genesis narrative is introduced not because *kephalē* denotes man's creational priority but because it is this which gives the passage its ontological and scriptural grounding.[12]

Neither 'authority' nor 'source'

The question of the man's authority, therefore, has no bearing on this issue; and the theme of origination ('woman from man') is introduced only as a supporting argument (woman is the glory of the man *because* she was created from man), not as an interpretation of the idea of headship.[13] In describing the man as head of the woman in this passage Paul has in mind either the glory or the disgrace that might be brought upon the most prominent figure in the household by the woman's appearance and behaviour in worship (*cf.* Liefeld 1986a: 139–143; Keener 1992: 35). The only absolute, creational component in this argument is that the woman was created from the man and for the sake of the man. This is made the basis for the view that woman is the glory of the man, which, I think, should be understood in terms of the non-hierarchal sexual 'complementarity' of man and woman. More will be said on this point later. But exactly what constitutes seemly behaviour in worship and in what sense the woman brings glory to the man may be recognized as culturally influenced issues without distorting Paul's argument. The scriptural objection is to the disgrace, not to the particular actions that give rise to it. 'Nature' no longer teaches us so clearly that it is a disgrace for a man to have long hair or for a woman to have short hair. But it is still appropriate for women to take responsibility for their appearance in worship; men are no less prone to distraction, or to self-glorification, than they were in Paul's time.

Christ as 'head': Ephesians and Colossians

The figure of the man as head of the woman in Ephesians 5:23, by contrast, has no connection with literal usage. Instead it is set alongside a parallel description of Christ as head of the church: 'a husband is head of the wife as indeed Christ is head of the church, he himself being the saviour of the body'. Readers have tended to suppose that the metaphor of Christ as head is a reference to his sovereignty or lordship over the church, and that in Paul's eyes a similar relationship of authority had been ordained between the man and woman. So, for example, G. W. Knight (1991: 170) writes: 'It is virtually

[12] The fact that there is no mention of Christ in verses 7–9 makes it unlikely that the statement 'Christ is the head of every man' is to be understood in creational terms (*cf.* Wolff 1982: 70). Nor, for reasons already given, can we understand the headship of Christ as presenting him specifically as 'source' of the new creation (as Fee 1987: 504–505).

[13] Gritz solves the conundrum by suggesting that by *kephalē* Paul meant both that the man was the source of the woman and that the woman should be submitted to the man (Gritz 1991: 84–85).

certain that in comparing the headship of the husband over the wife to the headship of Christ over the church, the apostle is using the term *kephalē* for the husband as he does for Christ, namely, as one who has authority and is the leader.'

It can be argued, however, that when Paul speaks of Christ as 'head' in Ephesians and Colossians, he is not thinking of the 'authority' that Christ has over the cosmos or over the church; nor does he conceive of Christ as the 'source' of things. The reference is rather, in keeping with the normal metaphorical sense of the term, to his pre-eminence and primacy. In particular, there is a close connection between the thought of Christ as 'head' and the theme of resurrection and exaltation.

Christ as head above all things: Colossians 1:18 and Ephesians 1:20–23

> *Kai autos estin hē kephalē tou sōmatos tēs ekklēsias; hos estin archē, prōtotokos ek tōn nekrōn, hina genētai en pasin autos prōteuōn.*

> And he is the head of the body of the church; who is the beginning, firstborn from the dead, so that he might become in all things pre-eminent (Col. 1:18).

> . . . *hēn enērgēsen en tō Christō egeiras auton ek nekrōn kai kathisas en dexia autou en tois epouraniois* [21]*hyperanō pasēs archēs kai exousias kai dynameōs kai kyriotētos kai pantos onomatos onomazomenou, ou monon en tō aiōni toutō alla kai en tō mellonti;* [22]*kai panta hypetaxen hypo tous podas autou kai auton edōken kephalēn hyper panta tē ekklēsia,* [23]*hētis estin to sōma autou, to plērōma tou ta panta en pasin plēroumenou.*

> . . . which he worked in Christ having raised him from the dead and made him sit at his right hand in the heavens, [21]far above every rule and authority and power and dominion and every name that is named not only in this age but also in the one to come; [22]and all things he put under his feet and gave him as head above all things – for the church, [23]which is his body, the fullness of the one filling all in all (Eph. 1:20–23).

The connection between the exaltation of Christ and his designation as 'head' appears most clearly in Colossians 1:18; Christ as head of the church 'is the beginning, firstborn from the dead, so that he might become in all things pre-eminent'.[14] The verse does not speak of Christ's authority over the body; the

---

[14] The use of the relative pronoun (*hos estin archē*) suggests that verse 18b is an interpretation of Christ's headship rather than a new idea. A parallelism with verse 15, if *prōtotokos* explains *eikōn*, would add further support. Note the connection between 'firstborn' and the motif of exaltation in Ps. 88:28, LXX: 'I will set him as firstborn, exalted among the kings of the earth.'

point is rather that he was first to be raised from the dead and therefore has attained a position of pre-eminence in relation to the body. But the same thought is also evident in Ephesians 1:20–23. Although at first sight the assertion that Christ has been set 'far above every rule and authority and power and lordship' and that 'all things have been put under his feet' appears to imply that the exercise of authority is intrinsic to the notion of 'headship', careful examination of the passage suggests that this was not Paul's meaning.

1. It is not clear that the subordination (*hypetaxen*) of all things under Christ's feet in verse 22 is intended to interpret or explain his headship 'above all things for the church'. It is a common mistake of biblical exegesis to assume that the juxtaposition of two ideas always makes them synonymous or mutually explanatory. In Psalm 8:6–7, LXX (vv. 5–6 in English versions), which undoubtedly lies behind this passage,[15] a distinction emerges between two quite different thoughts. On the one hand, there is the theme of exaltation and glory: 'You made him a little lower than angels, you crowned him with glory and honour.' On the other, there is a statement about subordination: 'you set him over the works of your hands; you subjected all things under his feet . . .' Arguably the same distinction appears in Ephesians 1:22: all things have been put under Christ's feet, but he has been given to the church as head above all things. This supposition is strengthened further when we consider the Hebrew text of 1 Chronicles 29:11, where David prays, 'Yours is the kingdom, O Lord, and you are lifted up for all as head.' While 'kingdom' indicates divine rule, 'head' signifies that which is raised up, exalted, made prominent, pre-eminent; and as God is lifted up as head 'for all', so Christ is raised up and given as head 'to the church'. This brings us to the next point.

2. To whatever extent the idea of authority over others does form part of Paul's conception of Christ here, it is an authority not *over* the church, of which Christ is head, but over 'all things' *for* the church. If the traditionalists were in fact right in interpreting *kephalē* in the light of the subordination of all things under Christ's feet, then it would not in fact be the church that is subordinate – and this, of course, would entirely undermine the argument for the subordination of women on the basis of the analogy with Christ's relationship to the church (Eph. 5:22–24). We should also bear in mind that in the Old Testament the idea of putting things under someone's feet carries strong overtones of subjugation, in some contexts the subjugation of enemies (*e.g.* Ps. 110:1). This would be quite inappropriate as an understanding of Christ's headship with regard to the church or of the husband's headship with regard to the wife.

3. But Christ is head *hyper* all things. The preposition *hyper* used here with

---

[15] See *e.g.* Lincoln 1990: 65–66.

kephalē means 'over and above, beyond, more than',[16] that a thing exceeds or surpasses some other thing. It is not normally used to define a relationship of 'authority over', for which we should expect *epi*.[17] This is also true of *hyperanō* in verse 21: the preposition indicates only that Christ has been exalted *above* 'every rule and authority and power', and so on, not that he has authority *over* them.[18] Similarly, in Colossians 2:10 the description of Christ as 'the head of all rule and authority' does not mean that he has 'authority over' these things: he is 'head of', not 'head over'. The idea is only that he is foremost or pre-eminent in relation to all rule and authority.

4. What about the description of Christ seated at the right hand of God (v. 20)? Does this not signify the investiture in him of authority over others? Again, I think that we are closer to Paul's intention in this passage if we read this motif as a rather restricted expression of Christ's exaltation to a position of honour. Although Psalm 110:1–3 (109:1–3, LXX), to which Ephesians 1:20 presumably alludes, describes the exercise of dominion over enemies, this does not necessarily mean that the invitation in verse 1 ('sit at my right hand') signifies the bestowal of authority. The subjugation of the enemies does not accompany the exaltation to the right hand of God but is expected some time later: 'sit at my right hand *until* I make your enemies your footstool . . .' Elsewhere in the Old Testament the thought behind the image of being seated at the right hand of a ruler appears to be one of acceptance or approval, the conferment of honour (*e.g.* 1 Ki. 2:19; Ps. 45:9).[19]

The New Testament picture is more complex, but the general emphasis is the same. In the majority of cases the motif of being seated at the right hand of God marks either the culmination of the process of Christ's exaltation or the close association of Christ with God in heaven (Mt. 26:64 and parallels; Mk. 16:19; Acts 7:55–56; Rom. 8:34; Col. 3:1; Heb. 1:3; 8:1; 10:12; 12:2). In

---

[16] Bauer-Arndt-Gingrich-Danker, *s.v. hyper* 2. Note also Sirach 49:16: 'Sem and Seth were in great honour [*edoxasthēsan*] among men, and Adam above [*hyper*] every living thing in the creation'; *cf.* Bel and the Dragon 2 (Theodotian).

[17] *E.g.* 2 Kingdoms 6:21: 'Blessed be the Lord, who chose me . . . to make me ruler over [*hēgoumenon epi*] his people'; and 3 Kingdoms 2:35: 'And the king gave Banaeas . . . over [*epi*] the army'. The difference between *hyper* and *epi* is illustrated by Ps. 96:9, LXX (Lord *over*, exalted *above*) and Dn. 6:4 (Theodotian) (it is Daniel's excellent spirit that raises him *above* the other two governors; the king then sets him *over* the whole kingdom).

[18] This is the consistent prepositional use of the word in the NT and LXX: Eph. 4:10 ('he who also ascended far above [*hyperanō*] all the heavens) and Heb. 9:5 ('above [(*hyperanō*) it [the ark of the covenant] were the cherubim of glory'); Ps. 148:4; Ezk. 43:15; Dn. 7:6; Jon. 4:6; Mal. 1:5. In a number of Old Testament passages *hyperanō* is used, as in Eph. 1:21, in connection with an exaltation motif; but in each case the idea is not one of 'authority over' but of prominence and glory: Dt. 26:19; 28:1; Ps. 8:1; Is. 2:2; Mi. 4:1.

[19] In a number of instances it is the Lord who is at man's right hand to help him (Pss. 16:8; 109:31).

none of these passages is there any explicit indication that the phrase denotes Christ's authority or rule over other powers;[20] and it is surely significant, too, that in none of these passages do we find the words 'till I make your enemies your footstool' from Psalm 110:1. This overtly bellicose idea might lead us to think that being seated at God's right hand in itself signifies the exercise of authority. But it is added only at Matthew 22:44 and parallels, where there is in any case no mention of resurrection or exaltation; at Acts 2:34–35, where it is explicitly quoted from the psalm and only indirectly applied to Christ; and at Hebrews 1:13, where the intention is to distinguish Christ from the angels. In other words, where Christ's resurrection and exaltation are described in terms of sitting at God's right hand, the New Testament apparently prefers to avoid the connection – natural in view of the importance of Psalm 110:1 for New Testament Christology – with the theme of subjugation and rule. The reason for this is quite simple: the subjugation of Christ's enemies was felt to belong not to the present but to the future (*cf.* 1 Cor. 15:24–28). So it is unlikely that the reader is meant to recall the words 'till I make your enemies your footstool' at verse 20 or, consequently, to interpret the verse as a statement about the attribution to Christ of a particular 'authority over . . .'

Christ as head and the growth of the church: Ephesians 4:15–16 and Colossians 2:19

> . . . *alētheuontes de en agapē auxēsōmen eis auton ta panta, hos estin hē kephalē, Christos,* [16]*ex hou pan to sōma synarmologoumenon kai symbibazomenon dia pasēs haphēs tēs epichorēgias kat' energeian en metrō henos hekastou merous tēn auxēsin tou sōmatos poieitai eis oikodomēn heautou en agapē.*

> . . . but, speaking the truth in love, we might grow towards him in every way, who is the head, Christ, [16]from whom the whole body, joined and knit together by every joint of support, according to the working in measure of each individual part makes the growth of the body for the building up of itself in love (Eph. 4:15–16).

This passage has provided one of the strongest arguments for an interpretation of *kephalē* as 'source': Christ as head is the source of the body's growth. But if this definition is as uncertain as lexicological analysis appears to indicate, we should consider carefully whether this is how Paul meant the word to be understood in this context.

The character of the 'growth' described here needs to be examined closely. C. F. D. Moule (1977: 79) argues that 'what is intended is the actual bringing

---

[20] 1 Pet. 3:22 is a possible exception, but even here *hos estin en dexia theou* is separated from *hypotagentōn autō angelōn, etc.* by the participle clause *poreutheis eis ouranon.*

into existence, and ultimately the completion, of a corporate entity which does not previously exist at all' – in other words, that the growth of the body consists in the addition of believers. It is clear, however, from Ephesians 4:4 that believers are 'one body' already by virtue of their calling; and in verse 16 it is the '*whole* body' that grows, so that the emphasis is on the participation of all in the growth. It is not, therefore, the physical or numerical extension of the body that Paul has in mind. In order to understand precisely what he means by this relationship of growth between head and body we need a more comprehensive grasp of his argument in the letter.

The leading theme of Ephesians 2 – 3 is the preaching of the gospel to the Gentiles (through the ministry of Paul in particular) and the reconciliation of both Jew and Gentile 'in one body to God through the cross' (2:16). When Paul says at the beginning of chapter 4, 'I beseech you, therefore, a prisoner in the Lord, to live in a manner worthy of the calling with which you were called', he is alluding quite specifically to that condition of reconciliation in one body. The oneness of the Spirit, which the Ephesians are exhorted to preserve (4:3), is in this context the foundational unity of Jew and Gentile. This is not to say that the 'one body' of 4:4 is a reference *only* to the unity of Jews and Gentiles. What we find, rather, is exactly the same sort of overlapping that is present in 1 Corinthians 12:13, where the original unity of the body not only overrides the old social divisions ('whether Jews or Greeks, whether slaves or freemen') but also finds expression in a new charismatic diversity ('all were given one Spirit to drink'). But at this point there is an important divergence between the two passages.

The various 'gifts' which are said in Ephesians 4:11 to have been given to the church are of a particular and probably select type; they are what might be called the 'offices' of the church: apostles, prophets, evangelists, pastors and teachers. Behind this selection lies a concern that formed no part of Paul's purpose in 1 Corinthians 12: namely, that the church should move from its foundational unity in the Spirit towards a 'oneness of the faith and of the knowledge of the Son of God' – from a shared experience of the power of the Holy Spirit poured out on Jew and Gentile alike to a condition of doctrinal stability. (The Corinthians, by contrast, being 'babes in Christ', their unity in the Spirit jeopardized by 'jealousy and strife' [3:1–3], were not in a position to make this sort of progress.) The diversity of gifts in this case is dealt with not as a source of conflict and rivalry, as in 1 Corinthians 12, but as the comprehensive means by which believers are 'prepared' and 'the body of Christ' is built up (v. 12).

The goal of this process is expressed in two ways. The first speaks of attaining to 'the oneness of the faith and of the knowledge of the Son of God, to mature manhood, to the measure of the stature of the fullness of Christ' (v. 13); the second of growing 'towards him in all things who is the head, Christ, from whom the whole body . . .' (vv. 15–16). The emphasis on 'all' in verse 13 ('until we all attain . . .') and the contrast with 'children' in verse 14 indicate that in both cases it is the maturity of each *individual* believer that is in view, not the general condition of the whole.

When Christ is designated as 'head', therefore, the reference is not, in the first place, to his relation to the church as a body[21] but to the process of growth in faith and understanding to the point where each believer is no longer susceptible to the trickery and error of human doctrine (v. 14). What Paul means in verse 15, therefore, is not that we should grow '*into* him', as though to become united with him, but that we are to grow, as children grow towards adulthood, *towards* him, who is the head. The idea runs parallel to the thought in verse 13 about attaining 'to a mature man, to the measure of the stature of the fullness of Christ'. Christ as 'head', from this angle, is the model for Christian maturity.[22]

It appears, therefore, that neither 'ruler' nor 'source' is an appropriate connotation for *kephalē* here. The point so far is that Christ is 'foremost, pre-eminent', one who has gone first, who 'has ascended far above all the heavens', the exalted Son of God (v. 13), who represents the measure of maturity towards which believers collectively should aim.

The question still needs to be asked, however: how does the growth of the 'whole body' in verse 16 relate to the head? Even setting aside for a moment the participle clause ('joined and knit together . . .'), the form of expression in verse 16 is packed, convoluted and problematic: '. . . from whom the whole body . . . makes the growth of the body for building up itself in love'. Why is the process of growth reflexive (the body makes the growth of the body)? What is the relationship between growth and 'building up'? In what sense is the growth *from* the head or *from* Christ? Would it not make good sense here to interpret Christ who is 'head' as the source of the body's growth?

A first step towards clarification is taken if we recognize here the interplay between the parts and the whole in the growth of the body. The phrase 'according to the working in measure of each individual part' is an unmistakable allusion to the statement in verse 7 that 'to each one of us the grace was given according to the measure of Christ's gift'. This suggests that it is through the exercising of individual gifts by the *parts* of the body that the body as a whole grows – hence the reflexive form of verse 16. This in turn gives rise to the supposition that the words 'for building itself up' are added as a direct allusion to the work of the apostles and other 'ministers' in 'building up

[21] Against Schlier 1965: 680.
[22] Likewise, the corporate aspect of the singular form *andra teleion* corresponds to the unity of the head, not that of the body; but the 'mature man' is not simply Christ; it is, in contrast to children, 'the measure of the stature of the fullness of Christ', a measure of collective Christian maturity.

the body of Christ' in verse 12. To say that 'the whole body . . . makes the growth of the body' is, therefore, effectively to restate *in corporate form* the process described in more individual terms in verses 13–15.

What then of the 'from whom'? Why should bodily or corporate growth be *from* Christ when individual growth is *towards* Christ? There are two problems here. The first concerns the apparent link between body and head; the second concerns the sense in which the growth of the body is 'from Christ'. Commentators[23] have drawn attention to the fact that it is the masculine pronoun (*ex hou*) that is used here, agreeing with 'Christ' rather than with the feminine noun *kephalē*, and that this has the effect of dissociating 'head' from 'body'. The fact that 'Christ' has been inserted *between* 'head' and the relative clause confirms this. The growth of the body, therefore, is from Christ, not from the 'head'. The use of the periphrastic expression 'makes the growth' rather than the simple form 'grows' points in the same direction: 'from whom' indicates the basis of an activity – namely, the work of the apostles, prophets, and so forth – that results in 'the growth of the body', not the immediate source of the growth.

This brings us to the second problem. If the periphrastic form of the verb emphasizes the active collaboration of individuals (either all believers exercising their gifts or the particular 'ministers' listed in verse 11) in the process of bodily growth, rather than the intransitive idea of the body growing, then it seems unlikely that 'from whom' is meant to point to the source of the growth in anything like a vital or organic sense. Paul is not saying that Christ, as head, is the source of the life of the body.[24] The connection, of course, may only be a loose one; but in the context a more precise explanation presents itself – that 'from whom' recalls the giving of gifts by Christ to the church, generally in verse 7, more specifically in verse 11.

The form of expression is somewhat terse, but the reason for this may be that verse 16 is intended as a highly compressed recapitulation of the preceding passage. So the phrase 'the whole body' is an allusion to the baptismal unity of Jews and Gentiles in one body and one Spirit (vv. 1–5). The participle clause 'joined and knit together by every joint of support', which describes the means by which this original unity is maintained, corresponds to the virtues of humility, gentleness, patience, and forbearance listed in verse 2.[25] The

[23] *E.g.* Moule 1977: 75; *cf.* Ridderbos 1975: 380.
[24] Bedale argues that *kephalē* in these contexts has in effect the force of *archē* and should be understood as 'source' or 'origin' (Bedale 1956: 70–71; *cf.* Lightfoot 1879: 200; Best 1955: 128; O'Brien 1982: 147–148). But apart from the objection that *archē* does not mean 'source', it is the 'whole body' as a unity that grows, and it is difficult to see how that growth can be referred to Christ as the body's origin; since the body already exists, the question of origin is irrelevant here.
[25] It may be significant that the word *syndesmos* ('bond') is found in Col. 2:19 ('the whole body, through the joints and bonds supported and knit together . . .'); and even more so that

'working in measure of each individual part' is the exercise of the different charismata given by Christ (vv. 7–11) to the body for the 'building up of itself in love' (*cf.* v. 12). And finally, this collective activity 'makes the growth of the body', which is the growth of each individual towards the maturity of faith and knowledge represented by the fullness or headship of Christ (vv. 13–15).

Turning next to Colossians 2:19, the impression one receives is that we have here essentially an abridged version of Ephesians 4:16 adapted to a rather different context.[26] It is important to understand how this adaptation has taken place. The immediate context is the warning (2:4–18) against being taken captive 'through philosophy and empty deceit according to the traditions of men, according to the elements of the world, and not according to Christ' (v. 8). In particular, the Colossians should be wary of those who insist on the value of participation in whatever obscure mystical activities are described in verse 18, for in their self-conceit such people do not 'hold fast to the head, from whom the whole body, by the joints and bonds supported and knit together, grows with the growth of God' (v. 19). The designation of Christ as 'head' appears to have much the same function as in Ephesians 4:15, though the point is made negatively rather than positively; the head is the goal or pattern for individual maturity in terms of faith and understanding.[27] By 'holding fast to the head' or by 'growing towards the head' we avoid being led into error. Christ as head is the one in whom 'all the fullness of the deity dwells bodily', the 'head of all sovereignty and authority' (2:9–10), with whom we have been raised (2:12–13; 3:1), who is seated at the right hand of God, and who will appear in glory (3:1, 4).

The man is head of the woman as Christ is head of the church: Ephesians 5:23

> . . . *hoti anēr estin kephalē tēs gynaikos hōs kai ho Christos kephalē tēs ekklēsias, autos sōtēr tou sōmatos.*

---

synarmologoumenos ('joined') is used in Eph. 2:21 to denote the foundational unity of Jew and Gentile.

[26] The interpretation of Eph. 4:16 given above effectively requires the temporal priority of Ephesians over Colossians, at least at this point: if the letters were written at the same time, it is quite possible that the literary influence was two-way. As a recapitulation of the preceding passage Eph. 4:16 has much stronger verbal and thematic connections with its context than Col. 2:19.

[27] Although the relative pronoun is still masculine (*ex hou*), there is no longer the intervening 'Christ', and the body's growth from the head is expressed more directly. This may be a consequence of the borrowing; the verse has been condensed further because it does not have quite the same contextual relevance. The 'from whom' is retained, apart from the charismatic context, for the sake of convenience; it constitutes a formal rather than a logical connection.

> . . . a husband is head of the wife as also the Christ is head of the church, he himself being the saviour of the body (Eph. 5:23).

It appears, therefore, that when Paul speaks of Christ as 'head' in these letters, he has in mind two basic and closely related thoughts. First, by his resurrection Christ has been exalted to a position of pre-eminence above all things. Secondly, Christ is 'head' in relation to the church because he is, in the words of Colossians 1:18, 'the beginning, firstborn from the dead': in his resurrection and exaltation Christ has preceded those who eventually will be raised in him.[28] Paul does not make use of the metaphor of headship in 1 Corinthians 15:22–23, but the idea is exactly the same: 'in Christ shall all be made alive, but each in his own order: Christ the first fruits, then those of Christ at his coming'.[29] There is thus not only the spatial dimension but also an important temporal aspect underlying the idea of Christ's headship in Ephesians and Colossians. This has been modified in the context of what is said about church growth in Ephesians 4:11–15 and Colossians 2:18–19, but only to the extent that Christ, who in his resurrection is the perfect forerunner, has also become the measure of the church's maturity.

If we now turn to Ephesians 5:23, it should be apparent that the description of Christ as 'head of the church' is in the first place a recollection of this double theme of exaltation and precedence in the order of resurrection, though the point of the statement will become clear only as we consider the development of Paul's argument in these verses.

Such an understanding of the headship of Christ obviously has implications for how we interpret the headship of the man in this passage. One of the central convictions about the relationship between man and woman that Paul draws from the creation narratives is the fact that man was created first (1 Cor. 11:8; 1 Tim. 2:13). In 1 Corinthians 11 this theme is closely connected with the statement that 'the head of the woman is the man', and it is at least conceivable that the creational priority of the man provides part of the rationale for Paul's description of the man as head in Ephesians 5:23. The temporal aspect, however, has no particular significance for Paul's argument in

---

[28] Note the association that the terms *kephalē* and *archē* have with the idea of the 'firstborn' in the Old Testament. There is a hint of this in Je. 38:7, 9 LXX: Israel is 'head of the nations', and then 'Ephraim is my first-born' (*cf.* Ex. 4:22; 4 Ezra 6:58–59; Jubilees 2:20). The eldest son in the Hebrew Scriptures is the 'head' of the tribe (*cf.* 1 Ch. 23:8, 16–20; 24:21). In 1 Ch. 5:12 the Septuagint has 'firstborn' for *rō'š*. Jacob says to Reuben: 'You are my firstborn, my strength and the beginning [*archē*] of my children' (Gn. 49:3, LXX; *cf.* Dt. 21:17). In the Hebrew text of 1 Ch. 26:10 it is said of Simri that he was 'the head though not the firstborn, yet his father made him the head'.

[29] *Cf.* Rom. 8:29: it is the resurrected 'image' of Christ as 'firstborn' to which believers are foredestined to be conformed; and Acts 26:23: Christ is the 'first [*prōtos*] from the resurrection of the dead'.

this passage and is in any case less pronounced in Ephesians than in Colossians. We should probably take the emphasis, therefore, to be primarily on the socially perceived prominence of the man in relation to the woman. Indeed, it seems likely, bearing in mind both the fact that *kephalē* is not usually used to describe the relation between two individuals and the broader focus of the *household* code here, that the headship of the man with respect to the woman is in part an inference from his headship in relation to the patriarchal household.[30]

Therefore, as far as can be deduced both from the normal metaphorical usage of the word and from its particular application to Christ, I would say that *kephalē* here describes not the authority of the man but his position or status within the ancient social order. It remains essentially a spatial image, signifying the man's place at the front or at the top. It is the man who participates in public life, who is conspicuous, visible, prominent, while a woman may be praised for staying at home.[31] It is the man whose beliefs and opinions are determinative for the marriage relationship. It is in the man that legal power and responsibility are invested; the woman derives her legal status either from her father or from her husband. Certainly this entailed the man's authority over his wife in some form, but it is the effect or appearance of this authority that is denoted by *kephalē*, the position and importance that it gives the man, not the authority itself. These are generalizations, of course, and a glance through the history books will uncover exceptions and qualifications. But in seeking to understand Paul's use of the metaphor we are concerned as much with the popular image of male–female relations as with actual social reality.

We shall consider in the next section whether this judgment needs to be amended in view of the close association of *kephalē* with the argument for subordination in these verses.

The argument about submission in Ephesians 5:21–24

. . . *hypotassomenoi allēlois en phobō Christou,* [22]*hai gynaikes tois idiois andrasin hōs tō kyriō* [23]*hoti anēr estin kephalē tēs gynaikos hōs kai ho Christos kephalē tēs ekklēsias, autos sōtēr tou sōmatos;* [24]*alla hōs ekklēsia hypotassetai tō Christō, houtōs kai hai gynaikes tois andrasin en panti.*

. . . being subordinated to one another in fear of Christ – [22]wives to their own husbands as to the Lord, [23]because a husband

---

[30] This may also be true of 1 Cor. 11:3. The expression 'head of the household' is found in Hermas *Similitudes* 7.3.

[31] For example, a first-century BC Roman burial inscription reads: 'Here lies Amymone wife of Marcus best and most beautiful, worker in wool, pious, chaste, thrifty, faithful, a stayer-at-home [*domiseda*]' (H. Dessau, *Inscriptiones Latinae Selectae* 8402, Berlin 1892–1916; translated in Lefkowitz & Fant 1992: 17).

is head of the wife as also the Christ is head of the church, he himself being the saviour of the body. [24]But as the church is subordinate to the Christ, so also wives to the husbands in everything (Eph. 5:21–24).

We should be careful not to underestimate, or misconceive, the extent to which women belonged effectively to a social sub-group, a lower caste, in the ancient world. Opinion and practice regarding the value and role of women were by no means uniform, and, at the time of Paul, were in a state of flux. Still, powerful legal, cultural and social forces contrived to drive a wedge between the sexes and to confine women to a position of inferiority and subordination. According to Aristotle, 'the male is by nature superior and the female inferior, the male ruler and the female subject' (*Politics* 1254b2 [1.2.12], Loeb). The comedian Philemon (*c.* 361–263 BC) wrote: 'It is a good wife's duty, O Nikostrate, to be devoted to her husband, but in subordination; a wife who prevails is a great evil' (No. 132 [vol. 2, 519, Kock], quoted in Dibelius & Conzelmann 1972: 47). Josephus, the voice of diaspora Judaism, is forthright in his views on the status of women: 'The woman, says the Law, is in all things inferior to the man. Let her accordingly be submissive, not for her humiliation but that she may be directed; for the authority has been given by God to the man'. (*Against Apion* 2. 201, Loeb). Plutarch's advice is rather more enlightened, but hardly egalitarian:

> Control ought to be exercised by the man over the woman, not as the owner has control of a piece of property, but, as the soul controls the body, by entering into her feelings and being knit to her through goodwill. As, therefore, it is possible to exercise care over the body without being a slave to its pleasures and desires, so it is possible to govern a wife, and at the same time to delight and gratify her (*Moralia* 142E, Loeb).

While a handful of remarks from disparate ancient writers, taken out of context, does not amount to a social history, they are nevertheless highly suggestive and can reasonably be taken as illustrative of prevailing opinion.

It was, moreover, a basic principle of Roman law that all women should be under male guardianship because of the levity and weakness of their sex. A daughter grew up under the authority of the *pater familias*, who could choose to transfer her to another male guardian or to the power (*manus*) of her husband. Essentially the same situation prevailed in the Greek world, though the power of the *pater familias* was never as despotic as it sometimes was under Roman law. The legal subordination of a woman to a male guardian remained theoretically in force until the end of the third century AD, though from the time of Augustus onwards its power was progressively weakened and women acted with increasing independence. For example, the well-known *ius trium liberorum* ('law of three children') permitted freeborn women who had had three children, and freed women with four children, to engage in business without reference to a guardian. This and other factors, both legal and social, gave some women at least much greater freedom to manage their own wealth and property.[32]

With this general picture in view, we may turn to consider what Paul has to say about the subordination of women in Ephesians and Colossians.

It seems unlikely that when Paul urges the Ephesians to be 'subordinated to one another [*hypotassomenoi allēlois*] in fear of Christ' (v. 21), he is thinking of mutual subordination – an exegetical tactic commonly employed by those wishing to mitigate the hierarchalism of the subsequent passage.[33] On the one hand, the emphasis in the statement appears to be on the words 'in fear of Christ' rather than 'to one another', suggesting that we should not give the participle too strong an imperative force. Paul's point is almost: 'Inasmuch as you are of necessity subordinated to one another, be so in fear of Christ.'[34] Expressions such as 'in fear of Christ' and 'as to the Lord' (v. 22) seem inappropriate if the appeal is for mutual subordination. It makes more sense, surely, to regard them as a means of reinforcing and encouraging a type of behaviour which, though necessary as a matter of public relations and church order, was felt to contradict the unity of love and respect that believers experience in the Spirit.[35] Although *allēlois* would normally indicate reciprocal action of some sort ('to one another'; *cf.* 4:2, 32), this idea is certainly not reflected in the instructions to various household members that follow. It seems best to attribute any awkwardness in the manner of expression to linguistic constraints. The problem arises because Paul wants to designate

[32] Pomeroy 1975: 126–130, 150–155; Witherington 1988: 5–23; Meeks 1983: 23; Whelan 1993: 73–75.

[33] As against Evans 1983: 74; Bruce 1984: 382–383; Mickelsen & Mickelsen 1986: 108; Lincoln 1990: 365; Keener 1992: 168–172. Knight argues that in verse 21 Paul urges both mutual submission and the 'specific submission of wives to husbands' in verse 22 (Knight 1991: 167; but see the editorial reservation, 493 n.6). But since the verb is omitted in verse 22 it hardly seems likely that such a change in meaning is intended: the submission of women to their husbands must be an example of just the type of submission enjoined in verse 21.

[34] We do not meet in these parenetic statements about the subordination of women the reflexive formulation that is found in Plutarch, *Moralia* 142E (*hypotattousai . . . heautas tois andrasin*), which lays the emphasis more firmly on the deliberate action of the woman. The significance of the middle/passive appears to be that women should acquiesce in an existing state of affairs. Commentators have sometimes emphasized the voluntary element in the form of the verb (*e.g.* Delling 1972: 42; Knight 1991: 168).

[35] The same tension, more sharply articulated, is found in the address to slaves: 'Slaves, obey your masters in the flesh with fear and trembling in singleness of heart as to Christ . . .' (Eph. 6:5).

relationships *within* the fellowship, rather than towards outsiders, for which he could have used *allois*.[36]

The idea of mutual action, more importantly, is contrary to the basic meaning of the verb *hypotassō*, which presupposes an accepted order of things, whether established by force or by convention, within which there is submission and submissiveness.[37] As with the metaphor of headship, the word brings into view the structure or organization of things within the appropriate social context. It is not designed to draw attention either to the lines of authority and obedience that operate within this structure (as is the case with children and slaves) or to the inner attitude of the subordinate party (submissiveness).[38] To some extent, of course, this conflicts with the earlier, more personal and egalitarian exhortations that they should 'bear with one another [*allēlōn*] in love' (4:2) and 'be kind towards one another [*eis allēlous*], compassionate, forgiving each other' (4:32), but this only reflects the inevitable tensions faced by believers in a hierarchally organized society.

The particular emphasis of verse 21 extends into verse 22, where the omission of the verb indicates quite strongly, I think, that subordination within the household is more an accepted fact than a deliberate objective, and that it is rather the indirect object ('to their own husbands') and in particular the manner of subordination ('as to the Lord') that are of primary concern to Paul. So his argument is not, 'Be subordinate rather than equal or independent' but 'Be subordinate *as to the Lord*, rather than resentfully or from some less worthy motive'. He is not teaching them to be subordinate but how to deal with the subordination that society generally expected of them. N. Baumert (1996: 318) says, 'The actual ethical-theological statement of the apostle is probably: "accept the position appropriate to you under the contemporary circumstances".'[39]

---

[36] For the use of *hypotassō* with *allois* see Epictetus, *Discourses* 1:4.19; 4.4.1.

[37] *Cf.* Knight 1991: 493 n. 6: 'Although many people have claimed that the word can mean "be thoughtful and considerate; act in love" (toward another), it is doubtful if a first-century Greek speaker would have understood it in that way, for the term always implies a relationship of submission to an authority.' It is possible, of course, that Paul is using the word inexactly or figuratively: the submission of believers to one another should be *like* the submission of an inferior to a superior person.

[38] This is particularly clear in Rom. 13:1, where Paul urges submission (*hypotassesthō*) to the authorities that already 'have power over' (*hyperechousais*) and 'are ordained' (*tetagmenai eisin*) by God. Note Delling 1972: 41: 'In the NT the verb does not immediately carry with it the thought of obedience . . . To obey or to have to obey, with no emphasis, is a sign of subjection or subordination. The latter is decisive as regards the content of the word.'

[39] This principle has rather different implications where there is equality of rights for men and women (Baumert 1996: 319): 'let all persons voluntarily subordinate themselves in Christ to one another: the husband to his wife, and the wife to her husband (this is a spiritual invitation, not a legal command).'

The logical force of the emphasis on their 'own' (*idiois*) husbands is difficult to ascertain: *idiois* may have little more than a conventional or perhaps intensive significance. But it is possible to demonstrate a quite consistent *contrastive* use of the word in Paul's letters, and there is perhaps the implication here that women should be subordinate to their *own* husbands rather than to other men in the church, or perhaps even directly to the Lord.[40]

It is usually assumed that *idiois* in Ephesians 5:22 has no proper contrastive value.[41] J. A. Robinson (1922: 204) argues from the absence of the word in Colossians 3:18 that its insertion in such a context was a matter of indifference. But the Colossians passage is brief and it is in any case possible that the distinction was of less significance for the circumstances at Colossae. Robinson also observes that *idiais* is added in 1 Corinthians 4:12 ('working with our own hands') but omitted in Ephesians 4:28 (according to the best text) and 1 Thessalonians 4:11. But 1 Corinthians 4:12 has a background of controversy (with our own hands, rather than being supported by others; *cf.* 1 Cor. 9:3–18) that is missing from the other two passages. The word is never included in the instructions to children, presumably because they would have had no such choice.[42]

If it is the case that *idiois* implies a contrast with other men, then the injunction may reflect the sort of concern for the maintenance of good order that is voiced in 1 Corinthians 14:34–35: 'Let the women keep silence in the churches; for it is not permitted to them to speak, but let them be submitted, as also the law says. If they wish to know something, let them ask *their own* [*idious*] husbands at home; for it is shameful for a woman to speak in church.' In Titus 2:5 it is said that younger women should be 'subordinate to *their own* [*idiois*] husbands, so that the word of God might not be blasphemed'.[43] Likewise, Peter speaks of the women as 'being subordinate to *their own* [*idiois*] husbands, that indeed, if some disobey the word, they will be won without a word

[40] See Barth 1974: 611. 1 Peter 3:1, where the same wording is found (*hypotassomenai tois idiois andrasin*), is also important because it refers to wives of unbelieving husbands. Alternatively, we might view the injunction in the context of what is said about sexual immorality in Eph. 4:17–19; 5:3–12: the marriage relationship was under particular threat at Ephesus. Colossians, which has only an abbreviated household code for husbands and wives, also has much less to say on the subject of *porneia*. MacDonald (1996: 29) argues that it was a prominent theme in early pagan anti-Christian polemic that Christian women neglected their domestic duties and their responsibilities towards their husbands.

[41] See *e.g.* Bruce 1984: 384, who regards the 'exhausted' use of the pronoun as characteristic of the household code.

[42] In 1 Cor. 7:2, where the issue is sexual immorality, the same terms are used as in Eph. 5: *heautou* with 'wife' and *idion* with 'husband'.

[43] In 1 Tim. 6:1 it is clear from what follows that *tous idious despotas* refers to unbelieving masters, which makes it highly likely that a contrast is meant between these and Christian slave owners or leaders.

through the conduct of the women' (1 Pet. 3:1). As in Ephesians 5:21, the use of the participle in both these passages may suggest that subordination is as much an accepted state of affairs as an explicit requirement, and that the chief interest in the argument is in the person to whom women are subordinate. It is interesting to note that the parallel exhortation to the men in 1 Peter 3:7 also has the participle form, but it is clear that *synoikountes* ('living together') describes how things are, not how they should be; the point is not that they should live together rather than apart. It is the manner of living together, therefore, that is the point at issue – just as it is the manner of subordination, not the fact.

But whatever Paul's exact reasons for the inclusion of *idiois* in Ephesians 5:22, I would suggest that this emphasis on 'their *own* men' is not redundant and has a bearing on how we evaluate the argumentative force of these verses. For it underlines the perception that the subordinate condition of the woman is more an accepted social reality than an express apostolic regulation.

The requirement that women should be submitted to their husbands is supported by a chiastic argument in verses 23–24 in which the relationship between the husband and wife is set alongside that between Christ and the church:

A   23For a husband is head of the wife
B   as also Christ is head of the church,
C   he himself being saviour of the body;
B'   24but as the church is subordinate to Christ,
A'   so also the wives to the husbands in all things.

The development of this argument, however, has not generally been well understood and needs careful exposition at three points. First, what is the logical connection between the requirement that women should be subordinate and the assertion that the husband is head of the wife? Secondly, what is the relation between the headship of the man and the headship of Christ? Thirdly, what are the grounds for what is said about subordination in verse 24?

1. I have suggested that the specific proposition of verse 22 ('wives to their own husbands as to the Lord') has to do more with the person *to whom* a woman should be subordinate than with the action itself. Even the words 'as to the Lord' reinforce this emphasis. In view of this, the first line of the chiasmus ('For a husband is head of the wife') functions as an argument not for submission but for submission *to the husband*, whether or not there is an intended distinction from other men. Both for lexical and for logical reasons, therefore, I would say that the idea of the man's headship is not introduced as the premise for the subordination of the woman. On the one hand, *kephalē* as a

metaphor does not normally denote 'one who has authority over another'. On the other, the ideas of headship and subordination are carefully dissociated in the development of Paul's thought, and we misread the passage if we simply suppose that *kephalē* is to be interpreted by the verb *hypotassesthai* ('to be submitted or subordinated'). That the man is head is not in itself an argument for the subordination of the woman. Paul is saying no more than that since, as things stand, the woman is socially subordinate, she should respect first of all the status and dignity of the man in the household. The fear might be, for example, that subordination to the leadership of the church (*cf.* 1 Cor. 16:16) would conflict with a woman's responsibilities towards her husband.

2. The statement about the headship of the man is correlated with a parallel statement about the headship of Christ: 'a husband is head of the wife as also Christ is head of the church'. Usually this is taken to mean that Paul puts forward the headship of Christ as a model or analogy that determines the nature of marital headship (*cf.* Knight 1991: 175–176). But the verse can – and I think should – be read differently. In both the New Testament and the Septuagint the simple comparative expression *hōs kai* ('as also', 'as indeed'), which links the two statements in verse 23, is used only to assert the existence of a similarity; it is not used predicatively to present, in the manner of analogy or metaphor, one situation *in the light of* another.[44] By way of illustration consider the following statement: 'The mouth is the entrance to the body, as the door is the entrance to a house.' This says only that two things are similar or comparable. It does not draw from the function of the door any conclusions about the function of the mouth, and is quite different from: 'Just as people enter the house by the door, so food enters the body through the mouth', where the analogy is used to say or explain or infer something about the function of the mouth.

No inference, therefore, about either the logical status or the character of the man's headship is drawn directly from the headship of Christ.[45] The argument is not, for example, that a man is head of the woman *because* Christ is head of the church, or that Christ's headship is a model for, or an endorsement of, the man's.[46] That the man is head remains in the context of the passage an unsupported assertion which arguably is descriptive in function rather than normative, an observation about how things *are* rather than a prescription of

[44] See *e.g.* 1 Cor. 7:7–8; 9:5; 16:10; Rom. 9:25; Eph. 2:3; 2 Tim. 3:9; *cf.* 2 Ch. 32:19: 'He spoke against the God of Jerusalem, as also against the gods of the peoples of the earth, the works of the hands of men'; also Ps. 55:9, LXX; 2 Macc. 2:9. In Eph. 5:29 *kathōs kai* has a similar function.

[45] This does not necessarily mean that the use of the word *kephalē* to define the status of the man is not in any way determined by the description of Christ as 'head': it is the logical rather than terminological independence of the first statement that is at issue.

[46] Against Ridderbos 1975: 381; Fiorenza 1983: 270; Witherington 1988: 59.

how they *ought to be* on the basis of some theological or scriptural principle.

3. It is in verse 24 that a direct inference is made concerning the relationship between the man and the woman: 'but as the church is subordinate to Christ, so also the wives to the husbands in all things'. The correlation now has a clearly analogical and inferential function, signalled not by the simple *hōs kai* but by the correlative construction *hōs . . . houtōs kai* ('as . . . so also').[47] The point of comparison has also shifted, from headship in the first pair of parallel statements to subordination in the second, a change of emphasis that is appropriately highlighted by the adversative conjunction (*alla*) that introduces verse 24: '*But* as the church is subordinate to Christ, so also wives to the husbands in everything.'[48] Not only is Christ head of the church *but* also the church is subordinate to him – because headship has to do with prominence and pre-eminence, not intrinsically with the idea of authority over others.

The thought behind this carefully constructed line of reasoning, therefore, is not that the woman should be subordinate because the man is head. It is important to note that formally the conclusion is established on the basis of the third proposition, that 'the church is subordinated to Christ'. Paul's argument is that if Christ's headship with respect to the church – understood not in terms of authority but either of priority or of prominence – is accompanied by the subordination of the church, then it is fitting that *as long as* the man has the sort of prominence that a patriarchal society attributes to him, the woman should be submitted to him. The submission of the woman, therefore, is contingent upon the accepted social status of the man.

We cannot say for certain that Paul consciously thought of the headship of the man as provisional in this way; and it is unlikely that he would have envisaged a situation in which the man was not socially dominant. But we can maintain that his argument does not require the headship of the man to be understood in absolute terms, or the subordination of the woman to be regarded as essential to the wife–husband relationship. He has closed the door, but he appears not to have locked it. We might reasonably suppose that he allowed a logical qualification of this sort to enter into his argument because at the back of his mind he sensed or knew that a culture in which women were obliged to accept a position of social and marital inferiority was not ideal. The possibility remains that under different circumstances the language of headship and subordination might not be the most appropriate way of describing the place of men and women in the order of things.

[47] Paul appears to make use of a similar method of argument in respect of the man in the progression from the *kathōs kai* correlation in verse 25 to the *houtōs* of verse 28.

[48] The insertion of *alla* at this point has generally caused difficulties for commentators. See Abbott 1897: 166–167; Robinson 1922: 205; Lincoln 1990: 370, 372; Knight 1991: 494 n. 12.

Submission in other passages

In the corresponding passage in Colossians the subordination of the wife to the husband is expressed in simpler terms: 'Wives, be subordinate to the husbands as is fitting in the Lord' (3:18). This encapsulates the basic practical requirement of Ephesians 5:21–24 without the subtleties of argumentation that appear to acknowledge the determinative influence of the social context. The two statements do not contradict each other; it is only that in Colossians 3:18 the contingent character of the parenesis has not been made visible.

Even taken on its own it is not certain that the verse requires an interpretation in absolute terms. The expression 'as is fitting' (*hōs anēken*) presupposes a frame of reference by which the suitability of the prescribed behaviour is to be judged. But what is this frame of reference? While it may be established in very general terms in the prepositional phrase 'in the Lord', this is not obviously the function of the phrase; 'in the Lord' defines the general context in which it is appropriate to make this sort of demand, not the specific standard of reference.[49] It is likely, therefore, that Paul has in mind the appropriateness of submission according to the accepted standards of marriage: commentators have sometimes detected Stoic overtones in the phrase 'as is fitting' and this may be an example of Paul's sensitivity to the prevailing ethos.[50] The language, moreover, simply does not convey the sense of theological necessity that would compel us to treat this as an absolute and universal requirement.

The subordination or submission of women is also mentioned in two passages (1 Cor. 14:34–35 and 1 Tim. 2:11) that will be considered in detail in later chapters. In both cases it is likely that it is not specifically to *male* authority that a woman is expected to submit but to the *teaching* authority of the church. There is passing reference to the theme in Titus, where the older women are instructed to 'train the young women to be husband-lovers, children-lovers, temperate, pure, housekeepers, kind, being subordinate to their own husbands, so that the word of God might not be blasphemed' (2:4–5). As with Colossians 3:18, the contingent character of the injunction is not made explicit. But, as has been argued already, the use of the present participle and the insertion of *idiois* suggest that subordination is as much an accepted and unavoidable state of affairs as an express command. In addition, there is a manifest concern in these verses and in the pastoral letters generally for the

[49] In the same way, it could be argued that in the clause 'as it is fitting [*kathōs prepei*] for the saints' (Eph. 5:3) the standards with reference to which 'fornication', *etc.*, are considered inappropriate types of behaviour are not defined by the words 'for the saints', which determine instead the context of application, but are implicitly, and perhaps explicitly in verse 5, the standards of the kingdom of God.

[50] *E.g.* Wicker 1975: 145: 'The phrase "as it is fitting" reflects the influence of the Stoic notion of duty in discussing the mutual relations of husband and wife'; O'Brien 1982: 222.

maintenance of domestic order and stability so that the gospel is not brought into disrepute in the eyes of the world. We shall return to this theme in chapter 6, but it at least raises the question of whether subordination here is invoked as a theological universal or as a pragmatic response to the problem of maintaining the credibility of the gospel in a strongly patriarchal culture.

Conclusions

In 1 Corinthians 11:3 the headship of the man is not put forward as a theological premise on the basis of which certain conclusions are drawn about the manner in which women should worship. The central premise of the argument is rather that woman is the glory of man. On the one hand, this reflects a well-attested Jewish tradition that a virtuous wife brings glory to her husband; and, on the other, it is supported by appeal to the priority of the man in creation and to the fact that the woman was created as a helper for him. What is said about the headship of the man is essentially a restatement of this idea in a figure that does two things. It reinterprets the Jewish idea of glory in terms of social position; and it makes a play on the practical significance of 'head' for the argument and the idiomatic association of the head with certain moral and spiritual qualities.

The interpretation of *kephalē* in terms of prominence rather than authority or source is also valid for Ephesians and Colossians, though the use of the term for Christ, who is the firstborn from the dead, has also brought into view the idea of temporal priority. Paul's argument in Ephesians 5:21–24 is formulated in such a way that the headship of the man is not made the immediate reason for the subordination of the woman. The conclusion is drawn indirectly: because the church is subordinate to Christ, and since both Christ and the man are 'head', the woman should be subordinate to the man. But, as in 1 Corinthians 11:3, the headship of the man is not put forward as a theologically determined premise. Both the subordination of the woman and the headship of the man stand in the argument as accepted social realities which must somehow be reconciled with the inner reality of Christian fellowship and the headship of Christ over his church. Elsewhere, it is true, subordination is prescribed in less equivocal terms, but in Ephesians 5:21–24 Paul has taken greater pains to argue his case and in doing so has revealed something of his underlying reservations.

The designation of the man as 'head' of the woman in 1 Corinthians and Ephesians, therefore, has nothing to do with abstract relations of authority or origination. The reference is to the prominence of the man as a sociological phenomenon and, underlying this, to certain fundamental and proper differences between the sexes. In view of the fact that man has this prominence – a prominence that is comparable to that which Christ has in relation to the church – and the various privileges that society has attached to it, both men and women should behave in a certain way: men should love their wives sacrificially; women should submit to their husbands and cover their heads when they pray or prophesy. In other words, the attitudes and behaviour advocated are contingent upon the nature of the relationship between the man and the woman; and if the balance of power and sexuality between men and women generally were to change, there is every reason to think that such attitudes and behaviour should also change. The important point, however, is that this is not merely a hermeneutical presumption; it is rooted in exegesis – in the choice of language and the development of Paul's argument.

3. The outstanding ministry of women

In his letters Paul makes reference on a number of occasions to the ministry of particular, named women in the churches. For the most part these references take the form of fleeting salutations and commendations, but they are affectionate and respectful, recalling the dedicated and sacrificial participation of these women in the work of the gospel. He applies to them the same terminology of collaboration that he uses for their male counterparts: they are 'co-workers', they have laboured greatly in the Lord, they have 'struggled together' with Paul in the gospel. Nothing is said to make us think that the contribution of these women was in any way different from or inferior to that of the men. They are not explicitly subordinated in their work to male colleagues or husbands; nor are they described as having performed only the womanly duties or 'good works' that Paul advocates elsewhere (*cf.* 1 Tim. 2:10; 5:9–10; *cf.* Scroggs 1972: 293–294).

As far as the matter of status and authority is concerned, these passages raise a number of important questions. What, for example, can be inferred from the description of a small number of women in the letters as 'co-workers'? What are we to make specifically of the designation of Phoebe as *diakonos* and *prostatis* or of Junia as 'apostle' (if this is the correct way to interpret Rom. 16:7)? In this connection, we might also ask whether the registry of widows that Paul mentions in 1 Timothy 5:9 constituted anything like a formal ministry or afforded these women authority in the church. Finally, does the reference to the church in the house of Nympha (Col. 4:15) imply that certain women held positions of leadership or authority in house churches?

Although Paul names no woman as a prophet, alongside the roles of co-worker and deacon this is likely to have been one of the most important activities in which women participated. We should look quite carefully, therefore, at the nature of the prophetic ministry and the significance and authority that it had in the early church. The relation of prophecy to teaching and the question of whether women ever had a teaching ministry also need to be considered.

Women as 'co-workers'

Paul describes Priscilla and Aquila as 'my co-workers [*synergous*] in Christ Jesus, who risked their own necks for my life' (Rom. 16:3–4). It is a measure of the standing and influence of this couple that not only Paul but all the churches of the Gentiles were thankful for whatever special service it was that they rendered to him, and perhaps for their ministry generally. The tendency to put Priscilla's name before her husband's (Acts 18:18, 26; Rom. 16:3; 2 Tim. 4:19) suggests that on account either of her social standing or of her involvement in Christian ministry she was the more prominent of the two. The status of co-worker also seems to be implied when Mary and Persis are said to have 'laboured [*ekopiasen*] greatly' or when (the sisters?) Tryphaena and Tryphosa are referred to as 'workers [*kopiōsas*] in the Lord'. Euodia and Syntyche, although they had since fallen out with each other, once 'struggled together' (*synēthlēsan*) with Paul and Clement and the rest of his 'co-workers' (*synergōn*) (Phil. 4:2–3).

Two particular conclusions have sometimes been drawn from the presence of women among Paul's co-workers. The first is that these women must have worked alongside male missionaries and church workers on terms of equality, since the same terminology is used to describe their activity. E. S. Fiorenza (1983: 169–170) argues from the use of *synēthlēsan* that Euodia and Syntyche worked with Paul 'on an equal basis'.[1] Certainly, the fact that Paul raises the matter of their disagreement so publicly and so anxiously indicates that these women occupied positions of some importance in the Christian community in Philippi (*cf.* Cotter 1994: 353).[2] The second conclusion is that when Paul urged the Corinthians to submit themselves to the household of Stephanas and to 'every co-worker and labourer [*panti tō synergounti kai kopiōnti*]' (1 Cor. 16:15–16), he naturally included female co-workers in the ranks of these church leaders (*cf.* Fiorenza 1983: 169; Witherington 1988: 111). The same assumption is made with regard to 1 Thessalonians 5:12: 'But we ask you, brethren, to know those who labour [*kopiōntas*] among you and are leaders over you in the Lord and admonish you, and to regard them beyond measure in love because of their work.'

These arguments, however, have their weaknesses (*cf.* Schreiner 1991b: 218–219). First, it is unlikely that *synergos* is meant to signify a position of leadership or authority. Although this is a favourite word of Paul's and is clearly used to demarcate a particular group of people, it remains essentially a descriptive term; they are simply those who were actively and prominently

---

[1] *Cf.* Hawthorne 1983: 180: 'There is also contained in the choice of this verb more than a hint of cooperation on the same level.' Fee (1995: 395) also argues that in this context the verb implies leadership. It goes beyond the scope of Paul's argument, however, to find in the phrase 'to be of the same mind' (*to auto phronein*) a reference to the concept of 'consensual legal partnership' (Fiorenza 1983: 170). Certainly there is no thought here of an original partnership of equality in the gospel between these two women and Paul.

[2] Note also the reputation of Macedonian women for liberated ways and the significant role women had in the founding of the Macedonian churches (Acts 16:14, 40; 17:4, 12); *cf.* Hawthorne 1983: 179; Witherington 1988: 112–113; Keener 1992: 243.

engaged in the same enterprise.[3] Paul speaks of himself and Apollos as God's 'co-workers' in 1 Corinthians 3:9, but this does not mean that they had the same authority as God (*cf.* 2 Cor. 6:1; 1 Thes. 3:2). Conversely, he says to the Corinthians that he, Silvanus and Timothy do not lord it over their faith but are 'co-workers' (with them) for their joy (2 Cor. 1:24) – again the word is used descriptively and need not imply an equality of status or authority. T. R. Schreiner (1991b: 219) makes the logical point: 'All church leaders would be fellow-workers and laborers, but not all fellow-workers and laborers are necessarily church leaders.'

Secondly, there is nothing in the description of these women as co-workers that is intrinsically at odds with the assumption that they operated principally within the boundaries of ministry to women or under male authority.[4] It seems quite likely that women were among those of the household of Stephanas and other co-workers to whom the Corinthians were urged to submit, but this need not have entailed the formal subordination of a man to a woman. Priscilla had a part, perhaps even a leading part, in instructing Apollos; she and her husband took him aside or welcomed him into their home and 'explained to him more accurately the Way' (Acts 18:26). This surely says something about a woman's *potential* competence to teach within the church; but it hardly constitutes evidence that women engaged in public, authoritative teaching in the New Testament period.

Women deacons

It is not an unreasonable assumption that Phoebe, whom Paul commends so warmly in Romans 16:1–2, was the bearer of the letter to the Romans, though, as E. Käsemann (1980: 411) remarks, it is surprising that nothing is said expressly to identify her as such, especially since it was Paul's purpose to introduce her to the community.[5] She is not described as a co-worker, but as a

---

[3] Paul frequently uses the word *kopiaō* to denote both the manual work he did to support himself and his work as an apostle. But the term indicates not the particular type of work involved but the effort with which it was done and the weariness it caused.

[4] Note Käsemann 1980: 413: 'Missionary couples, to whom we have express testimony in 1 Cor. 9:5, are a Christian variation on the Jewish practice of sending out two "yoke-fellows" . . . The wife can have access to the women's areas, which would not be generally accessible to the husband.' Also Witherington 1988: 116, with reference to J. Jeremias, 'Paarweise Sendung im NT', in *Abba. Studien zur neutestamentlichen Theologie und Zeitgeschichte* (Göttingen: Vandenhoek und Ruprecht, 1966): 132–139.

[5] Keener's (1992: 239) argument that Paul cites her church offices as evidence for her fitness to clarify the content of the letter is unfounded. The thought extends no further than that she deserves to be received by the church. Note also R. Jewett's speculation that Paul intended Phoebe to be the instrument through which he would inaugurate his mission to Spain (Jewett 1988: 142–61; also Whelan 1993: 70–73).

'sister', a *diakonos* and a *prostatis*. There is nothing particularly significant for our discussion in the Christian appellation 'sister',[6] but *diakonos* and *prostatis* require explanation.

The basic question with regard to *diakonos* is whether the word is used here in a quite general sense to mean 'servant' or 'minister', or whether it signifies the more formal level of appointed ministry indicated by 'deacon/deaconess'. If the former, then the word could in principle signify a level of authority comparable to that of Paul or Apollos or any other 'servant' or 'minister' in the New Testament; if the latter, then a more restricted and subordinate role would be in view: someone devoted to 'the practical service of the needy'.[7]

The description of Phoebe as *diakonos* 'of the church in Cenchreae' is exceptional in Paul; the *diakonos* is commonly defined in relation not to a church but to the gospel (Eph. 3:7; Col. 1:23; *cf.* 2 Cor. 3:6) or to the Lord (2 Cor. 11:23; Eph. 6:21; Col. 1:7; 4:7; 1 Tim. 4:6). Paul speaks of himself as a minister of the church in Colossians 1:24–25, but still this is not in relation to a local congregation. Undoubtedly the translation 'deaconess' here is anachronistic and betrays a certain patriarchal bias,[8] but it is probably also wrong to think of Phoebe as a 'minister' in the sense that Paul applied the term to himself or to his colleagues. It is not the word *diakonos* that conveys the idea of apostolic status but the qualifier: a servant *of the gospel* or *of Jesus Christ*. To be a servant *of the church in Cenchreae* is a different matter. Here we are rather closer in usage to Philippians 1:1 ('to all the saints in Christ Jesus who are at Philippi, with overseers and deacons'), where a particular congregation is in view, or to the regulations for 'deacons' in 1 Timothy 3:8–13.[9] The inclusion of the participle 'being' (*ousan*) also suggests that Phoebe's ministry had a publicly recognized character, though nothing like the ecclesiastical office of a later period.[10] J. D. G. Dunn's conjecture (1988: 2:887) that Phoebe had a ministry

---

[6] Dunn (1988: 2: 886) makes the point that the use of *adelphē* for members of religious associations is comparatively rare, which may indicate a special respect in the use of term in the church.

[7] The phrase is Cranfield's, quoted in Witherington 1988: 113.

[8] See Fiorenza 1983: 170; Keener 1992: 239; Whelan 1993: 69. Feminine forms of *diakonos* do not appear until the fourth century (*cf.* Stiefel 1995: 447).

[9] Against Witherington 1995: 34; and Fiorenza (1983: 170–171), who argues that 'saints, overseers, and ministers . . . are ascriptions of the whole community', and that the '*diakonos*, like the *synergos* . . . is a missionary entrusted with preaching and tending churches'. But we should keep in mind that *diakonos* means 'servant' and that Paul uses it for just that reason. A missionary or church leader may be described as a *diakonos*, but, in the absence of the development of any clear technical sense, it is absurd to suggest that the word *signifies* 'missionary' or 'leader'.

[10] *Cf.* Käsemann 1980: 411. Note Sanday & Headlam: 417: 'From the very beginning of Christianity – more particularly in fact at the beginning – there must have been a want felt for women to perform for women the functions which the deacons performed for men.

of hospitality in the port city of Cenchreae is credible, particularly in view of the use of the term *prostatis*. Indeed, it is likely that she was regarded as a *diakonos* principally on account of her personal standing and the effectiveness of her ministry.

Phoebe, therefore, constitutes rather strong evidence that women served in some sort of official capacity as deacons in the Pauline churches. The only other passage that may give support to this conclusion is 1 Timothy 3:11, where Paul inserts into a catalogue of the moral and personal qualities expected of male 'deacons' a statement about 'women'. But whom exactly does he have in mind? He is clearly not referring to all women at this point (unlike 2:9, where the same construction occurs), although the qualities listed are of a very general nature.[11] But does he mean the 'wives' of deacons or a separate group of women who are recognized as deacons? (*Gynaikas* can be rendered either 'wives' or 'women', Greek having no special word for 'wife'.) As has often been the case, there appear to be no decisive arguments one way or the other; but if we must get off the fence, the latter interpretation (women deacons) is probably the more attractive option, for the following reasons.[12]

1. The absence of either the definite article ('*the* women/wives') or a possessive pronoun ('*their* women/wives') on the whole weighs against the view that these were the wives of deacons. Schreiner (1991b: 505 n. 13) argues that elsewhere in the New Testament wives or husbands are signified without the use of the possessive.[13] But in the passages he cites it is invariably the direct relationship between husband and wife that is at issue, and in most cases the article is used.[14]

2. Since *gynaikas* is unqualified, the reader must look to the context for some indication of how the referent is to be delimited. The preceding paragraph (vv. 8–10) has spoken only of 'deacons', their character, and the manner of their serving; and since there is no explicit indication that these

---

Illustrations of this need in baptism, in visiting the woman's part of a house, in introducing women to the deacon or bishop, may be found in the *Apostolic Constitutions* . . . An office in the Church of this character, we may argue on *a priori* grounds, there must have been; but an order in the more ecclesiastical sense of the term need not have existed.'

[11] See Kelly 1963: 83; Stiefel 1995: 451.

[12] See also the arguments in Hurley 1981: 230–231.

[13] Schreiner is inclined, however, to accept that there were women deacons in the New Testament churches.

[14] Col. 3:18–19; Eph. 5:22–25; 1 Cor. 7:2–4, 14, 33; Mt. 18:25. When the nouns are anarthrous, it is usually in the case of a particular instance taken as illustrative of a general rule (Mk. 10:2; 1 Cor. 7:10–11; *cf.* also Mk. 12:19; Lk. 20:28; 1 Cor. 7:1). See also Stiefel 1995: 446; Blass-Debrunner-Funk §§252, 257(3).

women are in some way dependent on the deacons, this would be the obvious category by which to interpret them.[15]

3. Although here, as in verse 8, the word *hōsautōs* ('Women *likewise* . . .') serves primarily to recall the idea of a necessary qualification in verse 2 (*dei . . . einai*, 'must be'), it inevitably keeps in sight too the thought of verse 10: 'Let them also be tested first, then if they prove blameless, let them serve [*diakoneitōsan*].' This connection suggests that it is specifically women who 'serve as deacons' who are to be 'serious, not slanderers, and so on'.

4. If these are wives, why is nothing said about the wives of overseers in the preceding paragraph (3:1–7; *cf.* Swidler 1979: 309)? The implication, surely, is that Paul envisaged women deacons but not women overseers.

But if these women are 'deacons' in their own right, why are their qualifications listed separately and not subsumed under the general instructions? There is nothing especially 'feminine' in the qualities expected of the women: indeed they correspond closely to those listed for male deacons in verses 8–9 (*cf.* Lock 1924: 40). Arguably, the separation of the women from the male deacons in these instructions suggests that Paul regarded these women in a different light from the men and perhaps that he had in mind an inferior or restricted set of responsibilities. 'Faithful in everything' may simply be an abbreviated allusion to the fuller requirement given in verse 9: 'holding the mystery of the faith with a clear conscience'. But it may also indicate that Paul was more acutely aware of the need to hold the mystery of the faith in the case of the men than the women. Certainly, verses 12–13 give the impression that the men would have had more of a governing role and greater status than the women.

This represents something of a medial position: these women, even if they are classified as deacons, are regarded as somewhat less than 'deacons' in the sense in which this term might be applied to men; but they are more than simply wives. Even if we were persuaded that Paul had in mind the wives of deacons at this point, we should still have to reckon with the fact that the moral and spiritual qualities expected of them are essentially the same as those stipulated for the men. This suggests surely that they were closely involved in their husbands' ministry and bore a significant responsibility for it – and so we approach the same medial position from the opposite direction. It is certainly likely that male roles were more clearly defined than female roles in the early

---

[15] Stiefel suggests that *gynaikas* stands as an abbreviation for *gynaikas diakonous*, 'women deacons', an expression which Clement of Alexandria uses in reference to this passage (*Stromateis* 3.6.53; Stiefel 1995: 446–447). However, the text is part of a polemic against asceticism. Clement is speaking about the value that the New Testament attaches to marriage, and the reference to *diakonōn gynaikōn*, which follows on from a discussion of the wives of apostles, must be read as a further illustration of this: it means, therefore, 'wives of deacons'.

church, and that a woman's participation in ministry was, on the one hand, circumscribed by deep-seated social expectations and conventions and, on the other, more dependent on personal influence, character and prestige. This imbalance goes a long way towards explaining the disparity apparent in Paul's teaching in this passage between male and female deacons.

Phoebe the *prostatis*

The description of Phoebe as *prostatis* has provoked considerable debate. On the basis of the usage of the masculine equivalent *prostatēs* and the apparently related verb *proïstēmi*, three basic senses seem to be available: (1) one who leads, governs, presides;[16] (2) guardian, patron, protector; (3) helper, carer.

Some have argued that Phoebe was indeed a 'ruler' or 'congregational president' of the church at Cenchreae.[17] But it is highly improbable that Phoebe would have been a 'leader of Paul';[18] nor does it add any weight to the recommendation to say that Phoebe was a ruler 'of many'.[19] Paul's argument seems quite clearly to be that the Roman Christians should 'stand by' (*parastēte*) Phoebe in recognition of what she has done in the past (hospitality, provision of material needs, protection?) for many and for Paul himself (*cf.* Schreiner 1991b: 219). In other words, *prostatis* denotes function rather than office or status and essentially corresponds in meaning to *parastēte*; they should help her not because she is a ruler but because she in some way helped others. The aorist *egenēthē* ('she became', 'she was' [a *prostatis*]) refers more naturally to a time in the past when Phoebe was of great help to a number of believers, including Paul, than to a present position of authority in the church. The term does not necessarily designate Phoebe as 'a person in charge of the charitable work of the church' (Witherington 1988: 14). It simply brings into view what she did and the means available to her by which she did it.

[16] In the LXX *prostatēs* commonly means superintendent, overseer, officer, governor, captain (*e.g.* 1 Ch. 27:31; 29:6; 2 Ch. 8:10; 24:11; 1 Esdras 2:8; 2 Macc. 3:4; Sirach 45:24).

[17] *Cf.* Swidler 1979: 310; Koester 1982: 2: 139. The Kroegers claim that 'Phoebe's office as *prostatis* appears to imply authoritative responsibility similar to that of an elder' (Kroeger & Kroeger 1992: 91).

[18] *Cf.* Murray 1965: 227 n. 1; Schreiner 1991b: 219–220. The argument that *egenēthē kai emou autou* means 'she has been appointed, actually by my own action', which is the only way out of this dilemma, cannot be sustained (Kroeger & Kroeger 1992: 91). I can find no example – certainly not in the NT – of *ginesthai* used in this way with a genitive of the agent (usually the agent has a preposition, and then not with the sense 'ordained by'); see Bauer-Arndt-Gingrich-Danker *s.v. ginomai* I.2.a. Indeed, such a construction seems quite impossible. Besides, the assertion that she had been appointed to a position of authority seems a poor ground of appeal.

[19] The argument that *proïstamenous* in 1 Thes. 5:12 signifies those who 'rule' in the church is not entirely convincing (Swidler 1979: 310–311); at least, the concomitant sense of 'care for' must always be kept in view (*cf.* Reicke 1968: 701).

If *prostatis* means 'patroness', which seems closer to the mark, the attribution need not be technically exact;[20] Paul's point may only be that she performed the role of a *prostatēs* – or *patronus*, to use the Latin equivalent – towards many people. This would give the word a somewhat figurative sense, though the simple idea of 'carer, helper' is also available. This does not mean that Paul did not consider Phoebe his social superior, which seems very likely (*cf.* Whelan 1993: 83) – only that any social or financial dependence was probably of an informal nature and, if the aorist is taken seriously, limited to a particular period in time. One could well imagine however, that by virtue of her social standing, education or wealth Phoebe exercised a *de facto* leadership role in the church, and that it was only convention or caution that kept Paul from employing more explicit terminology.

The 'apostle' Junia

In Romans 16:7 Paul sends greetings to Andronicus and *Iounian*, who are *episēmoi en tois apostolois*, 'outstanding among the apostles'. There is now quite substantial support for the view that *Iounian* is the accusative form of a woman's name – *Iounia* or Junia[21] – presumably the wife of Andronicus; and that this woman is described by Paul as an 'apostle'. The philological arguments for this are complex but are worth at least summarizing here.

1. The evidence of the early translations of the Bible, particularly into Latin and Coptic (dating from around the third and fourth centuries AD), suggests strongly that the translators understood *Iounian* to be a female name.[22] J. Thorley (1996: 23) argues, for example, that it is 'statistically 6 times more likely' that the Coptic translators understood *Iounian* to be a feminine name.

2. The masculine form *Iounias* is linguistically improbable. It is sometimes suggested that the name is a contraction of the Latin name Junianus.[23] But according to Thorley (1996: 24–25), we should normally expect the *-as* ending to be added to a consonant and the final *-i* in the stem omitted, thus

---

[20] There is some doubt whether *prostatis* could have been used at the time as an equivalent of *patrona* (Dunn 1988: 2: 888); and according to Käsemann (1980: 411) a woman could not have taken on the legal functions of a *patronus*. Against this Fiorenza (1983: 182) maintains, somewhat obscurely, that 'the motif of reciprocity stressed by Paul speaks for a juridical understanding of the title'. There is some discussion of the attraction of the role of patron for Christian women in Kraemer 1992: 155. Witherington (1995: 34–35) points to 'clear evidence that women in the Roman world could assume the legal role of *prostatis*'. Whelan (1993: 75–77) provides evidence that women acted as patrons of clubs and guilds. Barrett (1962: 283), however, says that Phoebe could not have been a *patrona* to Paul because he was born free.

[21] There is some manuscript evidence that the name was originally *Ioulias*, but this does not alter the general argument.

[22] Thorley 1996: 20–23. See also Plisch 1996: 477–478.

[23] Blass-Debrunner-Funk §125(2); Bauer-Arndt-Gingrich-Danker *s.v. Iounias*.

giving not *Iounias* but *Iounas*. In any case, whereas 'Junia' was a common Roman name, there is no literary or inscriptional evidence for the masculine form 'Junias'.[24] The only real basis for this view appears to be the presumption that Paul could not have described a woman as an apostle.

3. The opinion of the ancient commentators was that the name was *Iounia* and referred to a woman (*cf.* Fitzmyer 1992: 737–738). John Chrysostom commented: 'Why, how great was this woman's love of learning, as indeed to be thought worthy of the familiarity of the apostles!' (Migne, *Patrologia Graeca* 60, cols. 669–670). Piper and Grudem (1991: 79–80) draw attention to two ancient texts in which *Iounian* is interpreted as a male name. The first is a reference by Epiphanius (AD 315–403), bishop of Salamis in Cyprus: 'Iounias, of whom Paul makes mention, became bishop of Apameia of Syria' (*Index discipulorum*, 125.19–20). The relative pronoun *hou* ('of whom') in this statement is masculine, indicating that Epiphanius thought *Iounias* was a man. The second text is the Latin translation by Rufinus of Origen's commentary on Romans, in which the name is given as 'Junias', which is masculine. The translator, however, would have been faced with the same ambiguity that confronts the modern interpreter. Elsewhere, in fact, Rufinus uses the name 'Junia'; and we also find 'Junia' in a quotation of Origen in Rabanus Maurus, which rather tips the balance back in favour of the feminine form of the name.[25]

It is probably too much to say that it has been conclusively demonstrated that 'Junia' was a woman. Further research could well complicate matters further, and for the time being we must satisfy ourselves with the view that in all likelihood *Iounian* denotes a woman. But was she an apostle?

Paul provides four pieces of information about this couple: they were his 'kinsmen', which probably means only that they were Jews (*cf.* Rom. 9:3), though possibly that they were relatives; they had been his 'fellow prisoners'; they were 'outstanding among the apostles'; and they were in Christ before him.

The phrase 'outstanding among the apostles' is ambiguous; it could mean that these two were highly esteemed by the apostles, or that they were prominent members of the group of apostles.[26] The former sense cannot be entirely ruled out, but the majority of commentators are of the opinion that

[24] Dunn (1988: 2: 894) cites Lampe as listing more than 250 examples of Junia, and none of Junias. Piper and Grudem (1991: 79), however, found only one instance of the Greek form *Iounia* independent of Rom. 16:7.

[25] For the details see Fitzmyer 1992: 737–738.

[26] Note *Psalms of Solomon* 2:6: *en episēmō en tois ethnesin* ('. . . a spectacle among the gentiles': trans. R. B. Wright, in Charlesworth 1985: 639ff.); but the construction here is rather different. In 3 Macc. 6:1 we find 'A certain Eleazar, a man famous among (*episēmos . . . apo*) the priests of the country . . .'; but here we have *apo* rather than *en*. Chrysostom's

this phrase includes Andronicus and Junia among the apostles (*cf.* Fitzmyer 1992: 739). This was also the consensus among patristic writers. Their imprisonment may also constitute indirect evidence that they performed an apostolic function; and perhaps the comment that they were in Christ before Paul is an acknowledgment of their apostolic status. But there may be a more significant consideration: why should Paul want to commend them as well known to the apostles – rather than, say, well known among the churches (*cf.* Rom. 16:4)?[27]

In any case, it is clear that in Paul's estimation these were significant figures in the church. If they were 'apostles', then there is a strong likelihood that they were Hellenistic Jews who were among the larger group of apostles mentioned in 1 Corinthians 15:7, to whom the risen Lord appeared.[28] It is also likely, however, that they functioned essentially as a missionary couple, perhaps coming into the category of apostles accompanied by their wives, of which Paul speaks in 1 Corinthians 9:5.[29] Whether any woman would have been granted apostolic status independently of her husband is another matter. There is no ostensible reason to believe that their responsibilities would have been differentiated according to gender, but given the degree of separation between the male and female spheres of life in the ancient world, we should probably assume a similar degree of separation in the work of male and female missionaries.

The 'registry' of widows

The pastorals clearly envisage some sort of 'registry' of widows. Paul instructs Timothy, 'Let a widow be enrolled if she is not less than sixty years old, having been the wife of one man . . .' (1 Tim. 5:9; see Swidler 1979: 304–306). But these women can hardly be designated as 'members of the clergy' (Kroeger & Kroeger 1992: 91).[30] In the first place, the chief purpose of this official list was one of material support: the women to be enrolled are the 'real' widows (literally, 'widows who are widows') described in verses 3–5, who have been

---

statement is also ambiguous on this point. He says that Junia was thought worthy *tēs tōn apostolōn . . . prosēgorias*. Liddell-Scott-Jones define *prosēgoria* as 'friendly greeting, familiarity'; the verb *prosēgoreō* means 'to address'. Does this mean that she was included among the apostles, or only that she was familiar to, or addressed by, the apostles?

[27] Sanday and Headlam (423) argue that '*episēmos*, lit. "stamped," "marked," would be used of those who were selected from the Apostolic body as "distinguished," not of those known to the Apostolic body, or looked upon by the Apostles as illustrious'.

[28] Dunn 1988: 2: 894–895. Käsemann (1980: 414) prefers to think of them as 'delegates of Antioch'.

[29] *Cf.* Piper & Grudem 1991: 81. According to Clement of Alexandria the apostles took their wives with them as 'fellow ministers', through whom 'the Lord's teaching penetrated into the women's quarters without scandal' (*Stromateis* 3.6.53).

[30] *Cf.* MacDonald 1996: 75, 157–166.

left all alone (5:5), who have no family to support them (*cf.* vv. 4, 8), and who therefore should be 'honoured' (v. 3).[31] The church should not be burdened with the needs of widows who have family to support them, but should be free to give aid to widows in genuine need (v. 16).

Nothing is said explicitly about the duties of these widows. The list in verse 10 (good deeds, the rearing of children, hospitality, washing the feet of the saints, giving relief to those who suffer, and so on) stipulates the qualifications for the order, not the responsibilities that come with it, and certainly nothing is said that might give the impression that these women had any sort of authority in the church. What Paul expected of them is stated in verse 5, that they should continue in 'supplications and prayers night and day'. Such women, being relatively free from domestic obligations, might busy themselves instead with 'the things of the Lord, so as to be holy both in body and in spirit' (1 Cor. 7:34).

The church in her house

There is some slight evidence in Paul's letters that women were involved in the leadership of house churches.[32] The strongest indication is the reference to the churches that met in the house of Aquila and Prisca, both in Ephesus (1 Cor. 16:19) and in Rome (Rom. 16:4–5). It is very difficult to avoid the impression that this couple had joint oversight – 'overseers' *de facto* if not *ex officio* – of these groups of believers.

It has sometimes been suggested that the expression 'Chloe's people' (*tōn Chloēs*, 'those of Chloe') in 1 Corinthians 1:11 is a reference to members of the church that met in Chloe's house.[33] But while Chloe must certainly have held a position of considerable prominence, it is more likely that Paul means members either of her household or of her business (*cf.* Fee 1987: 54). The expression, which implies a certain sense of ownership or dependence, seems an inappropriate designation for a church.

The reference in Colossians 4:15 to 'Nympha and the church in her house' is beset with textual difficulties similar to those presented by the name *Iounian* in Romans 16:7. Here too, as it would have appeared in the original unaccented text, the name *Nymphan* could be the accusative form either of the feminine name 'Nympha' or of the masculine name 'Nymphas', which would probably be a contraction of a longer name such as 'Nymphodorus' (see Lightfoot 1879: 242). This ambiguity has left its mark on the textual tradition in the divergence between the feminine and masculine forms of the pronoun in the attached phrase: some manuscripts read 'and the church in *her* house',

---

[31] *Cf.* verses 17–18, where the 'double honour' accorded to the elders who rule well is almost certainly to be understood in financial terms.

[32] On the nature and organization of the New Testament house churches from this perspective see Witherington 1988: 104–111; Fiorenza 1983: 175–184.

[33] *E.g.* Swidler 1979: 296; Kroeger & Kroeger 1992: 92.

while others 'and the church in *his* house'. A third tradition has 'and the church in *their* house'. J. B. Lightfoot (1879: 243) maintains that the use of the plural *autōn* ('their') in the last instance constitutes a well-known classical construction signifying 'Nymphas and his friends'; alternatively, we might suppose that the reference to 'Nymphas' implicitly includes his wife.

The matter is not easily resolved. The plural variant ('in *their* house') is not generally considered by modern commentators, but cannot be ruled out entirely. The argument against the contraction that Thorley used with regard to *Iounian* does not apply in this case since the stem of the name (*nymph-*) does not end with *-i*. In favour of the feminine form is the fact that it would be the more difficult reading and therefore the one more likely to have been modified in the process of transmission.[34] On the other hand, it is possible that the copyist changed *autou* to *autēs* simply because he was unfamiliar with the masculine name.[35] Even if we could be certain that a woman is spoken of here, there is still the question of whether she exercised authority over the church that met in her house. Perhaps the most plausible scenario is that Nympha was a wealthy widow who opened her home to one of the groups of believers in the city. As such she no doubt enjoyed some influence, but one imagines that formally the church was guided and instructed by male elders.[36]

Finally, in the introduction to his letter to Philemon Paul writes: 'To Philemon our beloved co-worker, and the sister Apphia, and Archippus our fellow soldier, and to the church in your house . . .' (Phlm. 1–2). Does this indicate that Paul regarded Apphia as one of the leaders of the church along with Philemon and Archippus? Although the possessive pronoun 'your' is singular and presumably refers to Philemon, the obvious reason for singling out Apphia would be that she had some natural connection with Philemon and was part of his household. Archippus may be mentioned only because he is a 'fellow soldier', but there is a strong possibility that he too is related to Philemon. That Apphia is called 'sister' is at least a mark of affection, but it also serves to distinguish her from both Philemon ('our co-worker') and Archippus ('our fellow soldier');[37] and the fact that she is just '*the* sister' and not '*our* sister' further diminishes her significance.

---

[34] *Cf.* Fiorenza 1983: 51; Bruce 1984: 183 n. 64.

[35] Note Lightfoot 1879: 243: '*autēs* has arisen from the form *Nymphan*, which *prima facie* would look like a woman's name, and yet hardly can be so.'

[36] Fiorenza (1983: 177) quotes a passage form Juvenal's *Satires* (6.511–541), which speaks of the woman who is a 'religious fanatic' and who 'will fill the house with a coven of worshippers of strange oriental deities'. But the 'minister' is still male, just about: 'an enormous obscene eunuch, revered because he castrated himself with a jagged hunk of glass'.

[37] Cotter (1994: 351) is probably wrong in thinking that 'sister' is the more prestigious of the three appellations. The fact that the term is also applied to Phoebe (Rom. 16:1) certainly does not mean that these two women held similar positions or wielded similar influence.

We do not know whether women such as Priscilla, Nympha and Apphia were ever regarded as 'elders' in their churches. Given the Jewish background of the role and the lack of any clear indication that the early church diverged radically from Judaism in this, it seems unlikely. It has sometimes been argued that *presbytidas* in Titus 2:3 signifies women elders;[38] but the word simply means 'old women', just as *presbytas* in verse 2 means 'old men'. These two groups are clearly correlated and if Paul was thinking of 'elders', he would have used the standard word *presbyteros* for the men, as in 1:5 (*cf.* Schreiner 1991b: 220–221).

At this juncture we might also consider a more general issue related to the participation of women in church leadership. Especially in the pastoral letters a significant analogy is drawn between management of the church and management of a household. This raises the question of to what extent changes in the way a household (or for that matter any other social institution) is typically managed should, as a matter of course, lead to parallel changes in the way a church is managed. If the analogy is purely a figure of speech, then such an inference is not permissible. But there is a more practical correspondence – overseers, for example, should be able to manage their own households well (1 Tim. 3:4) – which suggests that it is appropriate to model the church after the family *as it is* or *as it works best*, which may not coincide with ancient practice. In other words, as long as the form of church governance does not compromise the gospel or the sovereignty of God, it should ideally reflect the best *locally acceptable* model of household management. While this sort of adaptation to cultural standards certainly needs careful handling, it at least allows women to assume the sort of authority within the church that they exercise within the family.

Women prophets

There is no question that women prophesied publicly in the Pauline churches.[39] This is an unavoidable inference from 1 Corinthians 11:5: 'every woman praying or prophesying with the head unveiled dishonours her head'. Prophecy, moreover, was a prominent element in the worship and ministry of the churches. Although some distortion in the overall picture arises from the exaggerated significance of this and related charismata in the church at

---

[38] *E.g.* Kroeger & Kroeger 1992: 91. The Kroegers maintain that Titus 2:3 'requires female elders to be "worthy of the priesthood"', taking *en katastēmati hieroprepeis* to mean something like 'in behaviour like a priestess' (rather than simply 'reverent in behaviour'). But even if the phrase could be understood in this way, to say that someone should behave reverently 'like a priestess' is not at all the same as saying that they belong to the priesthood. In 4 Macc. 9:25 a young man on the point of martyrdom is described as *ho hieroprepes neanias;* this does not mean that he belonged to the priesthood.

[39] *Cf.* Grudem 1988: 216–217. Note also Acts 2:17–18; 21:9.

Corinth, there is sufficient indication that it was accepted as a normal part of life in the Spirit in other churches (Rom. 12:6; Eph. 4:11; 1 Thes. 5:19; 1 Tim. 1:18; 4:14).

Prophecy appears to have been ranked highly among the gifts. Given the polemical character of Paul's teaching in 1 Corinthians 12 – 14, we should not place too much emphasis on the ordering of gifts in 12:28 ('first apostles, second prophets, third teachers . . .'), which probably has more to do with the subordination of prophecy to the authority of the apostles, and of the Corinthian prophets to the authority of Paul in particular, than with the existence of an intrinsic hierarchy within the gifts (*cf.* Fee 1987: 619–620). It is also important to recognize that what is said about prophecy in 1 Corinthians 14 has to do basically with the contrast between intelligible speech and speaking in tongues. Paul elevates the status of prophecy over unintelligible, perhaps ecstatic, speech: 'the one prophesying is greater than the one speaking in tongues, unless he interprets' (1 Cor. 14:5). Nevertheless, he makes it quite clear that prophecy is to be included among the 'greater charismata' and is a gift to be eagerly sought (1 Cor. 12:31; 14:1, 39). 'Do not quench the Spirit,' he urges the Thessalonians. 'Do not despise prophesyings' (1 Thes. 5:19–20).

The content of prophecy is accessed through faith (Rom. 12:6) and may find its origin in 'mysteries' (1 Cor. 13:2). Prophecy entails the revelation of things that would otherwise be hidden to the human mind (*cf.* 1 Cor. 14:6, 26, 30), though it provides only an imperfect and partial access to whatever truth it seeks to make known (1 Cor. 13:9). The 'mysteries' that are uncovered through prophecy range from the 'mystery' of Christ (Eph. 3:5) and, presumably, the events of the end times, to more practical and personal matters.[40] The purpose of prophecy is the 'up-building, encouragement and consolation' of the whole community (1 Cor. 14:3–4). Prophecy may be a 'sign' of judgment to believers, but an unbeliever may also find the secrets of his heart disclosed through prophecy and come to acknowledge the presence of God in the church (1 Cor. 14:22–25).[41]

The authority of New Testament prophecy

If we ask what sort of authority prophets had in the church, we notice in the first place that there was a significant degree of subjectivity and judgment involved both in the pronouncement and in the reception of prophetic statements. The gift of prophecy is to be exercised 'according to the proportion of faith' (Rom. 12:6). Each prophetic utterance is not to be

---

[40] Paul speaks of going up to Jerusalem 'according to revelation' (Gal. 2:2), which some would see as a reference to the prophecy of Agabus in Acts 11:28 (*cf.* Longenecker 1990: 47).

[41] Grudem (1988: 174–175) takes prophecy to be a sign of 'blessing' to believers, but this entails a confusing and improbable change in the meaning of the word *sēmeion* in the course of the verse (*cf.* Fee 1987: 682–683).

accepted uncritically but is to be weighed by others in the congregation (1 Cor. 14:29; 1 Thes. 5:21). Prophecy may be interrupted if a revelation is given to someone else (1 Cor. 14:30). It is subject to the control of the prophet and within the context of worship should be undertaken in an orderly manner (1 Cor. 14:31–32). It was not always clear whether someone had an authentic prophetic gift (1 Cor. 14:37).

We should be careful, however, not to underestimate the significance of prophets in the New Testament churches. Prophecy must have been an extremely influential activity, not just at the local level but also in shaping the theological basis for the nascent Christian faith – and the assumption must be, though there is little direct evidence for it, that women contributed at both levels.

Prophecy appears on occasion to have been of considerable – perhaps decisive – importance in giving direction to the church. This is particularly clear in Acts (11:27–30; 13:1–2; 21:10–11), but it is also apparent, for example, in the circumstances surrounding Timothy's ordination to ministry; it was 'in accordance with the former prophecies about you' that Paul entrusted to Timothy the responsibility for maintaining sound doctrine in Ephesus (1 Tim. 1:18; *cf.* 4:14).

More remarkable is the significance attributed in Ephesians to prophets, along with apostles, both in the foundation of the church and in the revelation of the 'mystery of Christ':

> So then you are no longer strangers and outsiders, but you are fellow citizens with the saints and members of the household of God, built upon the foundation of the apostles and prophets, Christ Jesus himself being the cornerstone . . . (Eph. 2:19–20).

> In accordance with this you can, as you read, perceive my understanding of the mystery of the Christ (which in other generations was not made known to the sons of men as now it has been revealed to his holy apostles and prophets by the Spirit), that the Gentiles are fellow heirs and one body and partakers together in the promise in Christ Jesus through the gospel . . . (Eph. 3:4–6).

The view that Paul is speaking here of the Old Testament prophets can be quickly dismissed; Ephesians 3:5 clearly distinguishes between these prophets and people of earlier generations, and 4:11 lists apostles and prophets among the gifts given by Christ to the church.[42] So these are contemporary prophets; but does Paul mean all those with the gift of prophecy, or is the group restricted in some way? Grudem (1988: 49–62) argues, for example, that the

---

[42] *Cf.* Grudem 1988: 47; Lincoln 1990: 153.

phrase 'apostles and prophets' refers only to one group of people, that is the apostles who are also prophets. The arguments are worth assessing, for if Grudem is wrong and it can be shown that Paul saw the gift of prophecy as in some way foundational to the church and instrumental in the revelation of the gospel, then, in principle at least, we have reason to think that women's voices contributed to this formative process.

Grudem maintains, in the first place, that it is perfectly acceptable grammatically to suppose that the phrase *tōn apostolōn kai prophētōn* in Ephesians 2:20 and the similar phrase in 3:5 refer to a single group of 'apostle-prophets'. The same construction occurs, he suggests, in 4:11: *tous . . . poimenas kai didaskalous*, 'pastor-teachers' (1988: 49–51, 57). But the omission of the article before the second term is not enough to indicate that the two words have the same referent; it points only to a close association between them.[43] The apostles and prophets are seen as one group, but within that group they remain distinct. Moreover, there is no indication elsewhere that the apostles were characteristically regarded as or functioned as prophets.

Secondly, while it is true that there is no direct evidence that prophets received the revelation of the inclusion of the Gentiles, this is hardly a decisive argument. It points only to the dominance of the apostles in the New Testament record. There are no recorded examples of non-apostles casting out demons, but this does not prove that this was a unique apostolic prerogative.

Thirdly, Grudem argues that the metaphor of the 'foundation' really makes sense only if it describes a closed group, which could not have included the ever-expanding ranks of the prophets. But Paul is thinking of the role of the apostles and prophets not in hierarchal but in functional terms: it is not because they belong to a privileged group but because they have understood and articulated the mystery of the gospel that they constitute the foundation of the church. Grudem's understanding of the metaphor of a 'foundation' is pedantic and too much under the control of a bureaucratic and authoritarian conception of the church.[44]

Similar objections could be raised to the fourth argument, that Paul and his

[43] *Cf.* Blass–Debrunner–Funk §252; Lincoln 1990: 250. J. Jeremias (1968: 497) says that the absence of the article before *didaskalous* shows that 'the pastors and teachers form a single group', not in the sense that they are identical but because 'they both minister to the individual congregation'. In Acts 15:2 we find *tous apostolous kai presbyterous*, where the reference is clearly to distinct, though perhaps overlapping, groups (*cf.* 16:4); elsewhere, however, the article is repeated (15:4, 6, 23), with the effect of differentiating more clearly between the two groups.

[44] The argument that the prophets must be excluded from the foundation of the church for the sake of consistency with the image of Rev. 21:14 is unconvincing (Grudem 1988: 58), not least because this would also exclude Paul himself from the foundation. The image of the 'foundation' is used in different ways in the New Testament (*cf.* also 1 Cor. 3:10–11).

readers could not have thought of the prophets in the churches as part of the foundation of the universal church. There is no reason why the inclusive nature of salvation in Christ should not have been grasped and articulated at a local level. Indeed, it would be entirely appropriate if Paul had meant to embrace both the universal and the local character of the church in this reference to the apostles and prophets. Again, we need to remind ourselves that Paul includes the prophets here not for who they are are but for what has been revealed to them.

This reminder essentially provides a response to Grudem's remaining arguments, which is that there is no reason to think that Paul meant *all* those with the gift of prophecy to be included in this category. His point is only that in so far as the mystery of the gospel has been revealed to and through prophets in the church, the 'prophets' as a group have been instrumental in expressing and clarifying the foundational truth, according to which Jews and Gentiles may now belong to the same household of God. The issue, moreover, is not one of 'authority' but of revelation; these verses are not an argument for the leadership role of prophets in the church but rather highlight the central historical importance of revelation in defining the new terms of membership in the household of God. The mystery that has been revealed has its own authority and does not depend on the existence of a special class of apostle-prophets authorized to speak 'God's very words with absolute divine authority', as Grudem (1988: 56) puts it. Arguably, this obsession with the question of authority, this preoccupation with the *status* of the messenger rather than the *content* of the message, has constituted one of the biggest obstacles to the participation of women in ministry – if not to the ministry of the gospel itself.[45]

Perhaps the strongest argument, however, for the view that in Ephesians 3:5 Paul has in mind both apostles and prophets and not simply the 'apostle-prophets' is to be found in his earlier prayer for the Ephesians, that God 'may give to you a spirit of wisdom and of revelation in knowledge of him, the eyes of your heart being enlightened, that you might know what is the hope of his calling, what the wealth of the glory of his inheritance among the saints' (1:17–18). Here he speaks of an understanding of the nature of the inheritance bestowed upon the Gentile Ephesians to be gained through 'a spirit (or the Spirit) of wisdom and of revelation'. Although Paul mentions only the charismata of wisdom and revelation, we are very close to the thought of 3:4–6 that it has been *revealed* to the apostles and prophets that the Gentiles are *fellow heirs* with Jewish believers. The important point is that in Paul's view this knowledge is generally available to the church by revelation through the Spirit; it does not need to be transmitted through the

---

[45] Note Fee's discussion of Grudem's thesis (Fee 1994: 891–892).

apostles.[46] This lends quite weighty support to the opinion that this fundamental truth was perceived and articulated in the churches not by the apostles alone but by many with the gift of prophecy.

Nevertheless, care should be taken in translating these observations into the modern context. If prophets, including women prophets, had such a foundational significance in the New Testament, it was because the revelation of the gospel was new and not well understood. The basic teaching of the church about salvation could be drawn from Scripture and from the traditions about Jesus. But to an extent that is probably difficult for us to grasp from a modern perspective, both the apostles and the churches would have been dependent on prophetic insight into the 'mystery of Christ' and the reconciliation of Jews and Gentiles in Christ's body.[47] Although the teaching of the apostles was undoubtedly normative in this process, Paul acknowledges that many with the gift of prophecy discerned and expressed, probably in the context of worship, the same things. But this situation has changed. The revelation given to the apostles and prophets has since been enshrined in the New Testament and, while Christ himself remains the cornerstone, it is this collection of documents that now definitively articulates the mystery of Christ and which therefore, in practice, constitutes the 'foundation' for the church. So in one important respect at least, the contemporary prophet does not have the same status as his or her New Testament forebears. If this provokes murmurings of discontent among the prophetic community, then we must again ask which is the more important, the messenger or the message?

Prophecy, teaching and authority

One other question specifically raised by the participation of women in prophecy has to do with the relation of prophecy to teaching. Grudem is of the opinion that teaching has greater authority than prophecy for governing the church, and that this explains 'why Paul was perfectly willing to have women as well as men prophesy in the assembled congregation, while he restricted the authoritative teaching functions to men only' (1988: 146).[48] The question of why Paul did not allow women to teach will be considered in the following chapters. We may, however, at this point, make some observations about the relative importance of prophecy and teaching.[49]

It is significant, in the first place, that it is prophecy and not teaching that Paul opposes to speaking in tongues in 1 Corinthians 14. The reason for this,

---

[46] See also 1 Cor. 2:6–16.
[47] Note, for example, the significance of Peter's vision in Acts (10:9 – 11:18).
[48] *Cf.* Schreiner 1991b: 217.
[49] *Cf.* Keener 1992: 244–245.

presumably, is that he saw prophecy as a gift that was widely available to the congregation (*cf.* 'if *all* prophesy . . .' 14:24) and therefore a more realistic alternative to speaking in tongues than teaching, which would have been restricted to the biblically literate, perhaps to the better educated, and possibly to men. Nevertheless, while Paul could have demanded more attention to the teaching of Scripture or the apostolic tradition in order to counteract the Corinthians' predilection for unintelligible and unedifying utterances, he encouraged them instead to prophesy.

The statement in 1 Corintians 14:3 that 'the one who prophesies speaks to people for upbuilding and encouragement and consolation' also gives prophecy considerable practical importance in the life of the church. The church can 'learn' from prophecy (1 Cor. 14:31). Prophets are always listed ahead of teachers (Rom. 12:6–7; 1 Cor. 12:28–29; Eph. 4:11; *cf.* 1 Cor. 14:6) and are given greater prominence in the work of upbuilding described in Ephesians 4:11–16.[50] When Paul mentions the various contributions that might be made to the worship service, nothing suggests that he thinks of 'teaching' as more significant or more authoritative than 'prophecy' (1 Cor. 14:6, 26). It is true that in some of the letters (notably Colossians and the pastorals) very little is said about prophecy and there is a much greater emphasis on teaching as a guiding force in the life and faith of the church. But the reason for this is to be found not in any supposed superiority of teaching over prophecy but in the particular threat to the gospel posed by false teachers at this time in Colossae and Ephesus (*e.g.* Col. 2:6–23; and generally in the pastorals).

One is led, therefore, to consider whether the elevation of teaching above prophecy does not simply reflect a bias towards the cognitive dimension of faith and, conversely, a prejudice against the more 'intuitive' gifts such as prophecy. Paul does not appear to accept such an imbalance. The exposition of Scripture appears as only one element in the process of building up the church, and there is no reason to attribute to it a higher value than gifts of prophecy or revelation. Paul seems at least as eager that believers should prophesy as that they should be taught the Scriptures; and this surely suggests that there should be a balanced approach to the governance of the church, not the subordination of prophecy to teaching. These very different gifts are better regarded as complementary activities. Whereas teaching has to do with what is established, prophecy tackles the unknown. Teaching entails the exposition of Scripture and the transmission of traditions; prophecy reveals things that have been hidden – the mystery of Christ, the secrets of a person's heart, the purposes of God for his people.[51] Teaching may give the church doctrinal

---

[50] *Cf.* Witherington 1988: 107; Keener 1992: 244.
[51] *Cf.* Friedrich 1968: 854.

stability, but prophecy testifies to the dynamic, interactive presence of God in the congregation (*cf.* 1 Cor. 14:24–25) in a way which teaching cannot.

Both are essential for the edification and guidance of the church; but, equally, both are open to abuse. Teachers have misinterpreted and misapplied Scripture no less than prophets have misrepresented the mind of God. The church, as Grudem (1988: 74–79) points out, does not uncritically accept the revelations made by prophets. But does it uncritically accept the pronouncements of Bible teachers? According to Paul's instructions to Titus, an overseer should 'hold to the sure word as it is taught, so that he might be able both to exhort by sound instruction and to refute those who contradict it' (Tit. 1:9). This critical attention to what is taught corresponds, in effect, to the 'weighing' of prophecy by the church. A false antithesis is created, therefore, if we contrast the authoritative words of Scripture with the uncertain utterances of the prophets. The correspondence is, on the one hand, between the words of Scripture and the mysteries revealed to the prophet, and on the other, between the exposition of Scripture by the teacher and the articulation and evaluation of what has been revealed to the prophet. But then if a prophecy is weighed and judged to be from the Lord, why should it be regarded as any less authoritative, within its particular sphere of relevance, than any other 'word of the Lord'?[52] Prophecy cannot contradict or amend Scripture, and must be consistent with Scripture; but if prophecy has any validity at all in the contemporary church, it is because it provides access to areas of knowledge and understanding that are beyond the competence and authority of the Bible teacher.

To say that the gift of teaching carries an authority that prophecy lacks is not, therefore, an explanation of why Paul allowed women to prophesy but not to teach.[53] Authority in the church rested with the elders and overseers. Some of these were teachers (*e.g.* 1 Tim. 5:17), but some, in all likelihood, were prophets (*cf.* 1 Tim. 4:14); and in making their decisions they would surely have listened to the voices of other teachers and prophets within the body of Christ. In that case, we must assume that prophecy was no less influential than teaching both in the edification and in the governance of the New Testament church.[54] Although inevitably, given the foundational

---

[52] Even the authority of the Old Testament prophets rests on the fact that their words were judged, in the light of history and the traditions of Israel, to be trustworthy: if nothing else, they were 'weighed' in the process of canonization. Grudem (1988: 17–22) argues, however, that in the Old Testament it is not the prophecy but the prophet that is evaluated.

[53] Against Grudem 1988: 144–145; *cf.* Schreiner 1991b: 217.

[54] There is perhaps evidence in the book of Revelation that prophets were extremely influential in the early church and constituted, contrary to Grudem 1988: 56–57, a distinct, authoritative group (Rev. 10:7; 11:18; 16:6; 18:20, 24); note Caird 1984: 129. Moreover,

significance of the New Testament itself for the church today, the sphere of the teacher has been enlarged, there is still no reason why the prophetic voice should not be allowed its own proper authority.

Women teachers

It is not impossible that Paul envisaged women contributing the sort of 'teachings' in the context of worship that he mentions in 1 Corinthians 14:6, 26. The context and format appear to be much the same as for prophecy and other gifts, and there is no immediate reason to think that Paul excluded women when he wrote, 'Whenever you come together, each one has a song, a teaching, a revelation, a tongue, an interpretation . . .' (v. 26). If this 'teaching' is undertaken as the recognized expression of a spiritual gift, then there may be no conflict with the prohibition against women speaking in 1 Corinthians 14:34–35. And if this sort of teaching is seen as a spontaneous contribution to worship rather than as the exercise of a more formal 'office', it may still be possible to reconcile it with the prohibition against women teaching in 1 Timothy 2:12. One gains in the pastorals a much stronger impression that teaching is an organized element in the worship service and the responsibility of specific individuals: teaching is more clearly the province of elders and overseers (1 Tim. 3:2; 5:17; Tit. 1:9); Timothy and Titus are specifically commissioned to teach (1 Tim. 4:11, 16; 6:2; Tit. 2:1, 7); the apostolic traditions are to be entrusted to 'faithful men' (*pistois anthrōpois*) who will continue the work of teaching (2 Tim. 2:2). It is only in the pastorals, moreover, that Paul expressly identifies himself not just as an 'apostle' and 'preacher' but also as a 'teacher' (1 Tim. 2:7; 2 Tim. 1:11). Possibly it is teaching in this capacity, rather than the more charismatic *modus operandi* found in 1 Corinthians 14 and perhaps Colossians 3:16, that is disallowed for women in the pastorals. The instruction that women should learn in 1 Timothy 2:11 also suggests that in these verses Paul has in mind women participating in organized teaching sessions rather than listening to impromptu expositions during the course of the worship service.

If these conjectures are correct, then perhaps the most important conclusion to be drawn would be that women should not teach *under certain circumstances*. In other words, it becomes essentially a practical question, albeit a complex practical question that must take account of the context and manner in which teaching is undertaken, the woman's competence to teach, and the social acceptability of women teaching. Here, however, I anticipate issues that will be discussed at length later.

---

the 'prophecy' contained in the book has an intrinsic authority *as prophecy* (1:3; 22:18–20); no claim is made for its apostolic status (against Grudem 1988: 44).

Apart from this, the (extremely limited) evidence of Paul's letters is that women taught other women and children. Timothy was probably instructed in the faith by his mother and grandmother (2 Tim. 1:5; 3:14–15).[55] The older women are to be 'teachers of what is good [*kalodidask-alous*], that they might train the young women to love their husbands and children, to be temperate, pure, housekeepers, kind, being subordinate to their own husbands, so that the word of God might not be blasphemed' (Tit. 2:3–5). There is no basis for the view of R. C. and C. C. Kroeger (1992: 81) that this instruction was 'not necessarily limited to women', particularly since in verse 6 Titus is separately given the responsibility of urging the 'younger men to control themselves'. It should also be noted that it is not doctrine but domestic responsibility that the women are to teach. The Kroegers also suggest that Paul has women as well as men in mind when he says in 2 Timothy 2:2 that the task of teaching is to be entrusted to faithful 'persons' (*anthrōpoi*) (1992: 82). It cannot be inferred from the use of this term rather than the unambiguously masculine *andres*, 'men', however, that Paul is using the term inclusively. There is a tendency for *anthrōpos* to be understood as male if circumstances require (*cf*. 1 Cor. 7:1; Gal. 5:3), and it would have to be shown on other grounds that in this instance the inclusive rather than the specific masculine sense is the more likely one. In any case, the verse offers no support for the view that Paul expected women to teach men.

Conclusions

Although some uncertainties remain, the evidence that we have considered in this chapter makes it abundantly clear that women had a highly visible, active and influential part to play in the life and work of the early church. First, as co-workers in the gospel some women were closely associated with Paul's missionary and church-planting activities; indeed, the term 'co-worker' tells us more about their relation to Paul than about what they actually did. It is important to keep this perspective in mind. The point is not so much that they did what Paul and the other apostles did as that they worked *with him*. Secondly, the ministry of a woman deacon was probably at this stage only an extension of the 'good works' expected of all pious women (*cf*. 1 Tim. 5:10). Nevertheless, it was a position that carried with it some honour and respect. Thirdly, charismatic participation in worship provided an area in which women might make a significant contribution. For all Paul's enthusiasm for prophecy, the prophets remain a curiously anonymous band in his letters; but

---

[55] It is not necessarily the case that Timothy was taught the Scriptures by these women (against Kroeger & Kroeger 1992: 82). It is also clear that Timothy received much of his instruction from Paul (2 Tim. 1:13; 2:2; 3:10).

in principle at least, women with the gift of prophecy could have had a determinative role in establishing the ideological foundations of Christianity.

Setting aside for a moment the preoccupation with the issue of authority, we may discern in these fleeting allusions a very appealing model for the unselfconscious, collaborative ministry of women. There is no apology for their work, no apparent segregation, no fussy attempt to demarcate their sphere of activity, no overt subordination of their work to male authority. How this activity meshed with the patriarchal structures that prevailed both in society generally and in the church is difficult to judge. Perhaps developments took place over time which led to a more formalized and exclusively male pattern of leadership. Perhaps the pragmatic 'authority' of socially and spiritually influential women continued to operate alongside the official government of the church by elders and overseers. Perhaps it was those women who had already to some extent been liberated from the constraints of patriarchy – unmarried or divorced women, widows, women of independent financial means – who most naturally took up these roles. In any case, we should not think that attitudes towards the participation of women in ministry were uniform throughout the church, or even that Paul himself worked according to a simple and consistent policy. It is not easy to reconcile the generous acceptance of female participation in the work of the gospel with those passages which impose quite rigorous restrictions on the involvement of women in church life. To these we must now turn.

4. Exposing the undercover agents
1 Corinthians 11:3–16

We have taken 1 Corinthians 11:3–16 as quite conclusive evidence that women prayed and prophesied vocally and publicly in the Pauline churches, and that Paul approved of the practice. That women prayed in church, moreover, appears to be confirmed by 1 Timothy 2:9. Although the verb 'to pray' (*proseuchesthai*) from verse 8 is not repeated and it is possible that Paul is speaking only of how women should adorn themselves (*kosmein heautas*), there are some indications that in the first place he is instructing women how to pray.[1]

First, the main theme of thze passage is prayer (vv. 1–2), not dress, and Paul's argument as a whole appears more coherent if we suppose that his concern in verses 9–10 is with the manner in which women pray rather than purely with their deportment. The very general terms in which men and women are addressed is explained by the fact that potentially *any* man or woman in the congregation might pray – or even perhaps that the congregation prayed collectively. Secondly, the verb *proseuchesthai* occurs before *tous andras* ('the men') in verse 8, giving the impression that it is also presupposed, in conjunction with *boulomai* ('I want'), before *gynaikas* ('women') in verse 9. Thirdly, there is a close parallelism between what is said about the men and what is said about the women, which also suggests that the same activity is in view:

> I want, therefore, the men to pray in every place
> > lifting up holy hands
> > > without anger and argument;
>
> likewise women
> > in seemly deportment
> > > with modesty and sobriety . . .[2]

The question that concerns us in this chapter, however, is: how should women pray? 1 Timothy 2:9–10 sets out two closely related requirements.

---

[1] Note Dibelius & Conzelmann 1972: 45.

[2] This reading assumes that *kosmein* introduces a new clause parallel to the implied *proseuchesthai*, developing the idea of the woman's appearance in prayer introduced by the words *en katastolē kosmiō*. *Cf.* Dibelius & Conzelmann 1972: 44–45.

The first is that in her demeanour and dress (the word *katastolē* may signify both) a woman should express decency, modesty and sobriety. The exact nuances of Paul's terminology here are difficult to pin down, but these are conventional female virtues and it is clear that Paul is anxious to avoid some of the conventional hazards associated with a woman's appearance.[3] The second is that a woman's attractiveness – and quite possibly Paul is thinking of the attention that a woman would draw to herself when she stood to pray or prophesy – should derive not from such external adornments as hairstyle, jewellery or expensive clothes, but from her reputation for performing 'good works'. Probably we should assume that Paul did not intend this as an absolute ban on the trappings of fashion; the thought is not couched in such terms. The basic argument is the positive one: 'I want women to adorn themselves through good works'; and these should be more apparent to onlookers in the congregation than anything that is worn on the outside.

No doubt decency and modesty of dress included the covering of the head that according to 1 Corinthians 11:5 is expected of a woman who prays or prophesies, since this was the practice in the churches of God (1 Cor. 11:16). At least this gives us a point of introduction to the much more difficult discussion in this passage concerning how women should pray and prophesy.

With uncovered head . . .

> *Pas anēr proseuchomenos ē prophēteuōn kata kephalēs echōn kataischynei tēn kephalēn autou.* [5]*pasa de gynē proseuchomenē ē prophēteuousa akatakalyptō tē kephalē kataischynei tēn kephalēn autēs.*
>
> Every man praying or prophesying having something on the head dishonours his head. [5]But every woman praying or prophesying with the head unveiled dishonours her head . . . (1 Cor. 11:4–5).

A woman who prays or prophesies, presumably in the context of corporate worship, with her head uncovered (*akatakalyptō tē kephalē*) 'dishonours her head' (v. 5). This statement, which parallels a seemingly antithetical assertion about the man in verse 4, raises three basic questions.

1. The first has to do with the practical circumstances. Is it only when a woman prays or prophesies that she should cover her head, or does the regulation apply throughout the time of worship? It is possible that Corinthian women remained covered while seated but were in the habit of uncovering themselves when they stood to pray or prophesy. But why did Paul not simply

---

[3] Kelly (1963: 66) argues that foremost in Paul's mind here is not female extravagance but 'the impropriety of women exploiting their physical charms on such occasions, and also the emotional disturbance they are liable to cause their male fellow-worshippers'. Philo says that a harlot knows nothing about 'modesty, chastity, and prudence' (*kosmiotēs, aidōs, sōphrosynē*: *De Specialibus Legibus* 3.51).

say that women should be covered at all times when the church was gathered for worship? Instead, he is quite emphatic that it is in connection with the activities of praying and prophesying that the issues discussed in this passage become critical (vv. 4–5, 13). The language of verse 6 ('if a woman does not cover herself . . .') makes more sense if Paul is thinking of an occasion when women should actively assume a head-covering in contrast to a prior condition of being uncovered. Otherwise, we might have expected him to say, 'If a woman *uncovers* herself . . .' 1 Timothy 2:9 may also imply that a woman's 'braided hair' would have been visible during the service, and so presumably uncovered. We should probably assume, therefore, that women were expected to cover their heads only when they stood to pray or prophesy.

2. Does the phrase 'dishonours her head' refer to her own head or, figuratively, to the man? Probably there is a deliberate ambiguity here; the woman dishonours both herself and her husband who is her 'head' – or dishonours her husband by bringing shame upon herself.[4] The language of male–female relations in the passage, however, is very general and it may be that not just the marital relationship but the broader interaction between the sexes is in view.[5] For a man the converse is true; a man dishonours his 'head', that is Christ, if his head is covered while he prays or prophesies (v. 4).

3. What exactly does Paul mean by the phrase *akatakalyptō tē kephalē*? It has been argued by a number of scholars that it is not the uncovered head but the unbound hair of a woman that is causing problems. J. Murphy-O'Connor, for example, is propelled in this direction in the first place by his assumption that the phrase *kata kephalēs echōn* (literally, 'having down the head') in verse 4 describes men with long hair, which is associated with effeminacy and homosexuality in the ancient world. He quotes Pseudo-Phocylides 212–214 (possibly 30 BC–AD 40): 'Long hair is not fit for men, but for voluptuous women. Guard the youthful beauty of a comely boy, because many rage for intercourse with a man.'[6] If, however, verse 4 is speaking of hair rather than

---

[4] Grammatically and logically the sense 'dishonours her husband' may be primary (*cf.* Hooker 1964: 410–411). While the head may represent the whole person in certain idiomatic expressions or formulae (typically in the form 'upon or over the head'), in the present context it is impossible to escape the identifications established in verse 3 (*cf.* Fee 1987: 506 and n. 56; against Murphy-O'Connor 1980: 485). But this does not preclude the other sense as a play on words.

[5] *Cf.* Fung 1987: 185–186; Wilson 1991: 448–449; Witherington 1995: 235.

[6] *Cf.* Philo, *De Specialibus Legibus* 3.37; Musonius Rufus, discourse XXI; Epictetus, *Discourses* 3.1.1. See Murphy-O'Connor 1980: 484–487; *cf.* Barrett 1971: 257; note also Scrogg's suspicions: Scroggs 1972: 297 and n. 38. The significance of what is said about the man in this passage is probably contrastive and illustrative; homosexuality is in the background, but it is not the issue at Corinth. The connotation of effeminacy may be relevant to verse 14, but Paul does not make the connection between long hair on a man and the issue of head-covering (v. 4) in the way that he does for the woman.

head-coverings, the same must be true for verse 5.[7] The immodest behaviour of both men and women at Corinth is attributable, in Murphy-O'Connor's view, to the 'over-realized eschatology' of many in the church. They had drawn the conclusion, on the basis of the sort of egalitarian ideology found in Galatians 3:28, that in Christ there was no longer any distinction between male and female and they were therefore at liberty to erase the outward marks of sexual difference.

Other scholars have provided different rationales for the same basic interpretation. L. A. Jervis (1993: 235–238) finds the source of the erroneous Corinthian theology in Hellenistic Jewish ideas of the 'genderless' image in which man was originally created, such as are found in Philo. E. S. Fiorenza's argument (1983: 227) is that the women of Corinth were praying and prophesying with their hair unbound and dishevelled in a manner reminiscent of the 'ecstatic worship of oriental divinities'. It is likely, she thinks, that this behaviour was reinforced by the special egalitarianism of the Isis cult, which was prominent at Corinth: 'For the Christian women at Corinth, such loose and unbound hair was a sign of their ecstatic endowment with Spirit-Sophia and a mark of true prophetic behaviour' (1983: 227).[8]

There is some linguistic support for this view, but there are also weighty objections to it. It is true that in certain Old Testament contexts the Hebrew thought of 'loosening' (*pāra'*) the head is translated in the Septuagint as an uncovering of the head (*akatakalyptos* in Lv. 13:45, LXX, *apokalyptō* in Nu. 5:18, LXX). But the implication here is probably only that the hair is loosened or made untidy by the uncovering of the head.[9] The basic meaning of *akatakalyptos* is still 'uncovered', and the present context does not demand that it be understood otherwise. On the contrary, Paul speaks quite unambiguously in verse 6 of a woman covering her head, while 'a man ought not to cover his head' (v. 7). In these verses the verb *katakalyptō* can only refer to the act of covering; a man with short hair could hardly bind it up. It is worth noting, moreover, that in discussing Roman customs (many of them connected with worship), Plutarch repeatedly uses similar language (*epikalyptō, apokalyptō, aparakalyptos*) in various contexts to refer to the covering or uncovering of the head by men and women (*Quaestiones Romanae* 266–267).

It has also been argued that *peribolaion* in verse 15, which is usually translated 'cloak', specifically denotes something which is 'wrapped around'. Therefore, since a woman's long hair has been given to her in place of such a 'wrapper',

---

[7] Murphy-O'Connor 1980: 488–490; *cf.* Fiorenza 1983: 227 and 239 n. 66; Padgett 1984: 69–86; Gritz 1991: 85–86; Jervis 1993: 241. Prior to Murphy-O'Connor similar arguments were presented by Martin 1970: 231–234; Hurley 1973: 190–220.

[8] But note evidence in Witherington 1988: 81 that women participating in the Isis cult at Corinth had their heads covered.

[9] *Cf.* Philo, *De Specialibus Legibus* 3.60. For further discussion see Schreiner 1991a: 126.

Paul must mean that she should have her hair wrapped around her head, perhaps in plaits as indicated in illustrations of the period.[10] But this, too, is somewhat forced. If a woman has been given long hair in place of a garment that is wrapped around the body (*cf.* Ex. 22:26–27; Is. 59:17), it is because, symbolically at least, long hair covers not just the head but the body also.[11]

The argument that *kata kephalēs echōn* ('having down the head') in verse 4 refers to men with long hair may also be contested. On the one hand, while the phrase is obscure and probably idiomatic, we are not left completely in the dark. In Esther 6:12, LXX, it is said that Haman 'went home mourning *kata kephalēs*', which translates a Hebrew expression meaning 'with head covered' (*waḥªpûy rōs'š*). Plutarch relates how Scipio the Younger, not wanting to be recognized, began to walk through Alexandria 'having the *himation* down the head' (*kata tēs kephalēs echōn to himation; Moralia* 200F); the *himation* was part of the toga, or perhaps a shawl.[12] On the other hand, there is a logical objection. The passage presupposes that the manner of head-covering was essentially optional: a man or woman could *choose* whether or not to cover his or her head. Whatever 'having down the head' means, it was something that was open for any man in the congregation to do, not just those who might have had long hair.

Finally, Murphy-O'Connor (1988: 268) maintains that 'no Jew of the period would have entertained the notion that to pray with covered head was to obscure the image of God, or that it was in any way shameful'. This is based on a Mishnaic tradition, going back to Exodus 28:4, 37–38 and Ezekiel 44:18, which states that priests wore a turban. But to cover the head with a turban is not the same as to wear a shawl or to cover the face or the whole head, which is perhaps the significance of the phrase 'having *down* the head'. While the priest's turban may signify honour, a man may also cover his head in such a way as to indicate shame. When the harvest in Judaea failed because of drought, Jeremiah said that 'the farmers were ashamed, they covered their heads [*epekalypsan tas kephalas autōn*]' (Je. 14:4, LXX).

Paul, then, is speaking of something on the head, not unbound hair. But what type of head-covering is in view is difficult to decide. On balance, both the internal and external evidence suggests that this was not a full-facial covering but either a shawl or a cloak pulled up over the hair, leaving the face exposed.[13] On the one hand, it is the woman's hair that is her 'glory' and so, by

[10] Murphy-O'Connor 1980: 489; 1988: 269.

[11] Note also Fee 1987: 529 n. 25; Martin 1995: 233.

[12] *Cf.* Fee 1987: 506–507. Witherington (1995: 233) also cites Plutarch, *Aetia Romana* 267C; *Vitae Decem Oratorae* 842B; *Pyrrhus* 399B; *Pompeius* 640C; *Caesar* 739D.

[13] *Cf.* Fitzmyer 1957: 54; Wilson 1991: 447, 458; Keener 1992: 22; Witherington 1995: 237. See also Hurley 1981: 254–271.

implication, only the hair needs to be covered; and although the precise significance of verse 15 is not altogether clear, the reference to the *peribolaion*, a garment that is 'thrown around' to cover the body, may also point to the idea of a cloak or mantle pulled up over the hair.[14] And how could Paul have proclaimed in 2 Corinthians 3:18, albeit figuratively, that 'we all with unveiled face' behold or reflect the glory of the Lord if women covered their faces when praying or prophesying? On the other hand, while it was not unusual for women in the Graeco-Roman world to wear a head-covering during religious ceremonies, there is little evidence that they commonly covered their faces.[15] It is perhaps more likely that Jewish women would have kept their faces hidden during worship, but there is no real evidence that this was the issue at Corinth.

Is the covering of the woman's head when praying and prophesying primarily of religious or of domestic significance? Roman women appear to have covered their heads when sacrificing,[16] but it seems unlikely that Paul would have conceived a very close parallel between Christian prayer and prophecy and Roman sacrifice. In the context of 1 Corinthians 11:3–16 the head-covering draws its significance from the relation of the woman to the man; a woman should cover her head because she is the glory of the man and would otherwise dishonour the man. Whether we can draw the inference, however, that in the absence of men women would have prayed and prophesied uncovered is unclear. Paul's rhetorical question in verse 13 ('Is it fitting for a woman to pray to God uncovered?') may suggest that there is something in the nature of prayer, and not just in the male–female relationship, that makes the head-covering for women culturally appropriate. But it could simply presuppose the context of mixed worship.

From a Jewish perspective the woman's head-covering certainly signified her married status (Keener 1992: 25). There must undoubtedly have been connotations of modesty, chastity, faithfulness, respectability, attached to the wearing of a head-covering.[17] These, moreover, are the sort of qualities that

---

[14] *Cf.* Fee 1987: 528; Witherington 1988: 82–83.

[15] Witherington 1988: 81; Keener 1992: 22. Oriental customs inevitably were more conservative. Dio Chrysostom at the beginning of the second century AD records among several long-standing customs practised at Tarsus a convention 'which prescribes that women should be so arrayed and should so deport themselves when in the street that nobody could see any part of them, neither of the face nor of the rest of the body, and that they themselves might not see anything off the road' (Dio Chrysostom, *Discourses* 33.48, Loeb).

[16] *Cf.* Witherington 1988: 81; Keener 1992: 28; Witherington 1995: 233. Note Plutarch, *Quaestiones Romanae* 266F, 267A.

[17] Tomson writes: 'an unmarried girl could occasionally go out with her hair uncovered, but the head covering of the married woman when appearing in public was an essential feature of the "Law of the Jews", violation of which was considered very serious' (Tomson 1990: 133; *cf.* Jeremias 1969: 359–360). Note also Gn. 24:65.

should embellish the prayer of a woman according to 1 Timothy 2:9. More importantly for this study, for a woman to go in public with her head uncovered would arouse the obvious suspicion that she desired to attract male attention to herself (Keener 1992: 29; 1993: 585).

D. B. Martin (1995: 233–236) pursues a more complex thesis, arguing that in Graeco-Roman culture the veil signified both the protection of a woman's sexuality and the protection of society from the dangerous sexual power of women.

> The practice of veiling served several functions: it made visible the ideological notion that the female was a possible locus of dangerous invasion; the veil itself provided protection against invasion and penetration, both for the woman and by extension for the social body; the veil therefore protected the woman's body from the dangers posed by external forces and protected the social body from dangers posed by the female body itself. We can thus see that the veiling of women in church, especially when they were in an extra exposed state of inspiration, functioned as prophylaxis against external penetration and pollution for the community, the church, the body of Christ (1995: 248).

This is an intriguing perspective, but it bursts the exegetical seams of the passage. It is not Paul's argument that the head-covering *protects* the woman in any way; its purpose is quite simply to *conceal* that which should not be seen when a woman is praying or prophesying. Nevertheless, Martin's discussion of the significance of veiling illustrates the complexity of a practice that had such diverse connotations within the various religious and cultural traditions of the ancient world. In the end, as with so many details in this passage, it is practically impossible to identify a single, unambiguous meaning. Within the passage the significance of the head-covering has to do with the dilemma of the woman whose status must still be defined in relation not only to God but also to her husband. This becomes apparent in the next stage of the argument.

Dishonour and glory

... *hen gar estin kai to auto tē exyrēmenē.* [6]*ei gar ou katakalyptetai gynē, kai keirasthō; ei de aischron gynaiki to keirasthai ē xyrasthai, katakalyp-testhō.* [7]*anēr men gar ouk opheilei katakalyptesthai tēn kephalēn eikōn kai doxa theou hyparchōn; hē gynē de doxa andros estin.*

... for it is one and the same as one having been shaved. [6]For if a woman does not cover herself, let her also have herself shorn; but if it is shameful for a woman to have had herself shorn or to have been shaved, let her cover herself. [7]For indeed a man ought not to cover

the head, being the image and glory of God; but the woman is the
glory of a man (1 Cor. 11:5b–7).

The disgrace incurred by a woman praying or prophesying with her head
uncovered is no different, in Paul's view, from the disgrace of being shaved or
having her hair cut short (vv. 5b–6).[18] Indeed, if a woman refuses to cover
herself, it would be an appropriate mark of her moral condition for her hair to
be cut. If that is unacceptable, then of course she should cover herself. Various
suggestions have been made as to why short hair or a shaved head might have
been shameful for a woman. Such an appearance might be associated with
lesbianism.[19] Or Paul's point may simply be that a woman with short hair has
become 'mannish'. There appears to be no evidence that either prostitutes
generally or a particular class of prostitutes had short hair or shaved their
heads;[20] but the adulteress was sometimes humiliated by having her hair cut
off.[21] According to Plutarch, 'in Greece, whenever any misfortune comes, the
women cut off their hair and the men let it grow' (*Quaestiones Romanae* 267B,
Loeb). Probably the precise connotations are unimportant. In the context of
the argument as a whole and of verse 14 in particular, the more significant
thought is that a woman who cuts off her hair has removed that which
constitutes her feminine 'glory' and has thereby defaced the 'glory' of her
husband.

This idea of 'glory' (v. 7) constitutes the pivot around which the contrasting
practices of men and women turn. A man should not cover his head because
he is the 'image and glory of God'; a woman, on the other hand, should cover
herself because she is the 'glory of a man'.[22] The woman, in other words,
brings glory to the man. What Paul means by this is partly explained by the
argument from nature that he puts forward at the end of the passage (vv. 13–
15). It is no more appropriate for a man to cover himself than for him to have
long hair; nature itself teaches that such a thing would be disgraceful. But for a
woman her long hair is a source of 'glory' – or, we may deduce from the
context, of 'honour'. There are two sides to this, closely related: on the one
hand, a woman's hair was the supreme manifestation and representation of her

---

[18] For the distinction between the two verbs used here see Fee 1987: 511 n. 82.

[19] *Cf.* Lucian, *Dialogoi Hetairikoi* 5.3 (*cf.* Murphy-O'Connor 1980: 490; Fee 1987: 511
n. 81).

[20] Fee 1987: 511 n. 80; Keener 1992: 24–25. In ancient Judaism, according to Tomson, 'a
shaven woman was repugnant and could be divorced' (Tomson 1990: 135).

[21] Dio Chrysostom, *Discourses* 64.3.

[22] 'Image' is included in the case of the man in order to indicate the creational basis for the
idea that man is the glory of God; it is omitted in the case of the woman not because she is
less than the image of God but because 'glory', not 'image', is the main element in Paul's
argument. It is the relationship of the woman to the man that is at issue and Paul cannot say
that she is the 'image' of the man (*cf.* Hooker 1964: 411).

virtue (*cf.* Keener 1992: 29); on the other, symbolically at least, her hair was a covering for her nakedness, her shame.

The precise point of the assertion that a woman's long hair has been given to her 'in the place of a cloak' (*anti peribolaiou*) has for the most part eluded commentators. The simplest explanation, if it could be demonstrated, would be that Paul here is thinking of the *peribolaion* as a typically male garment – or of the significance of the *peribolaion* for the man – and one that represents for the man this two-sided concept of honour. In place of the *peribolaion*, therefore, which visibly expresses the 'glory' of the man, the woman has her long hair. Perhaps the difference between these two symbols of honour reflects the assignment of the man to the public sphere, where he would wear his cloak, and the woman to the home, where her hair would be exposed.

The importance of the *peribolaion* for the man is indicated in the Septuagint: if a man's coat is taken as a pledge, it must be returned before sundown, for this is his only *peribolaion*, the only covering (*himation*) of his nakedness (Ex. 22:25–26; *cf.* Jb. 26:6). But there is also the positive aspect: fringes were to be attached to the four borders of a *peribolaion*, presumably as a mark of dignity (Dt. 22:12). The word is used in Enoch 14:20 for the 'gown' of God, the 'Great Glory', and in the *Letter of Aristeas* 158 for the clothes of Jewish men, which are said to bear a 'distinguishing mark as a reminder' of divine blessing. The verb *periballō* ('to throw around, to clothe, put on') is often used for the covering of nakedness (2 Ch. 28:15; Is. 58:7; Ezk. 18:7, 16) or with strong connotations of shame (*e.g.* Pss. 70:13, LXX [=71:13]; 108:19, 29, LXX [=109: 19, 29]; La. 4:5; Mi. 7:10) or glory (*e.g.* Ezk. 16:10; Baruch 5:2).

A. Padgett (1994: 187) has argued that there is a contradiction between this verse and verses 5–6, and infers from this that the first part of the passage (vv. 3–7b) represents not Paul's views but those of the Corinthians, which Paul then goes on to refute. His point is that Paul appears to be saying in verse 15 that a woman does not need a head-covering because she has been given her long hair instead. How then can he himself have argued that woman should cover their heads in worship? But when Paul says that the woman's long hair has been given to her in place of a cloak, his point is that her hair embodies the same fundamental values – honour, status, glory, dignity, and the concealment of nakedness – as a cloak does. In certain circumstances, especially when a woman becomes the centre of attention when she stands to pray and prophesy, some of these values – those associated with glory, beauty, sexuality, and so forth – come into competition with the glory of God, and then it becomes appropriate for the woman's hair to be concealed.[23]

---

[23] Note also Is. 59:17; Je. 15:12, LXX. Payne, following Hurley, thinks that *peribolaion* signifies a prayer shawl, in place of which a woman has her long hair (Payne 1986: 128; *cf.* Hurley 1981: 168–171, 254–271). But this interpretation makes sense only if we suppose

Behind the conception of the woman as the glory of the man we can probably also discern the traditional Jewish theme of the righteous wife, which is found, for example, in Proverbs 11:16, LXX: 'A gracious wife brings glory to her husband, but a woman hating righteousness is a throne of dishonour.' Other examples might be cited: 'a virtuous woman is a crown to her husband' (Pr. 12:4); women 'bring glory to men, and without women men cannot be' (1 Esdras 4:17).[24] These texts illustrate a basic cultural assumption, that a woman's appearance and behaviour reflect upon her husband either to enhance or to impair his reputation. C. S. Keener (1992: 36) writes: 'The idea that a wife could shame her husband by her behaviour . . . was common in the ancient world.' For the second-century BC Jewish sage ben Sirach this was axiomatic: 'Better is the wickedness of a man than a woman who does good; and it is a woman who brings shame and disgrace' (Sirach 42:14, RSV). The sensitivity to dishonour in marriage is also illustrated by a first-century BC Egyptian marriage contract: 'Apollonia is not to stay away for a night or a day from Philiscus' household without Philiscus' knowledge, nor is she to live with another man or to cause ruin to the common household or to bring disgrace on Philiscus in whatever brings disgrace to a husband.'[25]

Exactly what sort of behaviour would have been regarded as either virtuous or reprehensible in the context of the Corinthian community, and just why it was considered so inappropriate for a woman to pray or prophesy with her head uncovered, are not easy questions to answer. Perhaps the complexity and obscurity of this passage betray the fact that the more powerful motives driving Paul's argument were emotional and instinctive, connected with deep-seated cultural fears and expectations, rather than theological. Perhaps, too, as we shall see later, these were not merely Paul's concerns. We might also ask to what extent Paul's instincts were heightened by an anxiety about the public reputation of the church. In a recent study of pagan reaction to early Christianity M. MacDonald (1996: 146) argues that his teaching about honour and shame in this passage reflects an awareness of how the community of

---

that the problem with the men at Corinth was that they wore their hair long and unbound *and* wore a prayer shawl.

[24] *Cf.* also Sirach 7:19; 26:1–3, 13–16; 36:22–24; 40:19. Note *Gen. Rabbah* 47.1 (17:15): 'And God said unto Abraham: As for Sarai thy wife, thou shalt not call her name Sarai, but Sarah [i.e. Princess] shall her name be (XVII, 15). It is written, *A virtuous woman is a crown to her husband* (Prov. XII, 4). R. Aḥa said: Her husband was crowned through her, but she was not crowned through her husband. The Rabbis said: She was her husband's ruler. Usually, the husband gives orders, whereas here we read, *In all that Sarah saith unto thee, hearken unto her voice* (Gen. XXI, 12).' Hooker (1964: 411 n. 1) draws attention to Rashi on Is. 44:13, who interprets the phrase 'the beauty of a man' (the reference is in fact to a carved idol) as signifying the woman, who is the glory of her husband. On this theme generally see Keener 1992: 38–39; Moxnes 1993.

[25] *P. Tebtunis* I 104, translated in Lefkowitz & Fant 1992: 90.

believers was perceived by outsiders. 'Behaviour that might be judged by the outside world as shameful for women could dishonour men and bring disgrace on the whole community.' Such a motivation is more apparent in 1 Corinthians 14:34–35 and is certainly operative in 1 Timothy, but it may be implicit in the language of this passage too.

At issue, no doubt, in general terms is the perception and management of sexuality within the community. The words of ben Sirach may express something of the concern that prompted Paul's instructions: 'Turn away your eye from a beautiful woman, and do not consider another's beauty; many have been deceived by the beauty of a woman, and herewith love is kindled as a fire' (Sirach 9:8).[26] By standing to pray or prophesy a woman put herself on display, and one can imagine that in certain cases at least the effect on the church was less than edifying. Perhaps elaborately adorned hair advertised wealth and status. Perhaps, too, there was a fear that Christian women praying and prophesying with their heads uncovered might be too closely associated in the popular mind either with cultic prostitution or with the frenzied behaviour of celebrants in the mystery cults.[27]

But what the passage points to most clearly is not so much the negative overtones, whether sexual or religious, as the rather ambiguous problem that arises from the *prominence* that women would acquire through their participation in worship in this way. This is important because it brings us back to the meaning of the *kephalē* metaphor. On the one hand, the woman who prays or prophesies with her head uncovered acquires a prominence that conflicts with the prominence of the man, and so her action becomes a source of dishonour. On the other, she displays her own glory (her long hair), which is also, by virtue of the nature of the sexual relationship, the glory of the man, and this conflicts with the glory of God, which alone should be exhibited in worship. By covering her head a woman conceals her 'glory' (that is, her hair, her attractiveness, her sexuality, her reputation, her status), thereby making herself less conspicuous in relation both to the man and to God.

Authority on the head

> *Dia touto opheilei hē gynē exousian echein epi tēs kephalēs dia tous angelous.*
>
> For this reason the woman ought to have authority over the head because of the angels (1 Cor. 11:10).

---

[26] *Cf.* Sirach 25:21; 42:12; 1 Esdras 4:18–19. In the story of Esther, Queen Astin is said to have dishonoured king Artaxerxes because she contradicted or disobeyed (*anteipe*) him (Est. 1:16–22, LXX). The real offence, however, is the dishonour rather than the disobedience.

[27] *Cf.* Gill 1990: 255–256; Witherington 1995: 12–13.

Traditionally this has been taken to mean – by a sleight of indirect reference that is not entirely clear – that the head-covering is a sign of the man's authority over the woman.[28] But the expression *exousian echein epi* ought to mean that the woman herself has authority over her own head.[29] It should be possible, therefore, to give a more positive slant to this verse.

It could be that Paul regards the head-covering as a symbol of the woman's authority to prophesy. M. D. Hooker (1964: 415–416) has argued, in an article that has stood the test of time better than many, that the woman now takes part in prayer and prophecy – contrary to Jewish custom – because 'a new power has been given to her'. 'The head-covering which symbolizes the effacement of man's glory in the presence of God also serves as the sign of the *exousia* which is given to the woman; with the glory of man hidden she, too, may reflect the glory of God.'[30]

In *Recovering Biblical Manhood and Womanhood*, Schreiner (1991a: 135–136) has put forward a number of objections to Hooker's interpretation, which are worth examining because they are also used to reinforce the view that this passage teaches the subordination of women.

1. Schreiner argues that 'for this reason' (*dia touto*) at the beginning of verse 10 connects the verse with verses 8–9, which 'clearly show that the issue is a woman's proper role relationship to a man'. But within the passage, as we have seen, this relationship is interpreted in terms neither of authority nor of rule but of 'glory': verses 8–9 are an explanation of the statement in verse 7 that 'the woman is the glory of a man'. It is in any case doubtful that *dia touto* points back only to verses 8–9. The argument of the preceding passage centres on the two ideas of dishonour and glory, and more probably it is to one or both of these themes that *dia touto* refers.[31]

---

[28] *Cf.* Tomson 1990: 136; Schreiner 1991a: 134. Fitzmyer (1957: 52–53) hesitantly supports a devious interpretation first proposed by G. Kittel, that *exousia* corresponds to an Aramaic word (*šltwnyh*), which in turn is equivalent to a Hebrew word (*šbys*), the root of which (*šlt*) is identical to a common Aramaic verb meaning 'to have power, dominion over'. It is difficult to believe that many at Corinth would have understood a pun which involved knowledge of both Hebrew and Aramaic.

[29] See Fitzmyer 1957: 50–51. In Sirach 33:20 we find the statement: 'Do not give your son and wife, your brother and friend, authority over you [*mē dōs exousian epi se*] in your life.' But this presupposes the active sense, 'someone has authority over you'. Fung (1987: 189) proposes a mediating position: 'the *exousia* might be the authority which the woman exercises by virtue of her relationship to the man as her head – thus a kind of "delegated" authority'.

[30] *Cf.* Fiorenza 1983: 228.

[31] It is possible that verses 7 and 10 form a chiasmus (not simply a parallelism as Schreiner [1991a: 135] argues), within which verses 8–9 function as a parenthetic explanation for the statement that the woman is the glory of a man, in which case verse 10 rests directly on the assertion that 'the woman is the glory of a man'. Verse 7, however, is not necessarily incomplete because it connects with the closing words of verse 6: 'let her be veiled'.

2. The argument that the word 'ought' (*opheilei*) suggests obligation rather than freedom simply misses the point. The woman is free to prophesy but she is under an obligation (for the reasons given by Hooker) to do so with her head covered.[32] She *ought* to wear a head-covering as a sign of her authority to speak.

3. It is said that if verse 10 refers to the woman's own authority, it contradicts the whole tenor of the passage and specifically the argument of verse 3, which 'shows that Paul wants women to wear a head covering in order to show that they are submissive to male headship'. But this is not the meaning of the *kephalē* metaphor. It is not even clear that 'Paul wants women to wear a head covering because such adornment appropriately distinguishes women from men'. Women adopt the head-covering not to differentiate themselves from the men (though that is an inevitable side-effect) but to conceal the woman's glory and avoid disgrace. The point is almost the opposite of what traditionalists generally maintain: the head-covering serves to *conceal* the thing that in a public gathering would most noticeably distinguish a woman from a man – her long hair. What is shameful about women worshipping with uncovered heads is not that they are behaving like men,[33] but that by displaying their most visible and most attractive female attribute they bring glory – and so, paradoxically, disgrace – to the man.

4. What verses 11–12 correct is the possible inference from verse 9 in particular, and from the argument about 'glory' in general, that the Christian woman is dependent upon, or owes her existence to, the man. This has no bearing on the meaning of verse 10, however it is interpreted, and certainly does not require us to agree with Schreiner that Paul has just reasserted his belief that 'women should wear head coverings as a sign of submission to male headship'. Once again, ideas of subordination are simply alien to the context.

5. Schreiner's last three points may conveniently be considered together. In principle there is no reason why Paul should not have used the word *exousia* to signify a 'sign or symbol of authority': an author can do more or less what he likes with a word as long as it is intelligible within the context. But the fact that the Bauer-Arndt-Gingrich-Danker lexicon recognizes the possibility of a symbolic meaning is neither here nor there. On the one hand, 1 Corinthians 11:10 is the only instance of such a usage considered; on the other, the lexicon does not answer the question of whose authority exactly is symbolized. The example of the statue of the mother of King Osymandias, which had 'three kingdoms on its head, signifying that she was both daughter and wife and mother of a king' (Diodorus Siculus 1.47.5), provides no support for

---

[32] According to Foerster (1964: 574) the word *opheilei* signifies inner obligation rather than external compulsion: 'It is thus very probable that in this verse Paul is referring to the moral duty of a woman and not to any kind of imposed constraint.'

[33] *Cf.* Schreiner 1991a: 131. See also Keener 1992: 35–36.

Schreiner's argument, for the point is certainly not that these three kings had authority over the mother. In the end, we come back to our basic quarrel with Schreiner, which is that the passage simply does not make it clear that the issue in verse 10 is the man's authority over the woman.[34]

Hooker's interpretation, therefore, cannot yet be dismissed.[35] But we might still ask whether the word *exousia* is in fact meant to be read, in whatever way, as an indirect reference to the woman's head-covering. To put the question the other way round, is the head-covering really a sign of authority? After all, the basic significance of the head-covering in this passage surely lies in the fact that it *covers* something, not that someone (woman or man) is endowed with authority. Two other approaches, therefore, might be considered. One is to suppose Paul's point to be that since by nature the woman is the glory of the man, she should take responsibility for the appearance of her head in the context of public worship. In Baumert's view (1996: 188), the expression means 'to maintain control over the head, to hold the head in order'. But here the thought is less that a woman should take responsibility for her appearance than that she should not allow her hair to become loosened and unkempt. Either way the interpretation strains the sense of *exousian echein*.

A second possibility that has not, as far as I can tell, been seriously investigated is that the women are on Paul's side in this dispute. It has usually been assumed that the women of Corinth were radical feminists straining at the leash of Christian propriety. But what if they had adopted an essentially conservative stance?[36] Let us suppose that it is the men at Corinth who had been insisting that women should pray and prophesy, like the men, with their heads uncovered as a recognition of their new spiritual equality in Christ. If the women – or some of the women, perhaps particularly Jewish women in the congregation – had resisted this departure from custom, it may be that Paul's intention in verse 10 was principally to endorse the woman's right to choose to remain covered.[37] Then the

---

[34] Against also Fitzmyer 1957: 51.

[35] Martin (1995: 245–246) argues that 'in Greco-Roman culture, as in many modern veiling cultures, the veil a woman places upon her head functions as the proper "authority" over her person – an authority that she herself, to some extent, controls.' However, 'this cannot be allowed to mask the ideological significance of the veiling (at least in ancient culture) as symbolizing and effecting the subordination of the female'.

[36] Plato has the Athenian express the view that women could never be persuaded 'to take food and drink publicly and exposed to the view of all'. 'The female sex would more readily endure anything rather than this: accustomed as they are to live a retired and private life, women will use every means to resist being led out into the light . . .' (Plato, *Laws* 6.781C, Loeb).

[37] Note Hall 1990: 40: 'Paul's purpose would seem to be to establish the right of a woman prophet to do what she wished with her own head – i.e. in this context, to keep it covered'; but Hall develops the insight in relation to the debate over the nature of inspiration.

statement 'a woman ought to have authority over her head' would mean exactly what it says.

The verse, however, cannot be understood as a simple accession to the woman's right to choose. Paul does not regard the head-covering as optional. The argument of verse 10 is still that the woman ought to keep her head covered, but the form of expression indicates that this was in fact what some, perhaps all, of the women in the church wished to do. The language reflects the fact that Paul's preference and the custom of the other churches is also the preference of the modest women of Corinth.

This gives a rather different complexion to the rest of the passage. In the first place, it would make most sense if *dia touto* ('for this reason' or 'because of this') embraced not only the theme of the woman as the glory of man but also the idea of dishonour and shame (vv. 5–6) – not an unreasonable assumption given the logical and rhetorical importance of the statement in verse 5. In effect, it refers back to the whole argument in vv. 3–9, but within this argument the leading proposition is the one given in verse 5. So the underlying thought would be: because it is shameful for a woman to pray and prophesy with her head exposed, she should have the right to cover herself.

Then, it appears that certain aspects of the passage may be better understood if we imagine that Paul's argument was framed chiefly to persuade men rather than women. The programmatic statements of verse 3 can be read as a reminder to the men that in certain important respects men and women are not the same and should not be required to behave or dress in the same manner. The fact that the statement 'the head of every man is Christ' occurs first may be explained by Paul's wish to emphasize the significance of the ensuing argument for men in the congregation.[38] The woman whose head is uncovered dishonours herself, which is why the women have objected to the proposed changes; but she also dishonours her husband, in which case it may be that verses 5b–6 are deliberately framed as an appeal to male sensibilities: 'Would you want your wife to be shaved or shorn?'

One especial bone of contention in the exegetical debate has been the question of why so much space is given in the passage to the question of male attire and hairstyle.[39] But if we suppose that it is principally the men who favour the uncovering of women's heads, we have a concrete explanation for the mention of male practice without having to find something seriously amiss in the way men were worshipping at Corinth. Paul's point would be: yes, men

[38] The assertion that 'the head of Christ is God' probably serves principally to facilitate the transition from the man's relation to Christ to the idea that he is the 'image and glory of God' (v. 7).

[39] Murphy-O'Connor (1980: 483; *cf.* 1988: 266) assumes that both men and women were participating in worship inappropriately coiffured (*cf.* Witherington 1995: 238).

pray and prophesy with their heads uncovered, but that is because the head of a man is Christ and the man is the image and glory of God; woman has a different place in the scheme of things. By drawing the men's attention to the shame that they would naturally feel if they were forced to cover their heads (v. 4), Paul seeks to elicit sympathy for those women who do not wish to pray or prophesy with their heads uncovered.

Is it conceivable that women wished to cover themselves when praying and prophesying, yet failed to observe other standards of propriety by talking during the services (1 Cor. 14:34–35)? There is perhaps a superficial contradiction here. But the circumstances and values in each case are not the same: in 1 Corinthians 11:2–16 there are moral and theological issues at stake, whereas Paul's teaching in 14:34–35 appears to address only matters of disorder and indiscipline. One could imagine that women were anxious to preserve their modesty during the religiously important activity of praying and prophesying, but relatively unconcerned about the impression they made by talking out of place at other times. Alternatively, it may again have been men in the congregation who were encouraging the women to break with custom by participating in public discussion.

Because of the angels

If Paul is acknowledging the anxieties that women had expressed about praying and prophesying with their heads uncovered, the puzzling reference to the angels in verse 10 (*dia tous angelous*) may point to an argument used by these women. This would explain why the allusion is so brief; they knew exactly what he was talking about. We, however, can do little more than guess at the precise significance of this phrase.[40]

One popular view is that these were evil and libidinous angels who might be lured by the uncovered heads of women in worship.[41] It could then be argued that *exousia* refers to the magical power invested in the head-covering to protect the woman, who by nature is weaker than the man, from the malign attentions of evil spirits.[42] The view is not altogether implausible, but nothing in the passage suggests that Paul thought of the head-covering as having a protective function, least of all a magical one; nor is there any clear evidence elsewhere that he knew of the existence of evil angels. What, in any case, were they doing present at Christian worship?

A more positive interpretation sees these angels as general overseers of good

---

[40] The view that these were not angels but 'messengers' from the local synagogue (Kroeger 1993: 376) is historically plausible (*cf.* Acts 18:7), but it is hard to see how such an obscure reference could have any part in Paul's argument in this passage.

[41] Note *Testament of Reuben* 5:6. *Cf.* Hooker 1964: 412; Kittel 1964: 86; Foerster 1964: 574 n. 70; Theissen 1987; Tomson 1990: 136; Wilson 1991: 454; Martin 1995: 243ff.

[42] See Fitzmyer 1957: 52, 53–54 for the sources of this view and the objections to it.

order in the world and particularly in worship.[43] There is some evidence that Paul himself regarded the angels in this light: angels are observers of what happens on earth (1 Cor. 4:9; 1 Tim. 3:16; 5:21); the language of angels is perhaps the language of tongues (1 Cor. 13:1); some at Colossae mistakenly worshipped angels (Col. 2:18). In Jewish writings angels are sometimes seen as mediators of the prayers of the saints: 'I am Raphael, one of the seven holy angels who present the prayers of the saints and enter into the presence of the glory of the Holy One' (Tobit 12:15, RSV; *cf.* Rev. 8:3). The psalmist declares: 'I will sing psalms to you before the angels' (Ps. 137: 1, LXX). In 4 Ezra 16:66 the question is asked: 'What will you do? Or how will you hide your sins before God and his angels?' In some rabbinic traditions angels are an embodiment of the Shekinah, and thus of the presence and glory of God (see *e.g.* Urbach 1975: 135–137).

The argument has been given particular impetus by the discovery of texts at Qumran that speak of the exclusion from the gatherings of the congregation of a person who was unclean or injured or deformed in any way, because 'holy angels are present in their congregation' (*1QSa.* ii.3–11). Fitzmyer (1957: 57) draws the conclusion from this that 'the unveiled head of a woman is like a bodily defect which should be excluded from such an assembly, "because holy angels are present in their congregation" '.[44] For a woman to be uncovered, in Paul's view, is no different from her being shaved, which is an unnatural condition. In effect, therefore, Paul means that 'the unveiled head of a woman is like a bodily defect' and the angels present at sacred gatherings 'should not look on such a condition'. This latter aspect of the argument is unconvincing, but it is not impossible that behind the severe Qumran doctrine lies a popular belief in the presence of angels at worship that was known either to Paul or to the women of Corinth.

A third view associates the angels with the law. Murphy-O'Connor (1980: 496–497) argues that one of the functions of the angels was to 'report to God infringements of the Law'. Women had full authority to pray and prophesy, but in doing so they exercised a function that was essentially incompatible

---

[43] *Cf.* Hooker 1964: 412–413. Fitzmyer (1957: 55) quotes Moffat: 'Paul has in mind the midrash on Gen. i.26f., which made good angels not only mediators of the Law (Gal. iii.19), but guardians of the created order. Indeed, according to one ancient midrash, reflected in Philo, when God said, "Let us make man", he was addressing the angels' (J. Moffat, *The First Epistle of Paul to the Corinthians*, London: Hodder and Stoughton, 1947: 152).

[44] Note also Conzelmann 1975: 189 n. 87. Fiorenza (1983: 228) argues from a different perspective that unbound hair was a sign of uncleanness. Therefore, 'since the angels are present in the pneumatic worship service of a community that speaks the "tongues of angels," women should not worship as cultically unclean persons by letting their hair down but should pin it up as a sign both of their spiritual power and of control over their heads'. But, contrary to Martin (1995: 243–244), it is difficult to believe that Paul was so concerned about cultic purity.

with the law. For this reason 'they needed to convey their new status to the angels who watched for breaches of the Law. The guardians of an outmoded tradition had to be shown that things had changed.'[45] Certainly, there is a strong association of the law, and in particular of the giving of the law, with angels (Gal. 3:19; *cf.* Acts 7:53; Heb. 2:2). Hebrews 2:5 may imply that angels had authority over the old dispensation, whereas the 'world to come' is subjected to Christ. Angels are now subject to Christ (1 Pet. 3:22). The angels long to look into the things that have now been revealed through the Holy Spirit (1 Pet. 1:12). Perhaps then the angels are thought to have a special, if somewhat retrograde, interest in the preservation of the creation order as it appears in Paul's citation of the 'law' in verses 7–9. Perhaps, too, there is a connection with the reference to the law in 1 Corinthians 14:34. Does Paul see the law as having a residual, pragmatic value in certain contexts? This possibility will be explored further in the next chapter.

In the end it may be impossible, and even unnecessary, to arbitrate between these views. Perhaps we should expect a variety of colourful connotations to congregate in the popular mind around such a religious motif as the presence of angels, like butterflies around a flower. But before giving in too much to indeterminacy and poetic fancy, we should consider whether in fact 1 Corinthians 4:9 might not provide a stronger clue to the meaning of the phrase 'because of the angels'. The apostles, Paul says, have become like men sentenced to death, 'a spectacle to the world, both to angels and to men': 'We are foolish for Christ's sake, but you are wise in Christ; we are weak, but you are strong; you are esteemed [*endoxoi*], but we are without honour [*atimoi*]' (v. 10). Is the reference to angels here merely rhetorical, merely intended to express the scope of their humiliation? Or is there a more substantial connection with the theme of honour and disrepute? Are the angels a means of objectifying these values, perhaps before God? If so, there could be the same idea in 10:11, that a woman who prays or prophesies with her head uncovered is dishonoured and humiliated before the angels; the allusion marks the extremity of her shame.

Conclusions

When Paul says, at the beginning of this difficult passage, that 'the head of a woman is the man', he means only that it is the man who is affected by the way in which the woman behaves. Through her beauty, character and righteous behaviour a woman acquires glory for herself, but that glory is also transferred to her husband. By praying or prophesying with her head uncovered a woman brings dishonour upon herself, but in the same manner that dishonour is also transferred to her husband, who is her head. The extent

---

[45] *Cf.* Scroggs 1972: 300 n. 46.

of this disgrace is brought out by the fact that Paul equates it with the disgrace a women would suffer if her hair were cut short or shaved off.

Men and women, as Paul understands things, are different in this respect: a man's behaviour reflects not upon the woman but upon Christ, whereas the woman's behaviour reflects not directly upon Christ, but in the first place upon her husband. This is the imbalance of the patriarchal marriage relationship. But it has its origins in the creation of the woman from the man and for the sake of the man. What Paul means by this will be considered at length in chapter 7 below, but at this point we may observe that it has to do principally with sexuality, not with authority. While this fundamental ordering of procreative responsibilities between the man and the woman may assume the form of patriarchy, in which the woman is assigned a subordinate position in the marriage relationship, this is not a theologically inevitable development. It should be possible to preserve the essential creational differences within an egalitarian framework.

Because a woman who prays or prophesies with her head uncovered brings dishonour both upon herself and upon her husband, Paul says that 'the woman ought to have authority over the head', and adds somewhat too cryptically, 'because of the angels'. It does not at all fit the argument at this point to read this as an insistence on the subordination of the woman to the authority of the man; nor is such a reading linguistically probable. Possibly Paul means that by covering her head the woman demonstrates that she has authority to pray and prophesy. Alternatively, his intention may be to confirm the right of women to cover their heads when others have been urging them to abandon a custom that appeared to contradict the woman's new-found freedom in Christ. The reference to the angels, though its precise significance remains obscure, is a reinforcement, oriented towards God, of the assertion that it is shameful for a woman to pray or prophesy with her head uncovered.

Paul concludes his exposition with an appeal to what appears 'fitting' or 'natural'. These are not absolute categories; today, in the West at least, we should recognize that it is culture and fashion, not biology or ethics or theology, that primarily determine whether it is disgraceful for a man to have long hair, or whether short hair effaces a woman's glory. Still, it is not difficult to understand what Paul meant when he said that a woman's long hair is 'for her a glory'. In an argument that may well have been directed at the men in the congregation, he says that a woman's long hair is the equivalent of the cloak which for the man is both a covering of his nakedness and shame, and a symbol of his dignity. But if so much value is attached to the woman's hair, it is only proper, in Paul's view, that a woman should pray to God with her head covered.

5. Silence in church
1 Corinthians 14:33b–35

Hōs en pasais tais ekklēsiais tōn hagiōn [34]*hai gynaikes en tais ekklēsiais sigatōsan; ou gar epitrepetai autais lalein, alla hypotassesthōsan, kathōs kai ho nomos legei.* [35]*ei de ti mathein thelousin, en oikō tous idious andras eperōtatōsan; aischron gar estin gynaiki lalein en ekklēsia.*

As in all the churches of the saints [34]let the women keep silence in the churches; for it is not permitted to them to speak, but let them be submissive, as also the law says. [35]If they wish to know something, let them ask their own husbands at home; for it is shameful for a woman to speak in church (1 Cor. 14:33b–35).

On the face of it, Paul's argument in this short passage is very straightforward: women should not speak in church; if they have any questions, they should ask their husbands at home. But as soon as we begin to prod around a bit, we stir up a hornet's nest of exegetical and theological difficulties. Did Paul write this? Or is this, as a number of commentators think, the work of a reactionary Jewish Christian interpolator? If Paul did write it, does he not contradict what he has just written in chapter 11 about women prophets? What 'law' says that women should be silent and submissive? Is it really 'shameful' for a woman to speak in church? More to the point, is this really what it means to be 'one in Christ'? Is this the best that Christian women can aspire to in worship, that they should keep their mouths shut?

We will begin by considering two matters of a literary-critical nature: first, the very important question of whether it was in fact Paul who wrote these verses; secondly, the problem of knowing whether the words 'as in all the churches of the saints' (v. 33b) belong with the instructions about women or with the preceding passage.

Literary-critical difficulties
Are verses 34–35 a post-Pauline addition to the text?

The question of whether it was Paul or some later, more conservative redactor who wrote verses 34–35 is an extremely vexed one, but cannot be ignored. There is no unambiguous manuscript evidence that these verses were ever lacking from the text of 1 Corinthians. Nevertheless, some quite forceful arguments have been put forward by some quite influential commentators in support of the view that they are not original.[1] These need to be set out and evaluated.

1. In the manuscript tradition of the western church, verses 34–35 have been moved to the end of the chapter. It has been argued that this transposition can be properly explained only if we assume that they were not part of the original text but a very early addition in the margin of a manuscript, and that this addition was subsequently incorporated into the text in two different places. Supposedly it is more difficult to understand why a scribe should have moved the passage from its traditional position to its place in the western manuscripts after verse 40. Perhaps the most notable proponent of this view in recent years, certainly in evangelical circles, has been G. D. Fee.

Further evidence for the interpolation hypothesis has been found in the sixth-century Latin text known as Codex Fuldensis (Payne 1995: 240–250). In this important manuscript, which was revised and corrected by Bishop Victor of Capua, verses 36–40 are, curiously, repeated in the bottom margin. Payne argues, principally from the positioning of certain sigla or symbols in the margin of the main text, that this gloss was intended as a replacement of verses 34–40. So he concludes that Victor, who is known to have been a fastidious scholar, must have had good grounds – such as the existence of a manuscript that did not include these verses – for thinking that verses 34–35 were an interpolation.[2]

2. The argument in chapter 14 is felt to be more coherent if verses 34–35 are removed. On the one hand, the sardonic questions of verse 36 ('Or did the word of God come from you? Or did it come down to you alone?') appear to pick up the thought in verse 33 that worship is not a matter of disorder but of peace 'in all the churches of the saints'. On the other, the sudden interest shown in the behaviour of women seems out of place in a chapter that focuses not on particular groups of people but on the manner in which spiritual gifts are exercised.

Although there are linguistic connections with the rest of the chapter, on closer examination they prove to be quite superficial and contrived.[3] The verb

---

[1] See, for example: Scroggs 1972: 284; 1974: 533; Swidler 1979: 337; Murphy-O'Connor 1986: 90–92; 1996: 290; Fee 1987: 699–705 and other references in n. 4; Payne 1995.

[2] Payne draws attention to the fact that there appears to be no citation of 1 Cor. 14:33–34 in the apostolic and early fathers before Tertullian (AD 160–240?). He also argues that a text-critical siglum in the Codex Vaticanus indicates awareness of a textual problem at the end of 1 Cor. 14:33. Carson (1991: 141) interprets the marginal gloss in Codex Fuldensis as evidence that Victor knew of a placement of verses 34–35 that differed from the western tradition. However, he appears to have followed Metzger in mistakenly assuming that verses 34–35 were included after verse 40 in the text but added as a marginal gloss after verse 33 (*cf.* Payne 1995: 241–242).

[3] *Cf.* Fee 1987: 702; Payne 1995: 246–247.

'to speak' is used repeatedly in chapter 14, but only in verses 34–35 is it used in an absolute sense with no clarification of the type of speech intended. Silence is required of people speaking in tongues and of prophets (vv. 28, 30), but only under certain circumstances, not because such speech is wrong. Similarly, the idea of 'submission' is found in verse 32 but the thought here is very different from the submission required of women in verse 34. Moreover, the plural form 'in the churches' looks very much like a *universal* application of the command to silence. But why should this injunction be addressed to all the churches when the passage as a whole has in view the particular circumstances of the church in Corinth? It is difficult to argue that *en tais ekklēsiais* means 'in the congregations of Corinth' when this usage is found nowhere else in Paul and the more usual singular form (*en ekklēsia*) is found in verse 35. In fact, these verses read very well as a marginal gloss added by someone anxious to counteract what he feared was too much licence granted to the whole church in chapter 14.

3. Certain aspects of the argument and language of these verses have been judged foreign to Paul. In particular, the way in which appeal is made to 'the law' without citing the text appears quite uncharacteristic of his style of argumentation. Paul does not, it is said, invoke a precept of the law in this way 'to establish an ethical requirement for Christian behaviour or Christian worship' (Payne 1995: 247). Moreover, since no Old Testament text corresponds unmistakably to what is claimed here, the assumption must be that the allusion is to non-biblical Jewish tradition. The implication would then be that whoever wrote these verses, unlike Paul, represented the outlook of conservative Jewish Christianity. Commentators have also sometimes argued from the parallels with 1 Timothy 2:11-15 that the author of the marginal note in 1 Corinthians was dependent on the later text.[4]

4. There is the problem, finally, of reconciling the blunt interdiction against women speaking in church with the apparent assumption in 1 Corinthians 11:5, 13 that women habitually prayed and prophesied. If there is a contradiction here, the obvious explanation, in the view of some scholars, is that Paul did not write 14:34–35.

There are, however, difficulties with the argument that these verses are non-Pauline. One is that the gloss must have been extremely early to have found its way into every manuscript. The presence of these verses in every extant manuscript has persuaded most exegetes that they are authentic. Payne's argument from the Fuldensis manuscript requires more thorough and

---

[4] *Cf.* Payne 1995: 248. Commenting on the use of *epitrepesthai*, Conzelmann (1975: 246 n. 53) cites the argument of Weiss: 'The passive points back to an already valid regulation, such as we find in 1 Tim. 2:12.' More probably the passive refers to Paul's customary teaching in the churches. The inference that *epitrepetai* is dependent on 1 Tim. 2:12 is unnecessary.

informed appraisal than can be afforded it here, but we can at least note that an alternative explanation for the emendation is possible. If Victor had been aware of a text that did not include verses 34–35, we must surely ask why he did not simply mark these verses as being of doubtful authenticity. In the event, it seems at least as plausible that verses 36–40 in the margin were meant to be inserted before verses 34–35 and that after verse 35 the reader was expected to resume the passage at 15:1. This would indicate clearly enough that some manuscripts placed verses 34–35 at the end of the chapter.[5] In any case, the argument is unlikely to make much of a dent in the overwhelming textual evidence for the inclusion of these verses somewhere in the chapter.

If these verses are not an interpolation, then some explanation needs to be given for their transposition to the end of the chapter in the western manuscripts.[6] This is not impossible. On the one hand, the interpolation hypothesis has already argued that verses 34–35 appear to be logically out of place.[7] It is not inconceivable that a pernickety scribe came to the conclusion that the instructions addressed to women were an intrusion into a discourse on charismatic gifts. Paul's concluding words in verse 39 ('be eager to prophesy and do not discourage speaking in tongues') show no awareness of the digression. On the other hand, C. Niccum (1997: 254) has recently drawn attention to the fact that the manuscript evidence for the transposition of these verses is not nearly as strong as has usually been assumed: 'the transposition occurs in only a few, closely related MSS from northern Italy spread abroad in the Middle Ages by Irish monastics'.

But are these verses in fact as incongruous as they seem? While we must

---

[5] Payne (1995: 243–244) anticipates this explanation but argues that if this were the case, we should expect to find some indication at the end of verse 35 that the reader who has followed the marginal gloss should skip to 15:1. This is true, but equally there is nothing to stop us from reading verses 34–35 after the inserted text. If anything, it is more natural to think that having read the inserted verses 36–40 we should read through verses 34–35 (as in the western tradition) and then recognize the end of the section (or chapter) when we come again to verses 36–40, which have already been read. The alternative would have been to rewrite verses 34–35 and mark their insertion after verse 40; but then the reader would not know that he should ignore them after verse 33. It cannot simply be inferred from the positioning of the Roman numerals in the margin that the marginal gloss was intended to replace the whole of section Lxiiii: it is only coincidental that the inserted text falls at the end of a section.

[6] The possibility that the verses were moved from the end of the chapter and inserted after verse 33 is generally not considered by scholars.

[7] See Carson 1991: 142–143; Witherington 1995: 288. Fee contradicts himself here. On the one hand, he argues that no adequate reason can be found for moving these verses from their position after verse 33 to the end of the chapter (Fee 1987: 700). On the other, he maintains that better sense can be made of Paul's argument 'without these intruding verses' (701).

acknowledge that there is an abrupt change of subject in verses 34–35,[8] there are nevertheless significant thematic links with the rest of the chapter. The passage has to do with the disorder caused by people speaking out of turn. The exclusive focus on women is not totally unexpected. Although Paul's discussion of issues relating to sexuality in chapter 7 is even-handed, 1 Corinthians 11:2–16 makes it clear that women were acting, or were being encouraged to act, in worship in a way that was both culturally inappropriate and contrary to the practice of other churches (v. 16).[9] An explanation must be found for the apparent contradiction between the two passages, but the underlying concerns are very similar, and Paul's retort in 1 Corinthians 11:16 ('If anyone thinks to be argumentative . . .') expresses the same defiance that we find in 14:36–38. Moreover, the tone and rhetorical force of verse 36 seems more likely to have been provoked by verses 34–35, with their reference to the shame of women speaking in church, than by the more humdrum instructions of verses 26–33.

That the language of 'speaking', 'silence' and 'submission' has a different sense in these verses is hardly surprising, since the subject-matter is so different. The question is whether Paul had good reason to address the issue of women here. If he did, then we cannot expect him to use words such as these in exactly the same way. The meaning of *lalein* ('to speak') is determined by the immediate context. The objection that it is used in a qualified sense elsewhere in chapter 14 is irrelevant. The appeal to the law is problematic and must be considered at greater length later; but it does not present a fundamental objection to the authenticity of these verses. That there are parallels between this passage and 1 Timothy 2:11–15 is unremarkable given a natural continuity of theme and the conventional, stereotyped character of this sort of parenesis (*cf.* Ellis 1981: 214–215).

On balance, therefore, there is no compelling reason to regard these lines as an interpolation. In fact, properly understood, they are not out of place in the discussion of chapter 14 and are consistent with Paul's general concerns in the letter. This will become clearer as we proceed.

Where does verse 33b belong?

But if we accept that verses 34–35 are part of the original text, then a decision

---

[8] Keener (1992: 91 n. 20) suggests that digressions of this sort were a common feature of ancient rhetoric.

[9] In support of the interpolation hypothesis, Payne (1995: 247) argues that *aischron . . . gynaiki* ('shameful for a woman') is borrowed from 1 Cor. 11:6 but used in a way that is alien to the context. This is mistaken. It merely assumes that the freedom granted to women to pray and prophesy in chapter 11 is contradicted by the injunctions of 14:34–35. Otherwise, the disgrace of a woman praying or prophesying with her head unveiled is very similar in character to the disgrace of women speaking out of turn in worship.

needs to be made regarding the logical attachment of the clause 'as in all the churches of the saints' (v. 33b). Does it belong with the preceding argument about order in the exercise of charismatic gifts? Or does it serve as a preface to the instructions concerning women?

Textual evidence tends to favour the view that these words form part of the preceding discussion; at least, the editor who placed verses 34–35 at the end of the chapter certainly thought so. There is also the apparent redundancy that results if verse 33b is tied to verse 34: 'As in all the churches of the saints . . . in the churches.' Whether the clause actually makes more sense when read with verses 31–33a, however, is another matter. We have already noticed that the appeal to the practice of other churches is repeated in the questioning of the Corinthians' exclusivist attitude towards the word of God in verse 36. If verses 34–35 are authentic, therefore, it would be quite reasonable to connect verse 33b with this passage too. Added to this, we might argue that verses 33b and 36 fit the specific requirement of verses 34–35 better than they do the broad recommendations and assertions of verses 26–33.[10] When Paul appeals to common church practice elsewhere in 1 Corinthians, it is invariably in connection with concrete instructions or teaching (4:17; 7:17–19; 11:16). The theological statements of verses 32–33a do not fit this pattern of usage. The language of 1 Corinthians 11:16 is particularly instructive in this respect because the subject matter and Paul's attitude are so similar to what we find in 14:33b–38. While the repetition of 'in the churches' is inelegant, it may not be pointless. 'As in all the churches of the saints' would refer to common practice, wherever believers gather together; 'in all the churches', on the other hand, would specify the occasion – presumably in contrast to 'at home', where it was quite acceptable for women to ask questions.

Silence, prayer and prophecy: various interpretations

If verses 34–35 are authentic and we accept that Paul required women to be silent and not to speak in church, how are we to reconcile this with the participation of women in prayer and worship presupposed in 1 Corinthians 11:5? A wide range of solutions to the puzzle have been proposed, the most important of which need to be examined.

1. Some have argued that verses 34–35 represent a Corinthian position (and are perhaps a quotation from their letter; *cf.* 6:12–13; 7:1) rather than Paul's own views on the matter.[11] But this view, though ingenious, has not won many adherents. The main grammatical objection to this interpretation is that

[10] The force of this observation appears to be recognized in Conzelmann's (1975: 246) otherwise eccentric argument that the interpolation consists of verses 33b–36. See also Witherington 1995: 287.

[11] See Flanagan & Snyder 1981: 10–12; Odell-Scott 1983: 90–93; Evans 1983: 99. See further references in Carson 1991: 489 n. 28.

the particle *ē* ('or') that begins verse 36 cannot be read as introducing a refutation of what has gone before. D. A. Carson, who is exercised at some length by this question, makes the point emphatically: 'The brute fact is this: *in every instance in the New Testament where the disjunctive particle in question is used in a construction analogous to the passage at hand, its effect is to reinforce the truth of the clause or verse that precedes it*' (1991:151, his italics).[12] There are logical difficulties too. Why, for example, does Paul quote the Corinthian position at such length, with its supporting arguments, and then not take the trouble to refute it in detail or make alternative prescriptions? Why did the Corinthians write such instructions to Paul in the first place? Why is the attitude of the Corinthians towards women too liberal on the one hand (expecting them to pray and prophesy with their heads uncovered), but too conservative on the other (not allowing them to speak in church)? The interpretation can hardly stay afloat under the weight of such questions – particularly since it has already been holed by the grammatical objection.

2. One rather neat way to avoid the apparent contradiction between this passage and 11:5 would be to suppose that they refer to different types of gathering.[13] Perhaps women prayed and prophesied when the church met in the home, but in the larger public assemblies were expected to keep silent. This is not implausible,[14] but we must ask where the evidence is that the church at Corinth regularly met both in the homes of believers and in larger public congregations. More to the point, where is the evidence that 1 Corinthians 11:3–16 addresses the circumstances only of private worship? The requirement that women should cover their heads when praying or prophesying makes more sense in the context of public worship. The passage appears to envisage the same sort of public disgrace that Paul is anxious to avoid in 14:35. We must also ask why no distinction is made between men praying and prophesying and women praying and prophesying in 11:4–5 (*cf.* Witherington 1988: 100). The symmetry of Paul's teaching here strongly suggests that men and women prayed and prophesied in the same gatherings.

Baumert (1996: 195–197) has recently argued that 1 Corinthians 11:3–16 has in view the worship service, whereas Paul's regulations in the later passage address issues arising in the context of 'executive meetings' or teaching discussions. This corresponds to a distinction maintained in the mystery cults,

[12] *Cf.* Liefeld 1986a: 149): 'What Paul negates by his use of the adversative Greek particle *ē* is *not* the *command* in verses 34–35 but the assumed *disobedience* of it, just as in the structurally similar passage 6:18–19.' See also Murphy-O'Connor 1986: 91–92.

[13] See Grosheide 1953: 342; Ridderbos 1975: 462; Almlie 1982: 41–55.

[14] The objections cited by Carson (1991: 145–146) are not fully convincing. In particular, for women to pray and prophesy in the home does not remove them from the context of the whole church suggested by 11:16 and 14:23–29. It also seems rather dismissive of house churches to suggest that such meetings were 'outside the gathered messianic community'.

and Baumert assumes that, as was the case with the Greek civic assembly, women would not have been allowed to attend, let alone speak at, the executive meetings of the cults. But although it is possible to identify different activities that took place within the Christian assembly, it is not clear that these constituted separate meetings. We shall return to this issue later, but for now it is enough to point out that 14:34–35 appears to presuppose the same practical situation as the instructions about prophecy and tongues in the rest of the chapter.

3. Some have tried to argue that chapter 11 is a reluctant concession to the basic rule: only under the pressure of circumstances did Paul grant exemption from the rule expressed in 14:34–35 to women at Corinth who had acquired a taste for praying and prophesying. But this view cannot be sustained. Nothing in chapter 11 suggests that Paul was unhappy with the fact that women were participating in charismatic worship in this way.[15] If he really disapproved, why did he not jump on the failure of women prophets to cover their heads as evidence for their being by nature unsuited to this form of public ministry? Why correct the mistakes when the mistakes could have provided a justification for condemning the practice?

4. Fiorenza has argued that verses 34–35, far from being an interpolation, should be understood as an integral part of a sequence of teachings on church order: first, speakers in tongues (vv. 27–28), then prophets (vv. 29–33), and lastly 'wives' (vv. 34–36). Here is the crux of her interpretation: the injunctions in verses 34–35 apply not to all women but only to the *wives* of Christian men. What is assumed here is Paul's 'ascetic preference for the unmarried state' (1 Cor. 7:7–8, 32–40) and his view that, while the married woman is preoccupied with the needs of the family, the unmarried woman may learn to be 'holy both in body and spirit' (1 Cor. 7:34). This special holiness is attributed to the fact that the unmarried woman has not been touched by a man (*cf.* 7:1). 'We therefore can surmise that Paul is able to accept the pneumatic participation of such "holy" women in the worship service of the community, but argues in 14:34f against such an active participation of wives.' The general theological argument here has probably been derived, in Fiorenza's view, from 'Jewish-Hellenistic missionary tradition, which . . . had adopted the Greco-Roman exhortations for the subordination of wives as part of the "law"' (Fiorenza 1983: 231).

The suggestion that wives are principally in view in 14:34–35 may be right. But given the significance of the man–woman relationship in 11:3–16, and the reference to the creation of the woman 'for the sake of the man' (11:9), we

---

[15] Note Barrett 1971: 331: 'Only special pleading . . . can deny that chapter xi concedes the right of women (suitably clothed) to pray and prophesy in a public meeting of the church.' See also Conzelmann 1975: 246 n. 58; Carson 1991: 146.

must surely assume that wives are also in view – perhaps not exclusively – in this earlier passage. It has also been pointed out that in a patriarchal system the life of an unmarried woman was if anything even more circumscribed than that of a married woman.[16] It is hard to imagine that unmarried or widowed women, who would have been viewed as a highly potent source of moral disorder (*cf.* 1 Cor. 7:8–9; 1 Tim. 5:11–15), would have been allowed to draw attention to themselves by speaking while married women were obliged to keep quiet. Moreover, it is hardly conceivable that Paul, for all his preference for the celibate lifestyle, would have made this sort of special holiness a prerequisite for charismatic ministry. If a woman's unbelieving husband is 'sanctified through his wife' (7:14), surely the wife too is no less sanctified, no less holy, despite having been touched by a man.

5. If it could be demonstrated that 'speaking' in verse 34 denotes some form of speech that does not include prayer and prophecy, the conflict with chapter 11 would, of course, disappear. One suggestion has been that *lalein* ('to speak') is simply an abbreviated form of *lalein glōssais* ('to speak in tongues'), an expression which has been used frequently in this chapter. The situation envisaged is where women in the church have not quite shaken off their pagan past and are disrupting the service with their noisy babbling. In this case, the words 'let them be submissive' might be thought to convey the sense that *hypotassetai* has in verse 32 ('spirits of prophets are subject to prophets'); it is the disorderly spirits of these enthusiastic women that are to be kept submissive or under control. But this is hardly possible.[17] It is the women, not their spirits, that are to be submissive, and the absolute use of *lalein*, accompanied by the command to be silent, makes it very unlikely that the ruling is to be understood in such a narrow sense.[18] Moreover, Paul does not use *lalein* only in connection with speaking in tongues in chapter 14; for example, in verse 19 he says, 'In church I want to speak [*lalēsai*] five words with my mind, that I might also instruct others . . .'

6. Considerable scholarly weight has been thrown behind the view that 'speaking' here refers to the weighing of prophecies (*cf.* v. 29). For women to participate in the process of judging the truth of what had been spoken prophetically could put them in a position of judging their own husbands.

---

[16] Murphy-O'Connor 1986: 91; *cf.* Carson's virulent reaction (1991: 146), and his comments on the advantages that married women had over single women (151). According to Philo, 'maidens' were to be more closely confined than 'those who have reached full womanhood' and who presumably were married or on the point of being married (*De Specialibus Legibus* 3.169, Loeb).

[17] See Fee 1987: 704; Grudem 1988: 218–220; Keener 1992: 77–78.

[18] It cannot be argued that *lalein* means to 'babble' or 'chatter' as in classical Greek: any such connotations, if legitimate at all in Hellenistic Greek, would be quite lost in the context.

Carson (1991:152) argues that the weighing of prophecies falls under the 'magisterial function' that is prohibited to women in 1 Timothy 2:12. B. Witherington, basing his analysis largely on the work of J. B. Hurley, reconstructs the scenario as follows:

> During the time of the weighing of the prophet's utterances, some of the wives, who themselves may have been prophetesses and entitled to weigh verbally what was said, were asking questions that were disrupting the worship service. The questions themselves may have been disrespectful or they may have been asked in a disrespectful manner. The result was chaos. Paul's ruling is that questions should not be asked in worship. The wives should ask their husbands at home. Worship was not to be turned into a question-and-answer session (Witherington 1988:103).[19]

Such an interpretation places verses 34–35 firmly within the context of the chapter, but it lacks intrinsic credibility. If Paul had meant that women were not to judge prophecies, why did he not say so? Despite some claims to the contrary, there is no meaningful connection between these verses and verse 29b.[20] Was a woman really any more likely to exercise authority over her husband as a judge of prophecy than as a prophet? Does not 'in the churches . . . in church' suggest a wider situation than just the evaluation of prophecy? And why should the weighing of prophecy be described as asking questions? W. L. Liefeld (1986a: 150) argues that in the ancient world questions were a means both of teaching and of challenging. But it seems quite clear that the women were asking questions at Corinth not in order to challenge but in order to learn (v. 35)[21] – which brings us to a final line of interpretation.

7. It is puzzling that what would appear to be the obvious solution to the problem has so often been disregarded. As Keener (1992:81) points out, the

---

[19] *Cf.* Hurley 1981: 188–193; Ellis 1981: 216–218; Liefeld 1986a: 150; Fung 1987: 196–197; Grudem 1988: 220–224; Ellis 1989: 69–70; Witherington 1990: 175–176; 1995: 287; Wilson 1991: 449; Gritz 1991: 89.

[20] Grudem's (1988: 221) argument for a structural link cannot be entertained for a number of reasons (see Fee 1987: 703–704), not least of which is the fact that verses 34–35 are simply not marked logically as a restriction imposed on the positive exhortation to evaluate the prophecies given. The argument that Paul's injunction presupposes the particular context of judging prophecies in verse 29 is doubtful (Grudem 1988: 223–224). If this line is taken, then the obvious context would be the teaching about prophecy, which concludes in verse 33 and is summarized in verses 39–40: verses 34–35, therefore, would have to be read as a prohibition against women prophesying!

[21] It is possible that *hoi alloi* in verse 29 denotes 'the other prophets', in which case we can assume that women prophets were involved in the process of weighing prophecy. Grudem (1988: 70–74), however, rejects this interpretation. See Ridderbos 1975: 452; Fee 1987: 694 and n. 30.

only form of speaking specifically mentioned in verses 34–35 is that 'the wife should ask her husband questions at home, rather than continuing what she is doing'. This does not necessarily mean that women in Corinth were speaking *only* in order to learn something; the point of the instruction may only be that Paul recognized the desire to learn as a legitimate reason for speaking out. But we can probably assume that this is what he had principally in mind, and also that this practice led to noisy and unseemly confusion.

This must be the starting-point, but it is not fully adequate as an explanation of why Paul insisted that women keep silent in church. The fact remains that it is not explicitly the asking of questions that is considered shameful, but *speaking*. The reason Paul did not allow women to ask questions, no matter how commendable the desire to learn may have been, is that for women to speak at all in church, on the evidence of these verses, was unacceptable.

So although one of the main reasons, apparently, why women were speaking in the service was that they wanted to learn, it seems that if we are to do justice to the text, we must recognize that Paul imposed a more comprehensive ban on women speaking. In order to understand why he did so it would be helpful to consider the broader cultural and religious implications of women participating in public discussions.

The cultural context

The socio-cultural background to Paul's restriction on women speaking in church has been well documented and needs only to be briefly sketched here. It is important to keep in mind that any survey of cultural attitudes is bound to be impressionistic. The literary evidence that we have is fragmentary and unbalanced. It represents the view of a cultured, educated, dominant, male elite. It is rarely a matter of objective, historical description; we have to take into account the circumstances, the prejudices, and the polemical intention of the writer.[22] Plutarch features disproportionately in the surveys, and while we must be thankful for the insight he provides, we must also ask how far he can be relied upon as a fair-minded and representative commentator. Only to a limited extent can this bias in the literary picture be corrected by archaeological evidence such as inscriptions. The situation is complicated further by variations in custom – broadly speaking, the condition of women improved as one travelled west across the Mediterranean world – and by the extreme cosmopolitan character of Corinth in particular.[23] Paul's own peculiar cultural and religious background also needs to be kept in view.

[22] Brooten (1985: 69–79) discusses some of the historical and hermeneutical difficulties involved in the enterprise of evaluating the New Testament teaching on women against the background of Jewish and Graeco-Roman sources.

[23] *Cf.* Scroggs 1972: 289; Witherington 1988: 5–23.

Disapproval of women speaking in public gatherings

There was a general prejudice among Greeks and Romans against the participation of women in public life generally and, in particular, in the assembly.[24] Women were not permitted to speak or vote in the civic *ekklēsia* (Stegemann 1993:162). Some men preferred women not to speak at all; Aristotle voiced the opinion that 'Silence gives grace to a woman – though that is not the case likewise with a man' (*Politics*, 1.5.8). The woman's proper sphere was the home, where honour could be better preserved.[25] Plutarch explained to the undoubtedly intelligent and educated Eurydice that 'Pheidias made the Aphrodite of the Eleans with one foot on a tortoise, to typify for womankind keeping at home and keeping silence' (*Moralia* 142D, Loeb). Although there are numerous recorded examples of women venturing into the legal or political sphere, the unusualness and impropriety of the action are invariably noted by the writer. Livy, writing in the first century BC, records the horrified reaction of the consul Cato (234–149 BC) to the rampant behaviour of Roman women who opposed the Oppian law:

> If each of us, citizens, had determined to assert his rights and dignity as a husband with respect to his own spouse, we should have less trouble with the sex as a whole; as it is our liberty, destroyed at home by female violence, even here in the Forum is crushed and trodden underfoot, and because we have not kept them individually under control, we dread them collectively . . . I should have said, 'What sort of practice is this, of running out into the streets and blocking the roads and speaking to other women's husbands? Could you not have made the same requests, each of your own husband, at home? Or are you more attractive outside and to other women's husbands than to your own?' (Livy 34.2.1–2, 9–10, Loeb).[26]

Plutarch, more moderately, argued that it was as important for a woman not to reveal her inner self to the general public through speech as for her to

---

[24] *E.g.* Valerius Maximus, *Factorum et Dictorum Memorabilium Libri* 3.8.6 (first century AD); Thucydides, *History of the Peloponnesian War* 2.45.2. See also Baumert 1996: 196.

[25] See MacDonald 1990: 223–224; 1996: 30–41. See also Xenophon, *Oikonomikos* 7.22, 30. The wife did not, of course, spend her time in idleness. In this passage Xenophon portrays a wife trained by her husband to superintend the work of the household, manage servants, and handle domestic finances.

[26] *Cf.* Valerius Maximus, *Factorum et Dictorum Memorabilium Libri* 8.3 (trans. in Lefkowitz & Fant 1992: 151): 'We must be silent no longer about those women whom neither the condition of their nature nor the cloak of modesty could keep silent in the Forum or the courts.'

conceal her body by her dress: 'Not only the arm of the virtuous woman, but her speech as well, ought to be not for the public, and she ought to be modest and guarded about saying anything in the hearing of outsiders, since it is an exposure of herself; for in her talk can be seen her feelings, character and disposition' (*Moralia* 142CD, Loeb).[27]

Essentially the wife was expected to operate under the authority, and within the intellectual sphere, of her husband. Plutarch's *Advice to Bride and Groom* is again instructive: the wife should 'do her talking either to her husband or through her husband, and she should not feel aggrieved if, like the flute-player, she makes a more impressive sound through a tongue not her own' (*Moralia* 142D, Loeb). Likewise, she was to share her husband's friends and her husband's gods: 'it is becoming for a wife to worship and to know only the gods that her husband believes in' (*Moralia* 140D, Loeb). Undoubtedly these sentiments express an ideal rather than a realistic conception of marital relations; nevertheless, they are probably a quite accurate indication of what was generally considered proper and decent. This is important, because it is against these popular standards of ideal behaviour, not against the messy reality of domestic life, that the moral and social condition of the church would have been measured.

Women were not denied all opportunity for education or social advancement in the Graeco-Roman world.[28] It appears that the daughters even of less wealthy families could expect to receive some sort of formal education, though this naturally centred on the acquisition of domestic skills and in most cases would end when the girl married, usually around the age of twelve to fourteen.[29] Plato's attitude towards women was ambivalent, but on one occasion at least he argued that women should enjoy equality with men, even in military affairs.[30] Some women, notably from wealthy and influential families, studied philosophy,[31] participated in commerce and manufacturing, and became members of associations and clubs.[32] The Stoics could even

---

[27] Roman opinion was more liberal, as illustrated by Cornelius Nepos: '. . . what Roman would blush to take his wife to a dinner-party? What matron does not frequent the front rooms of her dwelling and show herself in public? But it is very different in Greece; for there a woman is not admitted to a dinner-party, unless relatives only are present, and she keeps to the more retired part of the house called "the women's apartment," to which no man has access who is not near of kin' (Cornelius Nepos, *Lives of Famous Men*, preface 6–7, Loeb).

[28] See Pomeroy 1975: 136–139, 170–176.

[29] Witherington 1988: 17–18; Keener 1992: 83. In a letter Pliny (first century AD) reports the death of a thirteen-year-old girl; among other virtues he lists the fact that she 'applied herself intelligently to her books' (Pliny, *Letters* 5.16.3, Loeb; see Massey 1988: 19–20).

[30] Plato, *Republic* 455DE; cf. Oepke 1964: 778; Witherington 1988: 7–8.

[31] Keener 1992: 97 n. 66. It is likely that women learned within the home from a relative (Keener 1992: 99 n. 83).

[32] Meeks 1983: 24; Cotter 1994: 363–366.

advocate a theoretical equality of men and women: 'Virtue is the same for women as for men' (Diogenes Laertius 6.12, Loeb).[33] And Musonius Rufus (*c.* AD 30–101) argued that since both male and female horses were trained for racing and hunting, daughters should be educated as well as sons.[34] But the widespread assumption must have been, particularly in the Greek world, that education and cultural sophistication were almost exclusively a male prerogative. Whatever exceptions there may have been, it was generally accepted as a natural state of affairs that women were educationally and intellectually inferior to men.

If it was difficult for common Greek or Roman women to get a good education, the obstacles to Jewish women studying the Torah were even greater, and there is only very limited evidence that they ever did so.[35] The colourful, and undoubtedly extreme, opinion of Rabbi Eliezer on the matter is well known: 'Whoever teaches his daughter Torah teaches her obscenity' (*M. Sotah* 3 [21b]). Barrett (1971:331) cites the commentary of Strack and Billerbeck (III 467): 'In gatherings for worship the ancient synagogue did not on principle forbid women to speak in public, but did so in practice.' The intelligence of women was not esteemed very highly: 'Ten qab of empty-headedness have come upon the world, nine having been received by women and one by the rest of the world' (*Qiddušin* 49b).[36] Women had a reputation, among the rabbis, at least, for being talkative, emotionally unstable, unreliable, greedy, even dishonest and treacherous.[37]

Not much information is available about the status of women within Hellenistic Judaism.[38] Excerpts from Philo and Josephus give a flavour but represent only a limited perspective. Philo endorsed the traditional distinction that allocated the public domain (marketplaces, council halls, lawcourts, and other large gatherings) to men and confined women to the domestic sphere. 'The women', he wrote, 'are best suited to the indoor life which never strays from the house, within which the middle door is taken by the maidens as their boundary, and the outer door by those who have reached full womanhood[39] . . . A woman, then, should not be a busybody, meddling with matters outside her household concerns, but should seek a life of seclusion. She should not

---

[33] Plato had said that 'the female nature is inferior with regard to goodness to that of males' (Plato, *Laws* 6.781B).

[34] Musonius Rufus 4 (the passage is given in Lefkowitz & Fant 1992: 52–54; see also Oepke 1964: 780).

[35] Witherington 1990: 6–9; Keener 1992: 83; Kraemer 1992: 97–99.

[36] Translation from Oepke 1964: 781.

[37] See *Gen. Rabbah* 45 on 16:5; *Šabbat* 33b.

[38] *Cf.* Scroggs 1972: 290.

[39] *Cf.* 4 Macc. 18:6–7. Jeremias (1969: 362) points out that, chiefly for economic reasons, ordinary families 'could not adhere strictly to the totally retired life of the woman of rank, who was surrounded by her household of servants'.

show herself off like a vagrant in the streets before the eyes of other men,
except when she has to go to the temple . . .' (*De Specialibus Legibus* 3.169,
171, Loeb). Philo took it to be commonplace knowledge that women are
'endowed by nature with little sense' (*Quod omnis Probus Liber sit* 117, Loeb).
The testimony of women, Josephus says, should not be accepted in the courts
'because of the levity and temerity of their sex' (*Antiquities of the Jews* 4.219,
Loeb).

The participation of women in religious activity

The extensive participation of women in the cults of antiquity is certainly of
relevance to any study of the expectations regarding the role of women in
the New Testament church.[40] Both the public cultus and the mystery cults
gave women their most significant sphere of activity outside the home,
though R. S. Kraemer (1992:90) warns that we should not be 'too quick to
equate service to ancient deities with power and authority'. Women took
part in public processions. Some festivals were only for women. Women
featured prominently in the cult of Dionysus as maenads – 'mad women'
inspired with ecstatic frenzy by the god. They served as priestesses both in
the public cults (for example, the Vestal Virgins) and in the mysteries: the
hierophants of the cult of Demeter at Eleusis, for example, or the priestesses
of Isis. The cult of Isis, in particular, promoted the equality of women and
men, at least as a matter of principle. One prayer to Isis reads: 'You have
made the power of women equal to that of men' (*P. Oxyrhynchus* 1380,
214–216). Women were especially recognized for their aptitude in making
ecstatic pronouncements: the Pythian oracle at a Delphi, always a woman, is
the outstanding example.

Historians and satirists often attributed the success of the mystery cults that
were rapidly infiltrating the Graeco-Roman world from the East to the
superstitious and credulous nature of women. Juvenal (early second century
AD) lampoons the excesses of female devotees in his famously derisive and
histrionic style:

On a winter day she will go down to the Tiber,
Break the morning ice, plunge three times into the current,
Wash her fearful head where the waves crest high, and then, trembling,
Naked, with bleeding knees, crawl out on the field of Mars.
If white Io commands, she will go to the borders of Egypt,
Fetch from the sun-warmed Nile water, and sprinkle the temple
Sacred to Isis, that stands near the polling booths of the city.

[40] *Cf.* Oepke 1964: 786; Pomeroy 1975: 205–226; Meeks 1983: 24–25; Witherington
1990: 15, 22–25; Kraemer 1992.

> She has no doubt that she's called by the actual voice of the goddess –
> What a fine soul and mind for the gods to talk with by nighttime![41]

A respectable woman, in Plutarch's view, would 'shut the front door tight upon all queer rituals and outlandish superstitions. For with no god do stealthy and secret rites performed by a woman find any favour' *(Moralia* 140D, Loeb).[42] W. A. Meeks (1983:25) writes:

> What seems most likely is that some of the newer cults, especially in the years before they became part of the municipal establishments, allowed considerably more freedom for women to hold office alongside men than did the older state cults. This freedom in turn fueled the invective of opponents, who portrayed foreign superstitions as an insidious threat to the proper discipline of the household, and therefore to the fabric of the whole society.

The problem should not be overstated. The participation of women in the cults was not always ecstatic; nor was ecstatic worship restricted to women (see Keener 1992:77–78). Paul does not specifically attribute frenzied behaviour to women, and there is every reason to think that men as much as women were responsible for introducing pagan habits into Christian worship *(cf.* 1 Cor. 12:2–3). It is probably not specifically this sort of behaviour, therefore, that Paul is seeking to curb in 1 Corinthians 14:34–35. Nevertheless, it illustrates how hazardous and disruptive it could be for a woman to participate actively in novel and exotic forms of religion, and how such participation might hamper the endeavour of a new religious movement to gain credibility.

In both Palestinian and diaspora Judaism women were afforded much less scope for religious activity. It is generally assumed that men and women were segregated in the synagogue, though some scholars have disputed this.[43] Women sometimes figure in inscriptions as benefactors of ancient synagogues, and there is evidence that occasionally they held office or at least played a

---

[41] Juvenal, *The Sixth Satire: Against Women* (translation: Humphries 1958: 85). *Cf.* Pomeroy 1975: 221; Fiorenza 1983: 176–177; MacDonald 1990: 229–230. See also Strabo, *Geography* 7.3.4.

[42] *Cf.* a third- or second-century BC Pythagorean treatise (quoted in Lefkowitz & Fant 1992: 164); 'Women of importance . . . keep away from secret cults and Cybeline orgies in their homes. For public law prevents women from participating in these rites, particularly because these forms of worship encourage drunkenness and ecstasy. The mistress of the house and head of the household should be chaste and untouched in all respects.'

[43] Jeremias 1969: 374. *Cf.* Fee 1987: 703 and n. 21; Tomson 1990: 134; Kraemer 1992: 106–107. In any case, it is likely that an informal segregation operated, as often is the case in less egalitarian (or less permissive) societies.

significant role in the life of the synagogue.[44] Whether women ever exercised a liturgical function, however, is uncertain (Tomson 1990:134). The Tannaim explicitly prohibited women from officiating during community prayers: 'One does not invite women to read out before the community' (*Megilla* 3:11).[45]

It appears, therefore, that there would have been widespread resistance to the idea of women speaking in church. Neither the public *ekklēsia* nor the synagogue provided a model for the Christian gathering that would allow the free, vocal participation of women. This left only the cults with their altogether unacceptable moral and religious associations. These circumstances must certainly be taken into account in any attempt to understand Paul's injunction against women speaking in church.

The interpretation of 1 Corinthians 14:33b–35

The argument of 1 Corinthians 14

The first part of chapter 14 (vv. 1–25) is concerned basically with intelligibility and purpose, the second (vv. 26–40) with order and decency. The church is encouraged to seek 'spiritual things', but especially the gift of prophecy (v. 1). For whereas speaking in tongues, unless interpreted, is unintelligible, prophecy is a means by which the church may be built up and encouraged. This practical distinction between speaking in tongues and prophecy is expanded upon in verses 6–12 through various musical analogies. Speaking in tongues engages the spirit, but prophecy engages the mind (vv. 14–15) and is therefore meaningful to 'the person occupying the place of the unlearned' (v. 16). So Paul insists: 'in church I would rather speak five words with my mind, that I might also instruct others, than ten thousand words in a tongue' (v. 19). This opinion is underlined in a rather difficult passage by the argument that whereas the unbeliever is likely to regard speaking in tongues as madness – possibly the ecstatic 'madness' that characterized the mystery cults (*cf.* Fee 1987:685) – he may be convicted by a word of prophecy and be led to worship God (vv. 20–25).

Verse 26 returns to the theme of upbuilding but pursues the argument in a different direction; here it is not the intelligibility of these 'spiritual things' that is at issue, but the manner in which they are exercised. A wider range of activities is also now in view: 'Whenever you gather together, each has a hymn, has a teaching, has a revelation, has a tongue, has an interpretation; let all things be for upbuilding.' This should not become an unseemly free-for-all; speakers should take their turn. If there is no-one to interpret, the one who

[44] See Brooten 1982: 27–30; 1985: 78. See also Jeremias 1969: 374 n. 79; Dunn 1988: 2: 888; Kraemer 1992: 117–123.
[45] Quoted in Tomson 1990: 134. Tomson (1990: 134) says that 'women attended synagogue but prayed silently and did not officiate'.

speaks in tongues should be silent; if something is revealed to a person sitting in the congregation, the person who has stood to prophesy should likewise be silent. Prophecy should be a disciplined activity; it is subject both to the prophet and to the judgment of the church. For, as Paul concludes, 'God is not of disorder, but of peace' (v. 33a). The whole argument is recapitulated in verses 39–40: 'So, brethren, be eager to prophesy and do not discourage speaking in tongues; but let all things be done properly and in order' – and presumably this concern for propriety and order also encompasses what is said in verses 33b–35 about women speaking church.

What is expected of women?

'It is not permitted to them to speak'

Women are instructed in the first place to 'keep silent [*sigatōsan*] in the churches'. The same verb is found in verse 28 (the person speaking in tongues, if there is no interpreter, should 'keep silent in church') and in verse 30 (a prophet should 'keep silent' if someone else receives a revelation). The prophet and the speaker in tongues, however, are obliged to keep silent only under certain circumstances and for the sake of decency and order. The argument against women speaking is of a rather different sort. On the one hand, it is framed as a comprehensive and unqualified prohibition, and on the other, it is rooted in the fact of womanhood, not in the activity of speaking.

So two questions arise. What exactly is prohibited here? And on what grounds? The second question will be considered in the next section. In order to address the first, we must return to the problem of how these verses are to be reconciled with the assumption that women prayed and prophesied in church. What is meant by silence if women were allowed to utter prayers and prophecies?[46] We came close to a solution with the observation that verse 35 appears to identify the sort of speaking that Paul had in mind. But the language in which the prohibition is couched is more comprehensive than this. The asking of questions is probably only one type of speech that is banned; Paul draws attention to it only because it is the most constructive and perhaps the most excusable.

The way forward may be to recognize a different dimension to the distinction between women praying and prophesying and women keeping enforced silence. W. Stegemann (1993:163) has argued that two principal activities took place in the Christian *ekklēsia*: 'cultic rituals (such as the prayers and prophetic utterances of 1 Cor. 11 and 14) and teaching debates'. It is the

---

[46] The suggestion that women prayed and prophesied silently (Tomson 1990: 137) is far-fetched. How is prophecy to be weighed? How is anyone to know whether a woman is praying or not?

participation of women in these teaching debates, he says, that is regulated in 1 Corinthians 14:34–35. 'As in the citizen assembly, women are not allowed to speak in the Christian *ekklesia*, because it is *shameful* (*aischron*) for them to do so.' Stegemann quotes Valerius Maximus (first century AD): 'What have women to do with the citizen assembly? If the custom of our fathers is observed, nothing' (*Factorum et Dictorum Memorabilium Libri* 3.8.6).

This is a constructive line of interpretation, but there are some difficulties. First, it is not apparent that any such clear distinction existed in the Christian *ekklēsia* between cultic ritual and teaching debates. No distinction is made between worship which is *en ekklēsia* (*e.g.* v. 28) and the unacceptable speaking of women *en ekklēsia* (v. 35). Secondly, verses 34–35 are set in the midst of instruction chiefly about speaking in tongues and prophecy; in other words, they relate to the same context of 'cultic ritual'. This is underlined by the fact that teaching is listed in verse 26 as one of several contributions to the edification of the church, not as a separate activity. Thirdly, Paul's demand for silence does not discriminate in quite this way; it appears to apply generally to the situation of the assembled community.

A clue to what may prove to be a more satisfactory solution is found in verse 30, which makes it clear that those who prophesied, and presumably those who prayed or spoke in tongues, did so *standing*: 'if something should be revealed to another person sitting, let the first be silent'. In view of this we might imagine that Paul expected women seated in the congregation to remain silent during the course of the worship service; but they were naturally exempted from this rule whenever they stood up to pray or prophesy.[47] If at this moment a woman covered her head, as I argued in chapter 4, this would further distinguish the authorized activity of prayer and prophecy from her otherwise silent and inactive participation in the rest of the service. The actual posture, no doubt, matters less than the fact that prophecy was a clearly defined activity subject to a different set of regulations. Whether women participated in the weighing of prophecy would then depend on how this was undertaken. If people took turns to stand and comment on what had been said, then perhaps women were involved in that, too.

So what exactly was prohibited to women? One can readily imagine that chattering among themselves in the congregation came under the ban, whether or not women were formally segregated in the churches. Asking

---

[47] Possibly *hai gynaikes* ('the women') in verse 34 denotes the women as a distinct group, perhaps segregated, in the congregation. Note also Oepke 1964: 787: 'The apostle is simply preventing women from taking the initiative in speaking, but allows exceptions where there is genuine pneumatic endowment.' Perhaps women standing participated in the 'spiritual' act of worship, edification, *etc.*; they were in the charismatic sphere. Women *in the congregation* (and men, too, for that matter) were subject to prevailing custom and mores.

questions of the speaker, offering (unsolicited?) opinions, and generally entering into discussions and debate would have been included. Spontaneous prophetic outbursts, without due respect for the sort of order prescribed in verses 29–31, would also have been regarded as inappropriate. Whether Paul would have debarred women from teaching at this point is uncertain. Perhaps a woman might have stood and delivered a 'teaching' (*didachēn*, v. 26) in the same way that she prayed or prophesied. But this is more speculative, and teaching raises a different set of problems.

'Let them be submissive'

In view of the general preoccupation of the chapter with church rather than family order and the fact that no indirect object is provided for *hypotassesthōsan* ('let them be submissive'), it has been argued that the submission enjoined is not to the women's husbands but to the 'principle of order in the worship service'.[48] This is quite persuasive. The woman's submission is closely connected with the command not to speak; but women are instructed to keep silent not because their husbands are present but because they are in church. It is likely, therefore, that the need for submission is to be explained from the context of worship rather than from the woman's direct relationship to her husband.

In objecting to this interpretation Carson (1991:146) asks why women are singled out in this way when men surely would have been expected to submit to the 'ecclesiastical structures' instituted here; and he argues that *hypotassō* normally involves submission to a person or persons, not to an order or procedure. As regards the first point, the question that must be asked is: what *manner* of submission to the order of worship was appropriate for women? The submission of men to the 'ecclesiastical structures' would have been expressed differently and is not the issue here. Carson's second objection is unfounded. The verb *hypotassō* is used with an abstract indirect object in Romans 8:7, for example: 'the mind of the flesh is hostile to God, for it does not submit (*ouch hypotassetai*) to the law of God'.[49]

Since Paul does not make it clear to whom or to what women should be submissive, however, we probably do not need to define the idea too precisely. What Paul has in mind is simply the general demeanour and behaviour of women in worship, though any unruly behaviour on the part of a woman would undoubtedly have been regarded as an affront both to her husband and to church order. Perhaps we should think of submission to the husband as the underlying rationale for the more general submission to the order of worship.

---

[48] Witherington 1988: 102–103; 1990: 177; *cf.* Liefeld 1986a: 151.
[49] *Cf.* Rom. 10:3; *1 Clement* 34:5; Hermas *Mandate* 12, 5.1.

'Let them ask their own husbands at home'

The argument that women have no reason to speak in church because, if necessary, they can ask their own husbands at home appears to echo conventional expectations. We have already come across the question that Cato put to the rebellious women of Rome: 'Could you not have made the same requests, each of your own husband, at home?'[50] The idea is also expressed, more poetically and with greater condescension, in Plutarch's advice to Pollianus: 'And for your wife you must collect from every source what is useful, as do the bees, and carrying it within your own self impart it to her, and then discuss it with her, and make the best of these doctrines her favourite and familiar themes' (*Moralia* 145C, Loeb). Unmarried women, one imagines, would have asked their fathers or brothers.

Did Paul view this arrangement as a proper and deliberate means of educating women, perhaps even with the long-term goal of qualifying them to teach?[51] In this context the recommendation that women should ask their husbands at home sounds like an improvised expedient, a rather vexed response to an unforeseen practical difficulty. 1 Timothy 2:11 ('Let a woman learn in quietness in all submission') appears to reflect a more deliberate commitment to instruct women in matters pertaining to the gospel. But still, there is no good reason to think that Paul himself ever envisaged that women would eventually acquire the competence to teach in the church. The purpose is more likely to have been simply to keep women from spiritual and doctrinal error. The ubiquitous Plutarch regarded philosophical instruction as a safeguard against a wife becoming a dancer or believing superstitious nonsense. 'For if they do not receive the seed of good doctrines and share with their husbands in intellectual advancement, they, left to themselves, conceive many untoward ideas and low designs and emotions' (*Moralia* 145DE, Loeb).

Grounds for these requirements

What can be said about the reasons for these instructions? Why does Paul restrict the participation of women in worship in this way? And the more contentious question: were these regulations meant to be binding on the church throughout the ages?

First, some negative observations. No overt appeal is made to the order of creation, though we shall consider in a moment the possibility that the words 'as also the law says' allude to the creation narratives. No positive reason is given for keeping silent, such as the need to learn attentively – in contrast to 1 Timothy 2:11.[52] Nor is any specific practical justification provided, such as the

---

[50] Livy 34.2.1–14, quoted above, p. 114.
[51] *Cf.* Keener 1992: 112; 1993: 590.
[52] Against Witherington 1988: 102–103.

problem of women being put in the position of judging or opposing their husband's prophetic words.[53] The injunction appears quite undiscriminating and to be founded on very general assumptions about the status and condition of women.

Indeed, we should be careful not to place too much weight on the question of why women rather than men were not allowed to speak in the congregation. It is unhelpful, for example, to claim that 'Paul is opposing only the irrelevant questions some women have been asking during the teaching part of the service' (Keener 1992:85), because the obvious retort would be: 'So why does he prohibit *all* women from speaking?' It is difficult to mitigate the absoluteness of Paul's command here. Although women's lack of education and ignorance of the ways of the public assembly undoubtedly lie behind the prohibition, the principal reason has to do with the simple fact that they were women.[54] We should probably assume, on the basis of these directives, that it would have been acceptable for a man to ask an irrelevant or trivial question but not for a woman to ask an intelligent one. Male chatter may have been no less inane than female, but the implication of Paul's teaching is that what was prohibited for women was permissible for men. Decisive for Paul's argument are the issues of submission, shame and common church practice, not the relative merit of what women are saying. Investigations into the educational status of women in the ancient Mediterranean world may explain why Paul instructed women to learn from their husbands at home, but not – at least, not directly – why he imposed silence on them in church.

So much for what Paul does not say. What about the positive arguments? In a short space he makes use of a remarkable range of authority sources to support his demand that women should keep silent, from the practice of other churches to a 'command of the Lord'. Whether this reflects the strength of opposition at Corinth or the strength of Paul's feelings on the matter is not clear, but the arguments that he puts forward cannot be lightly dismissed.

'As in all the churches of the saints'

We have already seen that when Paul appeals to common church practice elsewhere in 1 Corinthians, the reference is to concrete instructions or teaching. Paul sent Timothy to Corinth to remind them of his 'ways' in Christ, 'as everywhere in every church I teach' (1 Cor. 4:17). In 1 Corinthians 7:17 Paul's 'rule in all the churches', that each believer should remain in the condition in which he was called, presupposes a particular circumstance, namely the strongly felt imminence of the end of the age: 'for the form of this

---

[53] Against Liefeld 1986a: 150.
[54] Against Jervis 1995: 69.

world is passing away' (v. 31). The question must surely be open whether, in the face of a rather different historical and eschatological horizon, the rule not to depart from the condition in which one is called still holds.[55] The word that Paul uses for 'rule' here (*diatassō*) is used in 1 Corinthians 9:14 of the Lord's 'command' that those who proclaim the gospel should gain a living from the gospel. But Paul himself disregarded this 'command': 'I have made no use of these things' (v. 15). He concludes his discussion of women's head-coverings in 1 Corinthians 11:3–16 with the combative assertion: 'If anyone is inclined to be argumentative, we do not have such a custom [*synētheian*], nor do the churches of God.' But still, it is only a custom and customs can change: Paul speaks in 1 Corinthians 8:7 of those who formerly 'by custom' (*tē synētheia*) were idol-worshippers. What this all suggests is that an appeal to common church practice is meant to indicate not so much an absolute and incontestable ruling as well-established guidelines for dealing with a current situation.

Paul's argument here, however, might also be considered from a different angle. The question of conformity to church practice is clearly of some importance to Paul, since in essence it is repeated in verse 36: 'Did the word of God originate with you, or did it come down to you alone?' In view of this, we might ask whether Paul's real concern is less to impose silence on women in church than to bring the Corinthian congregation into line with other churches. The fact that Paul refers to the law at this point may indicate that he has in mind particularly the more Jewish congregations and the churches of Judaea. Indeed, this may explain why the reference to the law is so imprecise; the reference is not so much to any specific text as to the practice of Jewish Christianity. From this perspective Paul's teaching has less to do with the intrinsic status of women than with Jewish–Gentile relations. We shall return to this point shortly.

'It is not permitted . . .'

The way the argument in verse 34 is constructed gives the statement 'it is not permitted' (*ou . . . epitrepetai*) greater argumentative force than the appeal to the law. In other words, it is the weight of apostolic authority that principally underpins the command not to speak. But what sort of weight does this denial of permission have? Apart from its occurrence here and in 1 Timothy 2:12 the sense in which *epitrepō* is consistently used in the New Testament is that of giving someone leave or permission to do something: demons are given leave to enter a herd of swine (Lk. 8:32); Paul is given permission by Agrippa to speak in his own defence (Acts 26:1). It is in every case related to a specific and

---

[55] This assumes that we can talk about the 'eschatological horizon' in a relative sense as well as an absolute and final sense. New Testament eschatology both transcends and is enmeshed in the immediate social and political circumstances.

limited set of practical circumstances, and authority is clearly located in an individual, not in a body of absolute truth. Even the permission to divorce granted by Moses (Mt. 19:8; Mk. 10:4), which comes closest to being the imposition of a theological principle, appears as a pragmatic concession and is implicitly restricted to the period of the law.[56] To deny someone permission to do something is to limit their freedom to act, but it does not necessarily mean that the action is intrinsically wrong; it is wrong given a particular state of affairs.

Schreiner (1995:126) argues that it is not the verb itself but the context which determines whether a universal or a contingent prohibition is in view. He gives a contemporary example: 'If I say to my daughter, "You are not permitted to drive the car one hundred miles per hour," it is obvious (or should be!) that this is a universal prohibition.' But is it so obvious? What if she moved to Germany where there are no speed limits on the motorways? What if she became a racing driver? What if in twenty years' time, as a result of technological developments, it became perfectly normal to drive at one hundred miles per hour? Or to consider the issue from a different perspective, would he have said to his daughter, 'You are not permitted to murder', or 'You are not permitted to commit adultery'? In these situations the language of permission must surely be inappropriate. Schreiner argues that the verb is used in the New Testament in contexts (1 Cor. 16:7; Heb. 6:3) where it is 'not necessarily limited to a specific situation'. But the expression 'if the Lord/God permits' is used in both these passages in relation to a particular set of circumstances. Hebrews 6:3 is especially interesting because clearly it would be a good thing for the recipients of the letter to leave the elementary doctrine of Christ and move on to maturity, but the writer entertains the possibility that the Lord will not permit this – surely for contingent reasons.

So, although this cannot be a decisive argument, it still seems likely that implicit in the use of *epitrepō* is an awareness on Paul's part that *certain circumstances* make it advisable to prohibit women to speak – or, in the case of 1 Timothy 2:12, to teach – in the congregation. The restriction is a matter of church governance, of practical and conditional, rather than theological and universal, authority.[57] There is, after all, no *a priori* reason why Paul should not impose a limited restriction in this way – or even, for that matter, why such a restriction should not be understood as a 'command of the Lord' (v. 37).

---

[56] Note that *epitrepō* is used in 4 Macc. 5:26 in connection with the law, but in this case it is God who gives permission (to eat certain foods).

[57] *Cf.* Gritz 1991: 130; Kroeger & Kroeger 1992: 82–83. Moo (1991: 184–185) is correct in saying that the present tense of *epitrepō* does not restrict the application of the injunction (as against Padgett 1987: 25; Redekop 1990: 242); the issue, however, is not the tense of the word but its usage, particularly in the New Testament.

'As also the law says'

Paul's reference to the law at this point ('. . . as also the law says') has been a confounded puzzle. Such an obscure and indefinite allusion to the law is uncharacteristic of Paul and has often been taken as evidence for an interpolation (*cf.* Fee 1987:707). This argument is inconclusive, but the difficulties are numerous. Does the 'law' in question say that women should be silent or that they should be submissive? Do we have here a reference to the Old Testament Scriptures, and if so, what is the text? Or does Paul have in mind oral tradition? A midrashic expansion of the creation narratives? Does he invoke the law approvingly, as proper justification for his instructions? Or is the point more incidental ('*even* the law says this') or illustrative ('the law *also* says this')?

The precise identity of the law is the immediate problem. It could be that Paul has in mind the words of Genesis 3:16: 'your turning will be to your husband, and he will rule over you'.[58] We would then have to decide whether he meant this 'law' to be understood positively or negatively, as a desirable or a regrettable state of affairs. Could he have reasserted the relevance of such a direct consequence of the fall for the redeemed community? If so, we must surely assume that he regarded it only as an unavoidable restriction in the face of the distortion of the created order. Just as women must accept the *biological* reality of painful childbirth in a fallen world (*cf.* 1 Tim. 2:15), so, in Paul's perspective, they must also accept the *sociological* reality of inequality and hierarchy in a fallen world. These are different aspects of human existence, but they have the same origin.

Alternatively, the absolute reference to 'the law' in verse 34 might be explained by supposing that Paul is referring back to a previous mention in the letter. This would have to be the allusion to the creation narratives in the argument of 11:8–9 that woman was created from man and for the sake of the man.[59] A close connection between the silence of women and the order of creation is also found in 1 Timothy 2:12–14. In many ways this is an attractive explanation. The problem with it is that Genesis 2:20b–24 does not 'say' that the woman should be silent or submissive; nor is it clear that in Paul's view these were implied in the order of creation.

A less precise referent might be found in the figure of the virtuous woman in Proverbs, who 'opened her mouth heedfully and subject to the law [*ennomōs*], and set order on her tongue . . .' (31:25, LXX); who 'opens her

[58] *Cf.* Robertson & Plummer 1914: 325; Grosheide 1953: 343; Barrett 1971: 330; Ellis 1989: 68–69. Objecting to this view, Fung (1987: 192) stresses that the pronouncement on Eve 'was not strictly a curse inflicted upon the woman, but a predictive warning, and in no sense a command'.

[59] *Cf.* Tomson 1990: 137; Carson 1991: 152.

mouth wisely and according to law [*nomothesmōs*]' (31:28, LXX). The connection between vocal restraint and the law in the text of the Septuagint may go some way towards explaining Paul's arguments in verse 34. Ben Sirach also placed high value on female reticence: 'A silent [*sigēra*] wife is a gift of the Lord, and there is nothing so precious as a disciplined soul' (Sirach 26:14). The wisdom-literature background probably offers a more satisfactory explanation than the view that Paul is citing a rabbinic formula.[60]

In the end it is difficult to identify a specific text. But do we need to do so? Quite possibly the reference is meant comprehensively, encompassing all these texts. Or if, as suggested above, Paul has in mind the need for harmony between the practice of Jewish and Gentile churches, it may be that 'as also the law says' is a general reference to the teaching of Jewish Christianity on the matter. The assumption is only that the practice of Jewish churches in this respect arises from Jewish Christian interpretation of the law. Of course, this is uncharacteristic of Pauline usage, but then so too is the failure to cite the actual text.

The more theoretical question that we face is whether Paul could have invoked the Old Testament law in support of his teaching on Christian conduct. This is a complex issue and can be treated here only in a somewhat rough and summary fashion.

There are clear statements in Paul's letters to the effect that the law has been abrogated as a determinative and controlling force in the life of the believer. 'Now we are discharged from the law, having died to that by which we were bound, so that we might serve in newness of spirit and not oldness of letter' (Rom. 7:6; *cf.* Gal. 2:19). The law that divided Jews and Gentiles has been abolished: Christ 'has broken down the dividing wall of the partition, the hostility, in his flesh abolishing the law of commandments in decrees' (Eph. 2:14–15).

The new life that the believer enjoys in the Spirit is not, however, completely *without law*. 'Do we abolish the law by faith?' Paul asks. 'By no means! But we uphold the law' (Rom. 3:31). In so far as the law is unable to make righteous and in fact serves only to accentuate human sinfulness and

---

[60] Note also Est. 1:20–22. On the possibility of an oral tradition see Aalen 1964: 513–525; also Fee 1987: 707 and n. 34. Wolff (1982: 144) suggests that the silence of women in temple and synagogue worship is derived from the Torah, citing Sipre Deut. on 22.16. Josephus makes a remarkably similar appeal to 'the Law': 'The woman, says the Law, is in all things inferior to the man' (*Against Apion* 2.201, Loeb). According to Tomson this is a reference not to the written law but to halakha, the interpretation and application by the rabbis of the principles of Mosaic law (Tomson 1990: 133 n. 199). In the same passage Josephus writes that 'The Law recognizes no sexual connexions, except the natural union of man and wife, and that only for the procreation of children' (199), but the latter restriction appears to be rabbinic rather than biblical (see note in Loeb edition, 373).

fractiousness, it has been abolished in Christ. But in so far as it expresses the will of God, it has been *fulfilled*: 'he who loves his neighbour has fulfilled the law . . . love is the fulfilling of the law' (Rom. 13:8, 10). Love does not make the commandments void; love is the means by which the requirements of the moral law are satisfied, because 'love does not do wrong to the neighbour' (Rom. 13:10). This law that is 'fulfilled' through love, through bearing one another's burdens, is now the 'law of Christ' (Gal. 5:14; 6:2). Not only love of one's neighbour but also the life in the Spirit is understood as a fulfilment of the law. Through Jesus God condemned sin in the flesh 'so that the requirement of the law might be fulfilled in us, who walk not according to the flesh but according to the Spirit' (Rom. 8:4). The 'law' and 'commandments' *of God* are still valid: 'circumcision is nothing, and uncircumcision is nothing, but keeping of the commandments of God' (1 Cor. 7:19); and if Paul became as one without the law among Gentiles, nevertheless he was not 'without the law of God but under the law [*ennomos*] of Christ' (1 Cor. 9:21).

But is this enough to demonstrate that Paul's appeal to the law at this point makes the demand for silence and submissiveness on the part of women in church a universally binding prescription? Or to put the question differently, does 'law' in verse 34 refer to the 'law of God' that Paul still acknowledges or to the 'law of commandments in decrees' that has been abolished? Carson (1991:148) points out that Paul makes use of the law as a basis for human conduct in 1 Corinthians 9:8–9 in his justification of the practice of making a living from the gospel: 'Do I speak these things according to man or does not also the law say these things?' But ironically Paul himself does not adhere to this rule (v. 12b). In Ephesians 6:2 Paul cites the commandment 'Honour your father and mother' in support of his counsel to children: 'Obey your parents in the Lord, for this is right.' But otherwise this sort of appeal to the law is rare in Paul, and not unambiguous. On the whole, he is more inclined to emphasize the characteristics of a righteous life, the fruits of righteousness (Phil. 1:11), without making any direct connection to Old Testament law.[61]

One important reason why the concept of 'law' was retained in Paul's teaching even though those in Christ are no longer 'under law' was the need to regulate at a practical level relations between Jews and Gentiles. The difficulties caused by conflict between these two groups constitute a minor but recurrent theme in 1 Corinthians (*e.g.* 1 Cor. 1:22–24; 7:17–19; 8:1–13; 9:19–23; 10:14–22, 23–33; 12:12–13; 16:1–4). Although the point is not made explicitly, it is likely that it is this specific problem, so central to Paul's

[61] See *e.g.* Rom. 13:9: the commandments are cited but transcended by the comprehensive and fundamental command to love one's neighbour. Sanders points out that in 1 Cor. 10 Paul goes to some trouble to argue both on typological and Christological grounds that idolatry is wrong, yet he fails to mention the first commandment (Sanders 1983: 95; *cf.* 107).

ministry, and not just an anxiety about what is socially and culturally acceptable, that lies behind the restrictions imposed in 1 Corinthians 14:34–35.

In general terms, we might ask to what extent Paul's teaching in the churches was aimed at maintaining fellowship between Jewish and Gentile believers. At the end of 1 Corinthians 10 Paul summarizes his teaching on the eating of food offered to idols, a subject of considerable importance for Jewish–Gentile relations: 'Whether then you eat or drink or do anything, do all things to the glory of God. Be unoffending to the Jews and to the Greeks and to the church of God, as I also strive to please all men in all things . . .' (10:31–33). He then urges the Corinthians to imitate him in this, as he imitates Christ (11:1), and praises them for remembering him in everything and holding fast to the 'traditions' that he had handed on to them (11:2). We might reasonably assume, therefore, that the wish to be 'unoffending to the Jews and to the Greeks and to the church of God' constitutes a significant part of the rationale for his teaching in the churches and, indeed, for the teaching of 1 Corinthians 11 – 14.

That women should pray and prophesy with their heads covered was certainly one element in these traditions – a 'custom' practised in all the churches of God (1 Cor. 11:16).[62] The requirement that women should keep silent in the congregation, as we have seen, was a matter of common church practice ('As in all the churches of the saints . . .') and so also formed part of this body of teaching. Earlier in the letter Paul referred to another 'rule in all the churches' (1 Cor. 7:17), which had to do principally with the status of Jews and Gentiles in the church: 'Anyone circumcised at the time of his call, let him not be uncircumcised. If anyone has been called in uncircumcision, let him not be circumcised' (7:18).

This gives us grounds for thinking that Paul imposed silence on women in the congregation in order to avoid offence – in particular, offence either to non-believing Jews who might enter the church (*cf.* 14:23) or to Jewish Christians who were already part of the church. Undoubtedly there were those among the Gentiles who also strongly disapproved of women participating vocally in public meetings, but Paul's instructions here are generally recognized to have a pronounced Jewish Christian character and in this matter at least indicate a bias towards accommodating Jewish opinion.[63]

---

[62] The point of 1 Cor. 11.3–16 is not that Paul omitted to pass on these instructions before. This is one of the traditions that they have held to, as is clear from the contrastive force of verse 17 ('In the following matter I do *not* praise you . . .'); but it has obviously been called into question by some who are disposed to be 'argumentative' (v. 16). Paul's aim, therefore, is to reinforce the custom, not to institute it.

[63] Tomson (1990: 132), for example, draws attention to the 'authoritative, Jewish-Christian character' of the language of 'traditions' and 'customs'.

Acts 18:1–17 illustrates both the Jewish Christian origins of the church in Corinth and the potential for misunderstanding and conflict. Whether this bias was pragmatically or personally motivated is not clear. Arguably, however, it provides a more significant explanation of why Paul restricted the participation of women in Christian worship than the fear that the church might be 'mistaken for one of the orgiastic, secret, oriental cults that undermined public order and decency' (Fiorenza 1983:232). It is likely, in fact, that verse 23 reflects a specifically Jewish distaste for the madness or *mania* of the cults.

If, on the other hand, we are to suppose that Paul saw good reason to insist, on the basis of the law, that women should keep quiet in church, how are we to reconcile this with a gospel of grace?

The law is specifically a means of dealing with the effects of sin, otherwise in Christ it is superseded by grace: 'Why then the law? It was added because of transgressions, until the seed might come to whom it has been promised' (Gal. 3:19). The believer has been discharged from the law (Rom. 7:6). Where there is no sin, there is no need for the law. Where there is sin – for example, the injustice of inequality – the law may be necessary. It is when we do what we know to be wrong that the law becomes valuable: 'If I do that which I do not want, I agree with the law that it is good' (Rom. 7:16). This is also made clear in 1 Timothy 1:8–9: 'But we know that the law is good, if anyone should use it legitimately, knowing this, that the law is not given for a righteous person but for the lawless and the insubordinate, for the ungodly and sinners . . .'

The question to be asked is: where is the sin? Is it sin for a woman to speak in church? Or is the sin the disorder or offence that women speaking inappropriately might cause in certain societies and cultures? Is it a matter of insubordination today if a woman voices an opinion in church, in the presence of her husband? If not, do we still need to invoke this 'law'? Is the 'commandment of God' any longer applicable? There is no unequivocal appeal to the order of creation here; for all the accumulation of authority sources, the issue appears to be entirely practical. Paul had good reason to curb the involvement of women in the worship service. The church today, particularly the church in the West, has to ask itself whether this is still the case. Do we have good reason to impose such restrictions on the freedom of believers?

'It is shameful . . .'

Although the concept of shame is in some ways an elusive and ambiguous one, it is quite apparent that it was highly determinative for behaviour in the cultural world of Paul's churches.[64] The various regulations and assumptions

---

[64] For a concise overview of the subject see Moxnes 1993.

regarding the status and behaviour of women that we have considered in this chapter are all underpinned, emotionally and socially, by a strong sense of what is honourable and what is shameful.

Shame has to do essentially with an awareness of public judgment on behaviour; MacDonald (1996:145) is broadly correct when she says that both passages dealing with the participation of women in worship in 1 Corinthians must be understood in the light of Paul's 'obvious sensitivity to the public visibility of Christian ritual'. Shame operates within the framework of a code of conventional social values; it has a moral dimension primarily within a sociological framework. To be ashamed of immoral behaviour (*e.g.* Rom. 6:21) is not simply to admit the intrinsic wrongness of that behaviour; it is to recognize that it is socially unacceptable. Indeed, in certain circumstances it is possible to be ashamed of something which according to one set of values is laudable but which according to another is judged despicable. When Paul writes that Onesiphorus was 'not ashamed [*ouk epaischynthē*] of my chains' (2 Tim. 1:16), we are made aware of the disapproval and contempt of the larger society in respect of the condition of the prisoner; but in the light of the gospel, and in the eyes of Onesiphorus, Paul's imprisonment was not at all shameful.

So when Paul asserts that it is shameful for a woman to speak in church, this is not in the first place a judgment on the essential rightness or wrongness of women speaking in church but a recognition of the public unacceptability of that action. This can be illustrated by considering the two other places in Paul's letters where the expression 'it is shameful to . . .' is used.[65] In 1 Corinthians 11:6 he says: 'If it is shameful [*aischron*] for a woman to have herself shaved or be shorn, let her veil herself.' This is clearly not directly a matter of behaviour that is immoral or contrary to divine law; at most, the shaving of a woman's head is *indicative* of an immoral character. In Ephesians 5:12 Paul says, 'it is shameful even to mention the things done by them in secret'. What is shameful here is not just the immoral deeds but also the act of speaking about them in public; these are not appropriate topics of conversation in polite society. It is quite possible, therefore, for an action to be shameful without being intrinsically wrong.

If shamefulness is primarily a matter of public acceptability, then we must allow for a measure of relativity in the judgment of what is shameful. This is necessary with regard not only to the type of action that in any culture is considered shameful but also to the intensity with which that shame is felt and expressed. Any attempt to translate these instructions into rules of behaviour for the church today must take into account the constraints of privacy and

---

[65] Note the similar *aischron . . . ei . . .* construction and the same connection with *public* disgrace in Judith 12:12; 4 Macc. 6:20; 16:17.

submission under which women in the ancient world lived and the extent to which such constraints were enforced by a powerful ethos of honour and shame. In most western cultures at least, it is not now shameful for a woman to speak in public. On the contrary, it may be considered shameful to deny women the opportunity to participate fully and on equal terms with men in the public process. Those who complain that in allowing women to lead and teach, the church is blindly conforming to the standards of the world, may simply be recommending instead blind conformity to the standards of the ancient world.

'A command of the Lord'

M. Harper (1994:64) argues that Paul's language in verses 37–38 is far too serious to be dismissed at the bidding of feminist self-interest. Paul is quite adamant that his instructions constitute a 'command of the Lord': 'If anyone thinks that he [or she?] is a prophet or spiritual, let him recognize that the things that I write to you are a command of the Lord' (v. 37).[66] Since he expects this command to be 'recognized' by those who are spiritually gifted, it is probably to be understood as a prophetically received command rather than an unknown saying of Jesus.[67] Are we bound to assume, however, that a 'command of the Lord' must be uncritically applied, regardless of the circumstances? Is there any reason why such a command should not be addressed to, and restricted to, a particular cultural situation? Is the Lord able to issue only absolute, and never contingent, commands? We should notice the strong connection (*hōste*) between the assertion that the instructions of this chapter are a command of the Lord (vv. 37–38) and the closing reiteration of the main practical theme, that all things should be done 'properly and in order' (vv. 39–40). The impression is surely given that something other than the universal condition of womanhood is at issue in this 'command of the Lord'.

This may well seem a hazardous path to take. It may appear that in principle all Scripture could be relativized in this way. But the assertion that what Paul has written is a command of the Lord, at least in so far as it refers to the instructions of 1 Corinthians 14:34–35, is intended only to reinforce a position that has already been established on other grounds. *Given that* it was considered shameful for women to speak in church, then it was entirely fitting that the

[66] In Paul's letters the 'word of God' (v. 36) usually, if not always, denotes the gospel rather than a specific command. The issue here appears to have to do with the spiritual authority that the Corinthians were abrogating for themselves rather than with the specific content of the 'word of God'. The phrase *ho logos tou theou*, therefore, is not equivalent to *kyriou . . . entolē*.

[67] *Cf.* Conzelmann 1975: 246. Tomson (1990: 138), however, finds here an appeal to a Jesus tradition.

solution proposed should be understood not merely as human opinion but as a command of the Lord.

Conclusions

If we are unwilling to dismiss this passage as post-Pauline, we must certainly take Paul's language seriously. It was clearly his ruling in the churches for which he had apostolic responsibility that women should not speak during the course of the worship service. The exception was when they stood, with their heads covered, to pray or prophesy and perhaps to participate in the other forms of charismatic ministry that are mentioned in verses 26–30. The formal reasons for this injunction are reasonably clear. The leading argument is that this is the practice in all the churches; and this practice is confirmed by apostolic authority. The submission, and perhaps the silence, of women in church is further supported by appeal to the Jewish 'law' in some form or other, and to standards of public decency. Finally, the whole argument, and perhaps the whole chapter, is presented as a prophetically inspired 'command of the Lord'.

These are the formal reasons; the underlying motivation is more difficult to discern. We can assume that the injunction arises partly out of concern for how the church was perceived within the prevailing culture of the ancient Mediterranean world; and anyone who has lived in a society in which the church is viewed with suspicion and barely tolerated will understand Paul's apprehension. On the one hand, there was prejudice against the participation of women in public gatherings; on the other, there was distrust of the outlandish and, in the view of many, subversive behaviour of women in many of the unofficial cults that were infiltrating from the East. Paul was unwilling for the oriental 'mystery' cult of Jesus Christ to be tarred with the same brush. Similarly, it would not help the cause of the gospel today for the church to be associated in the public mind with certain forms of radical feminism. This might be a strong argument in support of restricting the activity of women within the church; but it is still a contingent argument, not an absolute one.[68]

The other motive – perhaps the more important one – that has surfaced in the course of this investigation is Paul's natural desire to maintain good relations between Jews and Gentiles. One can easily imagine that the preference for silent women reflected certain personal instincts, but the

---

[68] Referring to Paul's exclusion of women from leadership in 1 Timothy, B. Barron (1990: 456) writes: 'One can see definite application to our own day, in which all too many women have brought the angry, divisive cultural baggage of radical feminism into their justifiable quest for a share of Church leadership. Perhaps, ironically, periods of feminist ideology are the times in which the church does need to consider temporary limitations on women in leadership.'

overriding consideration must have been pragmatic. If an unbelieving Jew would be offended by the unruly behaviour of women in a church service, then it was better for women to be silent. If Jewish Christians would find it difficult to worship in a church full of talkative women, then it was better for women to be silent. At the same time, this concern for order and acceptability did not prevent women from participating in the charismatic ministries of the worship service. This surely was also instinctive for the Christian Paul.

If this analysis is valid, then these underlying motives need to be taken just as seriously as the prohibition itself. It is highly unlikely that Paul saw the silence and submission of women within the church service as an inevitable inference from the creation order. In this case, we are obliged by the gospel itself to ask why he believed that such a restriction was necessary and whether such reasons are still applicable. Baumert (1996:198) points to the paradox that may arise as the church seeks to apply Scripture in changing circumstances:

> Behind all this stands a fundamental principle: if the situation should change, you should do whatever will be perceived as appropriate! Thus, following this same principle, today not only would Paul not be *against* such 'participation' by women in discussions, he would rather insist upon it! For otherwise our parish councils would be 'unbiblical.'

6. Leading him up the garden path
1 Timothy 2:11–15

Gynē en hēsychia manthanetō en pasē hypotagē; [12]*didaskein de gynaiki ouk epitrepō oude authentein andros, all' einai en hēsychia.* [13]*Adam gar prōtos eplasthē, eita Heua.* [13]*kai Adam ouk ēpatēthē, hē de gynē exapatētheisa en parabasei gegonen;* [15]*sōthēsetai de dia tēs teknogonias, ean meinōsin en pistei kai agapē kai hagiasmō meta sōphrosynēs.*

Let a woman learn in quietness in all submission – [12]I do not permit a woman to teach, *oude authentein andros,* but to be in quietness. [13]For Adam was formed first, then Eve, [14]and Adam was not deceived. But the woman having been deceived has come into transgression; [15]but she will be saved through the child-bearing, if they remain in faith and love and holiness with sobriety (1 Tim. 2:11–15).

The difficulties presented by the pastoral letters, and in particular by the teaching of 1 Timothy on the role and status of women within the church, are well known. Critical scholarship is still largely persuaded that these letters were written by a sincere but misguided imitator of Paul. The letters are thought to reflect developments both within the church and in ancient religious movements that belong to the second century. The language certainly differs in a number of respects from that of the undisputed letters of Paul and even evangelical scholars are inclined to concede that someone else – an amanuensis, perhaps Luke (*cf.* 2 Tim. 4:11) – had a significant hand in their production. The question of authenticity, however, cannot be resolved here, much as one might wish to throw scholarly caution to the wind and dismiss the arguments of the critics as so much dogmatism and pedantry. For the purposes of the present study[1] I shall identify the writer of the pastorals as 'Paul, the apostle', partly in faith, but partly also in the conviction that before long the critical scholarly consensus will have come more or less full circle anyway.

General emphases in the letter

Before we consider the specific regulations of 1 Timothy 2:11–15, certain

---

[1] See also a precursor to this chapter in Perriman 1993.

persistent themes in the letter, which are evident also in 2 Timothy and Titus, need to be recorded.

1. Paul repeatedly expresses his concern that false teaching should be curbed and 'sound doctrine' upheld. It is his principal charge to Timothy that he should remain at Ephesus to curb the influence of certain persons who were promulgating a different teaching (1:3). This exercise in damage control must have been the primary reason for the letter (*cf.* Fee 1984: 7). Characteristic of the heresy was a preoccupation with 'myths and endless genealogies' (1:4–7), 'the godless myths of old women' (4:7), the promotion of asceticism (4:1–3), 'a morbid craving for controversy and for disputes about words' (6:4, RSV).[2] As a result of this disruptive and, in Paul's view, demonic influence, many had 'been shipwrecked in their faith' (1:19–20; 4:1; 6:21). To counter it, he repeatedly instructs Timothy to 'hold faith and a good conscience' (1:19); to 'put these things before the brethren' (4:6); to 'attend to public reading, exhorting, teaching' (4:13); to hold to sound teaching, 'for by doing this you will save both yourself and your hearers' (4:16); to 'teach and urge these things' (6:2); to 'guard what has been entrusted' to him, avoiding 'the godless chatter and contradictions of what is falsely called knowledge' (6:20, RSV).

2. A large part of the letter is taken up with matters of church governance. Chapters 2 and 3 are devoted to the discussion of a range of practical issues: prayer, the attitude and deportment of men and women in worship, the participation of women in learning, the qualifications for overseers and deacons. Recommendations for managing widows in the church are set out at some length in 5:3–16; in 5:17–22 instructions are given concerning the rewarding and disciplining of elders, and in 6:1–2 there are guidelines for those under the yoke of slavery.

This material is broadly classified in the pastorals as 'teaching' (*didaskalia*) and, we may presume, corresponds roughly to the 'traditions' that Paul speaks of in 1 Corinthians 11:2 (*cf.* 1 Cor. 4:17).[3] A consistent distinction is maintained in these letters between the gospel (the truth, the words of faith)

---

[2] The exact nature and identity of the false teaching that Timothy met at Ephesus are not certain. The suggestion of Dibelius and Conzelmann (1972: 17; *cf.* 65–67) that we should think of 'early Jewish or Judaizing forms of Gnosticism' appears, however, to be generally accepted. Gritz (1991: 114–116) sees a link between this 'gnosticizing form of Jewish Christianity' and the Artemis cult (*cf.* Kroeger 1986: 225–244); the Kroegers see further connections with the role of women as purveyors of myths (Kroeger & Kroeger 1992: 62–66). These specifically feminist reconstructions of the background are criticized by Schreiner (1995: 109–111). Note also Fee 1984: 7–10; Padgett 1987: 20–21; Redekop 1990: 237; Barron 1990: 454.

[3] The context of 2 Thes. 3:6 suggests that the 'traditions' taught by Paul had to do with matters of conduct and lifestyle (*cf.* Col. 2:6–7). In 1 Cor. 15:3, however, Paul says that he passed on (*paredōka*) certain fundamental teachings about the death of Christ for our sins and the resurrection; and Ridderbos argues that one is not 'to restrict the activity of these

which is preached and the more expansive category of 'teaching' (1 Tim. 2:7; 4:6, 13; 5:17; 2 Tim. 1:11; 4:2). The content of the *didaskalia* is not the central tenets of the faith but more practical matters of attitude and behaviour, domestic and social morality, and church discipline. Paul closely associates his teaching with his own conduct and character (2 Tim. 3:10). Sound *didaskalia* stands in contrast to teaching which permits or promotes immorality (1 Tim. 1:10), to false teaching about marriage and eating (1 Tim. 4:1–3), and in particular to the sort of worthless religious speculation for which Paul expresses such contempt in the pastorals (1 Tim. 1:3–4; 4:6–7; 6:3–5). The purpose of the *didaskalia* is rather to promote 'love from a pure heart and a good conscience and a sincere faith', and to uphold the 'redemptive plan [*oikonomian*] of God which is in faith' (1 Tim. 1:4–5).

The practical teaching of 1 Timothy 2 and 3, including the prohibitions of 2:12, is explicitly classified as instructions pertaining to behaviour in 'the household of God, which is the church of the living God, the pillar and bulwark of the truth' (1 Tim. 3:15). The content of this 'truth', the 'mystery of the religion', is defined in verse 16: Christ, who was manifested in the flesh . . . and, significantly, 'preached' in the world.[4] The *didaskalia* ensures that the church remains a trustworthy proponent and guardian of the truth, which is the gospel of salvation. It determines and describes the sort of attitudes, behaviour, church structures, procedures and so on that are most consistent with and best express the person and salvation-historical agenda of Jesus Christ.

In this respect it is not inappropriate to speak of the pastoral letters as a 'church manual'; they are, or contain, a loosely organized handbook of applied gospel.[5] But there is no basis for interpreting Paul's words in 1 Timothy 3:15 to mean, 'This is how one should always behave in every respect in the household of God, regardless of the circumstances.' This verse gives Paul's teaching in the preceding chapters a practical and a pragmatic orientation; the question is: how should we behave in the household of God so as to ensure that it remains a viable and effective 'pillar and bulwark of the truth'? Or, as he expresses it earlier: 'the purpose of the command is love from a clean heart and a good conscience and sincere faith' (1:5; *cf.* 1:18–19; 6:11).

This goal-oriented character of Paul's parenesis should make us wary of absolutizing his practical instructions. In order to make concrete and real the

---

teachers to a certain part of Christian doctrine, for example, to the parenesis, but rather to extend it to the whole content of the proclamation' (Ridderbos 1975: 453). On the meaning of 'teaching' in the context of the pastorals see Wilshire 1993: 50–52; Saucy 1994: 81–84, 86–91; Fung 1987: 206–207.

[4] *Cf.* 1 Tim. 2:4–5, where the truth is that 'there is one God, and one mediator of God and men . . .'

[5] *E.g.* Knight 1977: 29–30; Hurley 1981: 195–197. Note also the discussion in Scholer 1986: 200; Padgett 1987: 20.

foundational truth of redemption and the fundamental response of faith and love, the *didaskalia* entails a sort of *negotiation* between the absolute, unchanging truth embodied in Christ and the complex social and historical circumstances of the Christian community. This does not merely relativize the *didaskalia*. In so far as the human condition remains constant – and this will include aspects of sexual differentiation – the *didaskalia* retains its significance in detail. But the circumstances of the community are fluid and to some extent the *didaskalia* must also be open to change. Otherwise, Christian teaching loses touch not only with the reality of the church but also with the fundamental purpose of the gospel.

3. At a number of points Paul urges Timothy to ensure the good opinion of outsiders towards the church: an overseer must have a 'good reputation among outsiders' (3:7);[6] younger widows should marry in order to 'give the enemy no occasion for reproach' (5:14); slaves are to respect their masters 'lest the name of God and the teaching be blasphemed' (6:1); the 'commandment' is to be kept 'spotless and irreproachable' (6:14). To some extent, at least, this explains the preoccupation with church order.[7]

The concern for 'sound' teaching also has in view the opinion of outsiders: *sound* teaching has less to do with what is revealed than with what is generally considered reasonable or appropriate. The point is made in the Bauer-Arndt-Gingrich-Danker lexicon: 'in accord with prevailing usage, Christian teaching is designated as *correct* instruction, since it is reasonable and appeals to sound intelligence'.[8] While the gospel itself may be an offence to human wisdom (1 Cor. 1:18–25), the teaching that governs the life and ministry of the church is 'sound' in so far as it accords with good public opinion, including Jewish opinion, with regard to what is morally and culturally acceptable. This, of course, raises a number of important questions about the *counter-cultural* impact of the kingdom of God, but at least we can say that Paul was at this stage noticeably sensitive to the manner in which the church was perceived by the larger community and anxious to avoid misunderstanding and unnecessary offence. Perhaps this is only a broader application of the quintessentially Pauline dictum, 'all things to all people' (1 Cor. 9:22).

The importance of the public reputation of the church may also be implicit in the sections that immediately precede the passage under discussion. The use of 'conscience' (*syneidēsis*) in 1:19 points to a concern with behaviour that is

---

[6] Stiefel shows how the qualities required of overseers and deacons are of a general and secular, rather than specifically Christian, nature and are easily paralleled in Hellenistic sources (Steifel 1995: 442–443).

[7] Note MacDonald 1990: 232; 1996: 154–165.

[8] Bauer-Arndt-Gingrich-Danker *s.v.* hygiainō 2. See also Dibelius & Conzelmann 1972: 24–25. *Cf.* Plutarch, *Moralia* 20F; Philo, *De Abrahamo* 223 a.1.; Josephus, *Against Apion* 1.222. Also Tit. 2:7–8 and other references in 2 Timothy and Titus.

publicly acceptable, conforming not just to specifically Christian standards but to general moral values.[9] Possibly, in 'delivering Hymenaeus and Alexander to Satan' (1:20), Paul handed them over to the civil authorities for punishment. Their misconduct was an offence not merely to God but also in the eyes of the state.[10] Similar concerns may lie behind the exhortation to pray for those in authority 'that we may lead a quiet and peaceful life in all godliness and reverence' (2:1–2).[11] The terminology here, which is the language of Hellenistic piety, strongly suggests an awareness of the public perception of the Christian faith.

The same is true of the reference in 2:10 to 'women who profess piety'. The word for 'piety', *theosebeia*, is found only here in the New Testament and is rare in the Greek Old Testament; it signifies an idea alien to biblical literature but common in the writings of Hellenistic (including Hellenistic Jewish) religion.[12] It expresses essentially a pagan religious attitude, almost as distinct from the attitude of biblical faith. It would be entirely appropriate *in the Lord* for women to adorn themselves with 'good works' rather than with expensive clothes and jewellery. But Paul's language suggests that his concern is also that the behaviour of these women should be consistent with the highest standards of Hellenistic piety. In his *Advice to Bride and Groom* Plutarch, for example, relates the story of how Lysander refused to accept expensive gifts of clothing and jewellery for his daughters, saying, 'These adornments will disgrace my daughters far more than they will adorn them.' He goes on to comment:

> For, as Crates used to say, 'adornment is that which adorns', and that adorns or decorates a woman which makes her more decorous. It is not gold or precious stones or scarlet that makes her such, but whatever invests her with that something which betokens dignity, good behaviour, and modesty (*Moralia* 141DE, Loeb).[13]

4. Finally, a particular anxiety about the conduct and influence of women in the church appears to run through each of these themes. The fact that Paul

---

[9] A similar distinction is made in Rom. 13:5; believers should be subject to the ruling authorities not only in order to avoid the wrath of God but also 'for the sake of conscience'.

[10] This explains the image of making shipwreck of their faith; they had compromised their faith, brought it into disrepute. These two men are perhaps mentioned again in 2 Tim. 2:17 and 4:14 – presumably after whatever punishment was imposed upon them by the state.

[11] This is not the bourgeois ideal of 'good citizenship', of Christian faith in harmony with the state (*cf.* Dibelius & Conzelmann 1972: 39–41). Although the delayed parousia expectation has certainly shaped the ethical and social teaching of the pastorals, the more immediate issue has to do, on the one had, with the impact of the gospel and the church on Graeco-Roman society, and on the other, with the disruptive influence of other religious movements, both within and outside the church.

[12] Bertram 1965: 124–126; *cf.* Dibelius & Conzelmann 1972: 39.

[13] *Cf. Moralia* 145EF. Note also numerous references in Keener 1992: 106.

differentiates between the respective obligations for men and women in worship already suggests a deep-seated division between the sexes in his understanding and an awareness of the special problems posed by each group. Women are to dress modestly; attending church should not be made an opportunity for ostentation and vanity (2:9–10). When reference is made to those false teachers who will forbid marriage in later times (4:3), part of the concern is undoubtedly with the social and spiritual problems created by unmarried women. Considerable space is given to the problem of widows (5:3–16), especially young widows, who are likely to become alienated from Christ by their sexual impulses (5:11), who 'learn to be idlers, going around the houses, and not only idlers, but also gossips and busybodies, saying things that they should not' (5:13). Some have already turned away after Satan (5:15).[14] Paul's advice is that these younger women should 'marry, bear children, manage the household, and give the opponent no occasion for reproach' (5:14).

The only evidence that some of the false teachers were women is Paul's prohibition against women teaching in 2:12. Given the nature of the letter there must have been some specific reason why Paul gave this instruction, regardless of whether we view it as universally applicable or historically conditioned; and the active involvement of women in the promulgation of false teaching would be the obvious inference. The danger is suggestively illustrated by the activities of 'the woman Jezebel' at Thyatira, no great distance from Ephesus and probably not much later, who 'calls herself a prophetess and who both teaches and misleads my servants to commit immorality and eat food sacrificed to idols' (Rev. 2:20). It is possible that Paul had in mind influential, wealthy, fashion-conscious (*cf.* 2:9–10) women, who would have been attractive quarry for the avaricious mystagogues who preyed upon the church and, when caught, amenable publicists for their teachings.[15] But this is not an inevitable inference, and it may have been the curiosity and vanity of these women rather than their wealth that lay at the root of the problem. It is also possible, of course, that Paul's injunction was more a preventive measure than a reaction to the current activity of women teachers in Ephesus.

It would be wrong to argue that it is only the teaching of error by women that is prohibited in 1 Timothy 2:12. Nevertheless, given his overall concerns in the letter, it seems certain that it was principally in order to avoid the further spread of false teaching that Paul denied women permission to teach in the

---

[14] Probably the same general situation is in view in 2 Tim. 3:6–7 in Paul's attack on people who 'worm their way into households and capture foolish women, loaded with sins, led by various desires, always learning and never able to come to a knowledge of the truth'. *Cf.* Acts 13:50; Ignatius, *Letter to the Ephesians* 16:1.

[15] *Cf.* Padgett 1987: 23 and n. 17.

church. He does not allow the women to teach either error or truth, at least in any formal capacity and at least in the context of the gathered assembly. But it hardly fits the practical purpose of the letter that in formulating this injunction his deliberate objective was to prevent women from teaching sound Christian truth. What motivated the policy was not the fear that women would teach truth but the fear that they would teach error.

Whether women were permitted to preach the gospel to men is unclear, though it is difficult to imagine Paul standing in the way of anyone preaching the good news of Jesus Christ, whatever the circumstances (*cf.* Phil. 1:18). It may be significant that Paul's female co-workers laboured with him 'in the gospel' (*e.g.* Phil. 4:2–3), though we cannot be certain that this description was meant to distinguish this work from the task of 'teaching'.

This is already enough to make it clear that Paul's instructions in 2:11-15 are directed at a specific set of problems that the church at Ephesus faced, and that they cannot be adequately understood and applied to the church today without taking that context into account. Undoubtedly, his apprehensions about the participation of women in worship and the teaching ministry of the church were rooted in a deeper concern about the reputation both of the gospel and of the Christian community in a deeply pagan culture. Women were to act and dress modestly in church for fear that worship of Christ would be confused in the public mind with the frenzied and disreputable worship of the mystery cults. Their new-found status and freedom in Christ were not to become a cause of domestic and social discord. It seems reasonable to assume, too, that either the false teaching or the false teachers had a particular attraction to women, and that this had a direct connection with the prohibition against women teaching – that and the fact that women teachers were hardly held in great esteem in the ancient world.[16] This was, after all, a time of religious and social upheaval, a time of consternation among those who regarded themselves as defenders of tradition and order, as they peered nervously over their parapets and saw the forces of disarray invading from the East – and in their vanguard a band of emancipated women.

Paul's regulations in this text, therefore, may have been prompted by the particular circumstances that prevailed at Ephesus, or even throughout the Mediterranean world. But does this mean that the church is now at liberty to discard them simply on the grounds that the circumstances have changed? The way in which Paul expresses himself in 1 Timothy 2:12 does not immediately suggest that he had only the situation at Ephesus in mind. He does not say, '*As long as* there is a risk of the gospel being brought into disrepute or misrepresented by the involvement of women in ministry, I do not permit

---

[16] See Sigountos & Shank 1983: 289–292.

them to teach . . .' If this is to be accepted as a legitimate inference, therefore, it needs more detailed exegetical support.

Interpretations of verse 12

Traditionally, of course, the verse has been understood as a straightforward prohibition: women should neither teach nor hold positions of authority over men in the church. The restriction cannot be understood to be socially or historically conditioned, it is argued, because it is grounded in the creation narratives: Adam was formed first (v. 13) and therefore occupies a position of authority or headship over Eve. In *Recovering Biblical Manhood and Womanhood* D. Moo reaffirms this position: 'We think 1 Timothy 2:8–15 imposes two restrictions on the ministry of women: they are not to teach Christian doctrine to men and they are not to exercise authority directly over men in the church. These restrictions are permanent, authoritative for the church in all times and places and circumstances as long as men and women are descended from Adam and Eve.'[17]

The biggest exegetical difficulty with verse 12 centres on the meaning of the verb *authentein*, which has traditionally been translated 'to have authority over'. The verb is found only here in the New Testament and is rare in ancient Greek literature – very rare prior to the first century AD. This makes it a difficult word to translate. L. E. Wilshire has surveyed more than 300 occurrences of the larger word group (*authenteō, authentēs, authentia*) from Homer to the Byzantine period, and has come to the rather unsatisfactory conclusion that at the time of Paul the word *authenteō* had 'a multiplicity of meanings' (1988: 124).[18] The drift of his analysis, however, despite certain reservations, is towards the view that the sense most appropriate to 1 Timothy 2:12 relates to the idea of exercising authority. In this he is essentially in agreement with the findings of a briefer investigation by G. W. Knight based on the citations given in the Bauer-Arndt-Gingrich-Danker lexicon.[19] A more recent attempt to validate the traditional interpretation of *authenteō*, based on an investigation of 'all currently known occurrences' of the verb, is presented by H. Scott Baldwin in *Women in the Church*.[20]

But there are still difficulties. What, for example, is the relationship between *didaskein* and *authentein*? If Paul was thinking simply of women being in positions of authority (as elders, for example), would it not have been more

---

[17] Moo 1991: 180; also Knight 1984; Fung 1987: 198–199; Bowman 1992; Saucy 1994.

[18] Wilshire's analysis is based largely on the *Thesaurus Linguae Graecae* computer database of the University of California, Irvine.

[19] Knight 1984. See also Perriman 1993: 135 n. 13.

[20] Baldwin 1995: 65–80 and Appendix 2. The material was gathered from two CD-ROMs: the *Greek Documentary* CD-ROM published by The Packard Humanities Institute, and the *Thesaurus Linguae Graecae* from the University of California, Irvine (see 72 n. 18).

logical to have placed that prohibition first, rather than the emphatic injunction against teaching? Does not the order of the sentence, if not the grammar, suggest that *authentein* is logically subordinate to, or consequent upon, *didaskein*? Why, in any case, does Paul use this obscure word and not the more usual *exousian echein* or *exousiazein* ('to have power or authority')? And how does it relate to verses 13–14? The idea that Eve had or might have had authority over Adam forms no part of Paul's brief synopsis of the story of her deception. Above all, despite the arguments that have been put forward in support of the traditional understanding of *authentein*, we must ask how well founded is the view that by using this word Paul simply intended to express his opposition to women holding positions of authority over men in the church.

Various attempts have been made to mitigate the patriarchal implications of the passage. It has often been suggested, for example, that *authenteō* has the more negative sense of 'to usurp authority' or 'domineer', so that what Paul objects to is the *misuse* of authority by women.[21] Keener (1992: 108–109) proposes as a translation: 'I am not allowing a woman to teach in such a way as to domineer over men.' Such an interpretation, however, is barely, if at all, warranted by the lexical evidence;[22] it is grammatically doubtful since the conjunction *oude* connecting *didaskein* and *authentein* cannot have the meaning 'in such a way as to';[23] and it makes little sense in the context of the passage. On the one hand, 'I do not permit' seems an inappropriate way to address such an abuse of the teaching ministry; and on the other, it is not the point of the Genesis story that Eve usurped Adam's authority or exercised authority over him in a domineering manner.

In a later article Wilshire (1993: 47) revised his interpretation of *authentein* in 1 Timothy 2:12 in favour of the idea of 'instigating violence', arguing that the dominant sense of the word group around the time of the New Testament had to do with 'self-willed violence, criminal action, or murder or with the person

---

[21] *Cf.* Evans 1983: 103; Fee 1984: 73; Scholer 1986: 205; Giles 1986: 44; Witherington 1988: 121; Pierce 1993: 348–349.

[22] See Knight 1984: 150–151. Baldwin lists only one passage where *authenteō* supposedly means 'to domineer' (Chrysostom, *Homilies on Colossians*, in Migne, *Patrologia Graeca* 62.376.1), but 'act independently or according to one's own purposes' would be more appropriate here. The arguments put forward by the Kroegers (1992: 88–89) for the meaning 'to usurp authority' are unconvincing because they have misinterpreted the two passages cited in evidence.

[23] *Cf.* Moo 1991: 187. If *authentein* is interpreted as signifying a domineering exercise of authority and *oude* is given its proper correlative sense ('I do not permit a woman to teach, nor to domineer over a man'), we have the problem of explaining how Paul could have conceived of a legitimate authority over men that was somehow *not* in conflict with the injunction against teaching ('I do not permit a woman to teach but she may have a non-domineering authority over a man'). Used in this way without any qualification *didaskein* cannot be restricted to false teaching.

who does these actions'. To cite just two of the examples given: Josephus speaks of the 'perpetrators [*authentas*] of the slaughter'; and the historian Diodorus Siculus (*c.* 60 BC–*c.* AD 20) relates Arses' intention to punish Baogoas, the 'author [*authentēn*] of the crimes'.[24] Wilshire suggests two ways in which the word might be understood in the context of 1 Timothy 2:12: either this is hyperbole, an 'exaggeration meant to lend power by overstatement'; or Paul may have in mind a particularly unpleasant incident in the life of the community at Ephesus, provoked perhaps by the influence of false teachers on the women.

Such an explanation, however, faces several objections. What possible connection, for example, is there with the prohibition against teaching? Would Paul have opposed such obviously unacceptable behaviour with the words 'I do not permit'? Why should he specify violence *against a man*? What has this to do with Eve's transgression, which was not one of violence towards Adam? The interpretation is also lexically doubtful in that the association of the word group with the idea of murder depends entirely on the use of the noun *authentēs* to denote the person who has committed a murder, the 'perpetrator of the deed'.[25] This does not necessarily mean that the verb can be used with a person as the object to mean 'to murder' or 'to act violently against'; in fact, there appears to be no evidence at all for such a construction.[26]

Others (*e.g.* Gritz 1991: 133–136) have argued that although the word in itself means simply 'to have authority over', without any negative connotations, in the context of Paul's teaching on women the frame of reference is implicitly restricted: women should not exercise authority over their own husbands. The question of precisely what type of male–female relationship Paul has in view here is not easy to answer. A number of elements in the passage suggest that he is thinking of the domestic situation. It would seem reasonable to assume, for example, that in verse 11 Paul enjoins submission to the husband in much the same way as he does in Ephesians 5:22 and perhaps in 1 Corinthians 14:34–35, and for similar reasons. The story of Eve's deception may suggest a marital relationship rather than the more general sexual

[24] Josephus, *Jewish War* 2.240.5; Diodorus, *Photian fragment*, 35.25.1.

[25] According to Moulton & Milligan 1914–30: 91, *authentēs* meaning 'murderer' derives from *autothentēs* (from *theinō*, meaning 'to strike'), while *authentēs* meaning 'master' is from *aut-entēs* (from a root meaning 'to accomplish'). Whether such a differentiation was known in Paul's day, however, cannot be ascertained. Wilshire records Chantraine's reservations about the work of Kretschmer on which Moulton and Milligan's conclusions were based (Wilshire 1988: 129). In any case, the meaning 'accomplish' is perfectly consistent with the interpretation of *authenteō* that I shall describe in this chapter.

[26] The participle *euthentēkota* in Schol. Aesch. *Eumenides* 42, which is cited as an instance of the use of the word to mean 'murder', has no object and only means that the murder described in the text had recently 'been perpetrated' (against also Kroeger & Kroeger 1992: 85–86, 185–188; Baldwin 1995: 73).

dynamic. Moreover, verse 15 clearly evokes the domestic context. Chapters 2 and 3, however, are otherwise entirely directed at the need for order and appropriate behaviour within the congregation as a whole; and Paul explains his purpose in writing these things in 3:15: 'that you may know how one should behave in a household of God, which is a church of the living God'. The repetition of *en hēsychia* in verse 12 also lends support to this view; the requirement that women should not teach but 'be in quietness' really makes sense only in the context of a corporate gathering.[27] It seems almost certain that in the absence of the sort of explicit qualification of *andros* that we find in 1 Corinthians 14:35 and Ephesians 5:22 ('*their own* husbands') we should understand the relationship in general terms: women should not teach or *authentein* men within the church.[28]

Some interpreters (*e.g.* Gritz 1991: 31–43, 129) have attempted to explain the restrictions imposed by Paul against the background of Ephesian religion. In general terms it has been argued that the mystery cults, and in particular the worship of the Great Mother, Artemis of the Ephesians, would have engendered just the sort of ideas and expectations regarding the role of women in worship likely to have provoked Paul's seemingly repressive response. These cults offered women a status and authority that were denied to them both by traditional Greek and Roman religion and by Judaism.

More specifically, and more controversially, it has been claimed that in the context of these new and exotic oriental beliefs the word *authenteō* assumes a special technical sense that casts an altogether novel light on the passage. In their book *I Suffer Not a Woman*, R. C. and C. C. Kroeger argue, first, that the primary sense of *authenteō* is one of originating or being responsible for something, 'to take something in hand or to take the initiative in a given situation'; and secondly, that a valid distinction can be made between 'being an originator and professing to be one'.[29] So, they believe, Paul is saying, 'I do not permit woman to teach nor to represent herself as originator of man.'[30] This is then to be understood in the context of an early form of Gnosticism that taught the precedence of Eve over Adam and specifically encouraged

---

[27] On the whole, the lexical evidence and usage in the New Testament favour the sense 'in quietness'. While it is conceivable that Paul preferred women to keep absolute silence while learning in church, this seems inappropriate in the general context, where the issue is not so much the disruption caused by women speaking out in church (*cf.* 1 Cor. 14:34) as the attitude of women in worship. If Paul had meant that women should keep silence, the verb *sigaō*, as in 1 Cor. 14:34, would have made the point less ambiguously. See Moo 1991: 183; Gritz 1991: 129.

[28] Also Tit. 2:5. *Cf.* Fung 1987: 200–201; Moo 1991: 188. But note Blass-Debrunner-Funk §257(3).

[29] Kroeger & Kroeger 1992: 101–103; also Kroeger 1986: 230–232.

[30] Kroeger & Kroeger 1992: 103. *Cf.* Kroeger 1986: 232; Barron 1990: 454–455.

women teachers. The statement in verse 13 that 'Adam was formed first, then Eve' is seen as a direct rebuttal of such claims.

The Kroegers' study is a fascinating foray into the background material, and should certainly be taken seriously in any attempt to reconstruct the features of the Ephesian heterodoxy. There are the inevitable methodological difficulties that come from trying to interpret the New Testament in the light of texts that originate from the second and third centuries AD, but one can hardly avoid the impression that some sort of historical trajectory existed between the Hellenistic Jewish false teaching that Paul confronted in Colossians and the pastorals and the full-blown Gnosticism of the later period. When it comes to explaining Paul's statement in 1 Timothy 2:12, however, the thesis is open to damaging criticism on two fronts. First, while it is quite possible that there were primitive Gnostic elements in the Ephesian heresy and that women played a prominent part in its dissemination, there are doubts about the validity of the Kroegers' reconstruction of Gnostic ideas relating to the role of Eve in creation. Secondly, can it really be claimed that *authenteō* here means 'to *profess oneself to be* the originator of someone'?

1. Although the Gnostic texts are difficult to interpret confidently and the comments offered here are somewhat tentative, it seems doubtful that we find the sort of background of ideas required by the Kroegers' interpretation – even supposing that these myths existed in embryonic form in mid-first-century Ephesus.[31]

In the first place, it is not so apparent that Eve is presented in the Gnostic literature as the originator of Adam. In the most important of the texts cited, *On the Origin of the World*, Adam is created by the seven rulers in the likeness of the pre-existent 'Adam of Light' (114.30–32).[32] Life is breathed into the inert body of Adam by Sophia Zoe, the daughter of Pistis Sophia, the force from which all things emanate (115.11–14).[33] Sophia Zoe is also called 'Eve of Life' and the 'female instructor of life'; she is responsible for creating the male instructor, known as the 'Beast', which is the serpent of the Genesis story. The earthly Eve, however, is only a 'likeness' of Sophia Zoe left behind after life had been breathed into Adam in order to deceive the rulers (116.26 – 117.14). A passage is also quoted from *The Hypostasis of the Archons* (89.11–17) in which Eve appears to give life to Adam. But in fact she only arouses him from the sleep into which he had fallen when the 'rulers' had created the woman from his side (89.3–11).

It appears, therefore, that both Adam and Eve were created as likenesses of pre-existent heavenly figures, but the earthly Eve still appears *after* the man. Of

---

[31] Kroeger & Kroeger 1992: 119–124; cf. Kroeger 1986: 232–242.

[32] For the texts see Robinson 1988.

[33] In *The Apocryphon of John* 19.21–33 it is Yaltabaoth who blows the spirit into Adam.

course, there is plenty of scope for confusion, and it is anybody's guess what form these myths took in primitive Gnosticism, if they existed at all. But at least the texts do not teach a reversal in the order of creation of the earthly Adam and Eve. The female principle of life preceded the creation of the man; but this is quite different from the idea that the woman preceded the man, and far removed from the claim purportedly made by the women of Ephesus that they themselves were 'originators of man'.

Secondly, it is argued that in the Gnostic texts it is Adam rather than Eve who is deceived, and that this distortion is directly refuted by Paul in 1 Timothy 2:14. In one story the rulers plan to trick Adam into believing that Sophia Zoe (the heavenly Eve) was created from his rib, so that he should be lord over her; their ruse is to bring a deep sleep upon him and instruct him in his sleep (*On the Origin of the World* 116.20–25). But the Kroegers overlook the fact that the deception does not actually take place. Sophia Zoe laughs at the rulers' decision; she puts a mist in their eyes, and then secretly leaves her likeness with Adam. At first the rulers pursue her, but she hides in the tree of knowledge, and eventually the 'blind creatures' flee. Later, the Beast, the 'wisest of all creatures', approaches the earthly Eve and persuades her to eat from the 'tree of *gnosis*', though, of course, this is depicted not as deception but as enlightenment (118.25 – 119.5).

2. Evidence from the Gnostic texts is bound to be inconclusive. Far more important is the interpretation of *authentein*, which in practice is the thread by which the whole argument hangs.

Much is made of the fact that in the Latin lexicons (*e.g. Thesaurus Linguae Graecae*, Scapula's *Lexicon Graecae–Latinum*) the phrase *praebeo me auctorem* is given as a definition of *authenteō*. The Kroegers translate this as 'to declare oneself the author or source of anything', but this is misleading. The basic meaning of *praebeo* is not 'to declare', but 'to put forward, present, offer, show'; according to the standard dictionary of Lewis and Short, the reflexive form means '*to show, approve, behave one's self* in a certain manner' (*cf.* the *Oxford Latin Dictionary*: 'to put oneself forward (in a given role)' or 'to behave (as)'). Two interpretations of the phrase, therefore, seem possible. The first is 'I show myself to be an author', which is of no use to the Kroegers' argument since it would entail the implicit recognition that woman really is the originator of man. The second is to suppose that we have here simply a means of converting *auctor* into a verbal form for want of a direct Latin equivalent for *authenteō* (just as in English we might say 'to act as author' rather than 'to author').

The textual support cited for the interpretation also appears on investigation to be illusory. In *Epistle* 51.1, Basil (fourth century AD) asks the question: 'Was I following others, or myself originating [*katarchōn*] and *authentōn* the bold deed?' The 'bold deed' (*tolmēmatos*) of which he has been accused is the slandering and condemning of his friend Dianius. His question contemplates two possible interpretations of the accusation: are they saying that he simply repeated what others had said, or is he supposed to have been directly responsible for the deed? The point is not whether he *professed* to have perpetrated the attack upon Dianius, but whether he actually did perpetrate it. This is clearly the sense of the Latin version in the *Patrologia Graeca*: *ipse incoeptor et auctor facinoris* ('was I myself the instigator and author of the deed?'). Here there is nothing at all of the idea of 'professing oneself originator'. The same is true for the two other passages, which the Kroegers only briefly paraphrase.[34] In neither case – again this is evident from the Latin versions – is there any need to introduce the idea of 'professing oneself to be . . .'[35]

Lastly, the Kroegers overlook one important feature of the use of *authenteō* with the sense 'instigate, originate', which is evident from all the instances cited, including those in which the word is reckoned to have the meaning 'to declare oneself to be the origin of something'. That is that the object of the verb is always an action or a state of affairs. One does not instigate or perpetrate a physical object, such as a man, so this makes no sense as the basis for an interpretation of *authenteō* in 1 Timothy 2:12.[36] This awkward fact must somehow be taken into account as we try to make sense of the passage.

If, therefore, none of the alternative translations commonly proposed for *authenteō* is convincing, we must go back to square one and re-evaluate the evidence for the traditional interpretation. For this purpose Baldwin's study, although analytically less thorough than the other lexicological investigations, will prove especially useful.

The meaning of *authenteō*

From his comprehensive survey of the use of the verb in ancient Greek literature, Baldwin (1995) concludes that 'the root meaning involves the concept of authority'. He then lists twelve distinct meanings, arranged under five main headings, not all of which he considers viable in 1 Timothy 2:12. The sense 'to rule, to reign sovereignly' is judged to be 'impermissible' in this

---

[34] The words *tēs de kriseōs authentei ho hypsistos theos* in the edict of Constantine (Eusebius, *Life of Constantine* 2.48, in Migne, *PG* 20.1025C) are translated in Latin as *improbitati autem dijudicandae ac puniendae praeest Deus altissimus*; the meaning of the Greek is 'the highest God is the author of judgment'. The phrase *dichonoian tina . . . Eutychous authentountos gegenēsthai* from the letter of Pope Leo (Leo, *Epistle* 30 in Migne, *PL* 54.788A) is rendered in Latin *dissensionem quamdam . . . Eutyche auctore generatam*, and in English roughly 'a certain disagreement came about with Eutychus being the originator or author'.

[35] All three passages are cited in Lampe 1961 *s.v. authenteō* under the sense 'be primarily responsible for, instigate; authorize'.

[36] The *Oxford Latin Dictionary* gives as one meaning of *auctor* 'The originator, source, author (of information, etc.)', but there appears to be no circumstance, normally speaking, in which one could be *auctor* of a person.

context, apparently because it implies an absolute authority. A number of other more specialized definitions are also disqualified without much discussion: 'to have legal standing' (middle voice), 'to domineer', 'to grant authorization', 'to act independently', 'to exercise one's own jurisdiction', 'to instigate', 'to commit murder'. This leaves, in Baldwin's view, four possible meanings: (1) 'to control, to dominate'; (2) 'to compel, to influence'; (3) 'to assume authority over'; and (4) 'to flout the authority of'. Rather surprisingly, the expression 'to exercise authority over' does not appear in Baldwin's summary, though later in the book Schreiner (1995: 130) takes this to be the most likely meaning.

Baldwin's study, with its appendix citing all the passages with translations, is of considerable value as we seek to make sense of what *authenteō* means and why Paul made use of it here. Three preliminary critical observations, however, may be ventured.

1. Only two of the texts cited pre-date the New Testament, two others are from the second century AD, one is from the third century AD, and the remaining 73 are from the fourth century and later. Baldwin (1995: 78) claims that there appears 'only limited historical development of the meaning of *authenteō* across fourteen centuries'. But it is quite apparent that the word acquired special prominence in the writings of the church fathers, and it would be very surprising if such a marked historical association had no significant impact on the usage of the word. Moreover, although there is some justification for the argument that we cannot uncritically assume that the verb *authentein* corresponds exactly to the sense of the cognate noun *authentēs* (Baldwin 1995: 76–78), it is surely a mistake to disregard the noun altogether in determining the meaning of the verb – particularly since *authentēs*, unlike the verb, not only is quite widely attested in pre-Pauline literature but also appears in Jewish texts of the period (Septuagint, Philo, Josephus) (see Wilshire 1988).

2. Very little consideration is given in Baldwin's analysis to the grammatical circumstances in which *authenteō* is used. The range of meanings presented bears witness to the difficulty of pinning down this highly elusive verb: the problem is that there is no simple English equivalent for *authenteō* and we are obliged to make use of a variety of expressions according to the context. But in order to understand what Paul is saying in 1 Timothy 2:12 we also need to take account of semantic distinctions that derive from the relation of the action of the verb to an object. Does *authenteō* have the same meaning when it is used intransitively as when the action is directed towards an object? What difference does it make for that object to be a person rather than something impersonal or abstract?

3. It appears that nuances have been extracted too freely from the general context and incorporated into the definition of *authentein*. On the one hand,

the passage has not always been accurately interpreted, which has led to the introduction of semantic components into the general definition that have dubious lexical relevance. On the other, the process has probably resulted in a more elaborate classification of meaning than is necessary. At least, we should look carefully for what is distinctive and consistent in the usage of the word in the various literary and grammatical contexts in which it occurs. Baldwin's conclusion that this has to do with the concept of 'authority' will prove inexact. In order to provide a guiding thread for our re-evaluation of his study, I would suggest that central to the meaning of the word, and consistent with the use of the cognate noun *authentēs*, is the thought of the *active* assumption or implementation of authority or responsibility or power in quite concrete terms.

The early texts

We should consider first, then, those texts that are closest chronologically to the New Testament period.

The translation of *authentēkotos* in the Egyptian papyrus 1208 (27 BC) already suggests something more active than simply having or being in a position of authority: 'I exercised authority over him [*pros auton*] . . .'[37] The sentence continues: '. . . and he consented to provide for Calatytis the Boatman on terms of the full fare, within the hour', which indicates that *authentēkotos* refers to a specific act of persuasion or command. Baldwin classifies this under the meaning 'to compel, to influence someone/something'.[38]

In a fragment from the *Rhetorica* of Philodemus (first century BC) we find the uncertain phrase *authent[ou]sin an[axin]*. As a translation for this Baldwin gives an expression from a paraphrase by Hubbell (published in 1920): 'those in authority'.[39] The text presents a number of difficulties, however. In the first place, as Baldwin acknowledges, it is quite possible that we should read *authentaisin* (from the noun *authentēs*) in the corrupted text rather than the verb *authentousin*. This uncertainty must make the passage a dubious witness to the meaning of the word. Then the word *anax* already means 'lord, master', which makes it unlikely that *authentousin* here simply means 'having authority'. In the Greek text the words *syn authent[ou]sin an[axin]* are set

---

[37] *Ägyptische Urkunden aus den königlichen Museen zu Berlin* 4, 1208.38f. (the translation is by J. R. Werner; see Knight 1984: 145).

[38] Baldwin (1995: 276 n. 5) appears disposed to accept Payne's arguments in favour of the translation of P. D. Peterson: 'when I had prevailed upon him to provide'. The Liddell-Scott-Jones lexicon cites this passage under 'to have full power or authority over'. Dibelius and Conzelmann (1972: 47), however, give the sense 'self-assured, firm conduct' for *authentēkotos* in this text.

[39] *Cf.* Knight 1984: 144–145; Wilshire (1988: 134 n. 5) suggests 'authorized rulers'.

within quotation marks, which is presumably meant to indicate that there is something odd or idiomatic about the phrase. According to Liddell-Scott-Jones *anax* is applied primarily to 'the gods', and in view of the vagueness of Hubbell's translation of the passage, which is in fact an extremely loose paraphrase, it is quite possible that *anaxin* here denotes not earthly rulers but the gods who actively 'influence' or 'intervene in' human affairs. It is not even clear that 'those in authority' in Hubbell's paraphrase is meant to be a translation of *authentousin anaxin*: the phrase 'powerful rulers' also appears in the text and quite possibly this is a more accurate rendering of the Greek expression. 'Powerful' suggests a more concrete and dynamic influence than is denoted by 'in authority'.

The verb appears in an astrological context in Ptolemy, *Tetrabiblos* III.13 (second century AD), where it is said that 'Saturn is household-master of the soul and *authentēsas* both Mercury and the moon'. In a technical text of this nature it is always going to be difficult to draw precise inferences about the use of the word in other contexts. Baldwin judges the meaning to be that Saturn 'controls' or 'dominates' Mercury and the moon. What needs to be made clear is that the verb refers to the direct, active influence or effect that Saturn has upon the other heavenly bodies. Knight (1984: 146) argues that *authenteō* corresponds in meaning to the preceding expression 'household-master [*oikodespotian*] of the soul'. But the inference is not certain: on the one hand, there is no reason why the relation of Saturn to Mercury and the moon should be the same as its relation to the soul; and on the other, as I have stressed before, the mere juxtaposition of two words or expressions does not make them synonymous.

Finally, the *Attic Lexicon* of the grammarian Moeris (second century AD) appears to regard *authentein* as the Hellenistic equivalent of the Attic *autodikein*, which is translated in Liddell-Scott-Jones as 'to have independent jurisdiction'.[40] This may simply be mistaken (if the verb was as rare at this time as it appears to have been) or it may reflect a usage for which no early literary evidence has survived. Perhaps this should be viewed as a specialized development of the more general idea of 'acting independently' or 'taking direct responsibility' for a matter.

The early evidence for the use of *authenteō* is too scanty and too difficult to allow us to make a confident pronouncement on its meaning. But there is reason, first, to question the assumption that the word signifies the possession of authority by one person over another, and secondly, to think that the idea of exerting an active influence over someone is nearer to the essential meaning of the word. This should become clearer as we consider what distinctions of

---

[40] The text has *autodichēn* and *authentēn*, which the editors take to be the infinitives *autodikein* and *authentein*.

meaning emerge when the instances of the verb listed by Baldwin are classified grammatically.

Grammatical classification

1. When used intransitively, that is without an object, *authenteō* means something like 'to act independently, act on one's own authority, take the initiative (in a matter)'.

The papyrus *PLond 1708* (sixth century AD) tells how a man called Psates not only defrauded his sisters of their inheritance but 'even *acted on his own authority* [*authentēsai*] and leased our ancestral home . . . ' (Baldwin's translation and italics). Another sixth-century papyrus, *PMasp 67151*, contains the will of a certain Phoibammon and the stipulation that his wife should, according to Baldwin's translation, 'not be able to seek anything further with regard to my heirs of any kind or joint heirs neither *to have authority* [*authentēsai*] in any fashion to detach outright goods of any kind from any manner of my estate'. This translation may be tolerable if we recognize that this is not an authority *over someone* but an authority *to act*. The translation of *authentousa* in the *De Magistratibus Populi Romani* of Johannes Laurentius Lydus (sixth century AD) as 'of its own initiative' points to a certain emphasis on the active taking or exercising of authority rather than the static condition of having authority; the construction of the passage indicates that *authentousa* refers to the specific application of authority by the magistracy, the taking of initiative in alleviating the tribute and making grants (Knight 1984:146). When Basil (AD 370, *Epistle* 69.45) says that, rather than seek a general synodical decree by which to take action, the bishop of Rome should *authentēsai* concerning the matter, there is no reason to regard this specifically as an appeal to the bishop's authority; he is saying only that the bishop should take responsibility or take the initiative in the matter.

Some of these intransitive constructions are taken by Baldwin to signify the exercise of rule, but the interpretation is questionable. For example, Epiphanius (AD 375) comments on the text 'he must reign until he should put all his enemies under his feet' (1 Cor. 15:25): 'the Son is doing all things and *authentountos* and exercising authority (*exousiazontas*) and handing over to the Father the ones who are in submission along with the kingdom' (Epiphanius, *Panarion* 224.2). Baldwin translates *authentountos* as 'ruling', but this is doubtful. It is more likely that the participle means 'acting independently' or 'taking the initiative'. Proculus Constantinopolitanus (AD 446) proclaims: 'How much is the difference between law and grace! How the one condemns, but the other unites; the one punishes, but the other saves completely; the one serves, but the other *authentei*; the one afflicts with sin, but the other utterly destroys' (*Oratio* VI, Migne, *PG* 65.692ff.). Again, Baldwin translates *authentei* as 'rules', but surely the point is not that grace has authority over people but that it is a dynamic, creative, initiating force, and that unlike the law it acts independently. This becomes clearer if we consider a similar passage from John Chrysostom (*c.* AD 390): 'Today we celebrate the universal feast together, fulfilling likewise the law and confirming grace, "because the law was given through Moses, but grace and truth came through Jesus Christ". Where there is a servant, there is a "was given"; but where there is freedom, there is a "came," because the servant serves, but the Lord *authentei*' (*On the Resurrection of the Lord*, line 42). The contrast is not between servanthood and lordship but between the predetermined character of the law ('was given') and the freedom that comes with grace to initiate and act independently.[41]

2. In a number of instances *authenteō* is used transitively with an impersonal object with the meaning either 'to instigate or perpetrate' a state of affairs, or 'to take charge of, take responsibility for' a matter.

We have already noted the phrase *katarchōn kai authentōn tou tolmēmatos* in Basil, *Epistle* 51: 'originating and perpetrating the bold deed'. Writing about the election of Matthias in Acts 1:15–26, John Chrysostom says that Peter 'first takes responsibility for the matter [*tou pragmatos authentei*], as having been put in charge of all of them' (*Homilies on the Acts of the Apostles*, Migne, *PG* 60.37.13; my translation).[42] Werner offers the translation 'assume authority over the matter' for *authentiseis tō pragma* in Christian papyrus Number 103 (sixth or seventh century AD, *BGU* I.103), indicating the active taking of initiative and responsibility in the particular instance. Baldwin (1995:75) understands this to mean that someone 'moves forward to fill the leadership role', but this is an unwarranted expansion of the meaning of the verb.

3. The verb *authenteō* occasionally appears in transitive constructions with a personal object.

The Egyptian papyrus 1208, which I have already considered, is one example: 'I exercised authority over him [*pros auton*] . . .' Eusebius (fifth century AD) instructs deacons 'not to exercise authority over the people [*eis ton laon . . . mē authentein*], but to do everything by the command of the elder' (*Sermons* 5, Migne, *PG* 86.348; Baldwin's translation). His meaning, however, is not that it is wrong for deacons to hold positions of authority but that in

---

[41] The same connection with grace appears in Eusebius, *On Ecclesiastical Theology* 3.5 (*c.* AD 325). Baldwin translates the clause *tou . . . patros authentountos kai dōroumenou tēn charin* as 'of the Father *ruling* and giving grace'. But this interpretation is certainly not demanded by the context, and it seems more likely that *authentountos* belongs with the thought of 'giving grace'; the Father initiates and provides grace.

[42] The *authentei* clause has been omitted in the translation given by J. H. Parker (*The Homilies of S. John Chrysostom on the Gospel of St. John,* Oxford, 1841: 43). Baldwin, however, appears to have taken the phrase 'as having been put in charge of them' to be a translation of *tou pragmatos authentei* and has included it under 'to control, dominate'. In fact, the phrase translates *hate autos pantas egcheiristheis*.

their ministry towards the people they should not *take the initiative or act independently*; instead they should act 'in accordance with the intention of the elder'.[43]

In some texts the personal object is in the genitive, as in 1 Timothy 2:12.[44] Commenting on Matthew 12:46–49 Chrysostom says that Mary 'wanted to show the people that she has power over and *authentei* her son' (*Homilies on the Gospel of St Matthew*, Migne, *PG* 57.465; my translation). To translate *authentei* here as 'has authority over' would not strain the sense of the passage. Nevertheless, we have a specific situation in which someone attempts to exercise authority or exert influence over another person (with the particular purpose of getting him to speak with her), and it would be quite appropriate to find this nuance in the use of *authenteō* here.

Didymus the Blind, in a polemic against Montanism, protests that 'we do not shun the prophecies of women', for there are many examples of women prophesying in the Bible. However, he goes on, echoing both 1 Corinthians 14:34 and 1 Timothy 2:12: 'we do not allow them to speak in church nor *authentein* men [*andrōn*] so that books be written in their name' (*Dialogue Between a Montanist and an Orthodox* 457). Baldwin translates *authentein* (both here and when the thought is repeated a few lines later) as 'to control', which underlines the fact that the word is used to refer to a particular set of circumstances in which women might exert an influence over men. The line might be translated: '. . . nor to prevail upon men to write books in their name'.

Joannes Philoponus (*c*. AD 520) says that 'ignorance rather than knowledge *authentei* souls [*psychōn*] in birth' (*About the Rational Soul* 487.12). He draws an analogy with healthy people who become sick when in a plague-infested country, which suggests that it is the active influence of ignorance on the soul that is in view, not any authority that ignorance may have over the soul. Ignorance does not 'rule' the soul, as Baldwin thinks, but affects, afflicts, influences it, determines its condition.

Finally, a twelfth-century Byzantine author, Michael Glycas, comments on the unusual situation among the Agilians, where 'the women *authentousin* the

---

[43] In three very similar passages (Joannes Malalas, *Chronicles* 291.12; 342.15; Emperor Constantine VII Porphyrogenitus, *About Strategy* 159.33), *authentēsas* occurs with the accusative *tēn sygklēton* ('assembly, senate'). In each case someone is made king in defiance of the senate, which strongly suggests that we have here a fixed form of expression meaning 'to overrule', referring, however, to a particular occasion on which action is taken.

[44] Werner's translation of the astrological text from Ptolemy, *Codicum Parisinorum: Catalogus Codicum Astrologorum Graecorum* 1.777.7 (a fifteenth-century manuscript) appears to be erroneous (see Baldwin 1995: 305). In the context it is more likely that *ton pantōn authentounta* means 'one who initiates or instigates *all things*' rather than 'one who exercises authority over all'. The passage describes a person 'who initiates all things in the trade and gains nothing (*mēden ktōmenon*)'.

men and commit sexual immorality as they desire' (*Annals* 270.10). As Knight (1984:149) has pointed out, a Latin translation of this text has *sua viros in potestate habent*: 'they have men in their power'. But even this should not be construed as a statement about women holding positions of authority; it means that they have power over men to influence them. In the context it seems highly likely that it is specifically in committing sexual immorality 'as they desire' that the women *act on their own initiative* and exercise power over men.

This has not been an exhaustive review of the texts collated by Baldwin, but it should be enough to demonstrate that it is not quite accurate to assert that the basic meaning of the word has to do with authority. The word certainly does not mean 'to have authority' or 'to hold a position of authority'. The translation 'to exercise authority' is nearer the mark since, as Schreiner (1995:132) recognizes, it focuses on the use, rather than the possession, of authority. But Schreiner underestimates the significance of this distinction. The word does not intrinsically presuppose that the subject has authority; a person requires no authority in order to take the initiative, act independently, and so forth; only the freedom to act.

Fundamentally, *authenteō* has more to do with 'authorship' than with 'authority'.[45] What the word brings into view is the particular occasion on which authority or responsibility is exercised, initiative is taken, an action is perpetrated. When the object of the verb is a person, the meaning would appear to be that one person actively exercises authority or exerts influence over another in a particular situation and with a particular objective in view. Implicit, then, in the use of *authenteō* is the thought that the person who is the object of the verb *does something* as a result. Many of the definitions listed by Baldwin already acknowledge the active aspect of *authenteō*. Where he has attributed to the word a meaning closer to the idea of ruling, there are strong grounds for questioning his translation, or at least for maintaining that this nuance is not required by the context.

This interpretation is consistent, moreover, with the basic meaning of the noun *authentēs* prior to and around the time of the New Testament – the author or instigator or perpetrator of a deed, often of a crime, particularly a murder or suicide.[46] The historian Polybius (200–118 BC), for example, speaking of a massacre at Maronea, describes Cassander as 'the author of the

[45] *Cf.* the Latin definition mentioned above: 'praebeo me auctorem' ('I act or behave as author'). E. A. Sophocles, *Greek Lexicon of the Roman and Byzantine Periods from B.C. 146 to A.D. 1100*, gives the sense 'to be the originator of anything', citing Athanasius, in Migne, PG 26.1180C: *authentousi . . . tēs asebeias*.

[46] See Wilshire 1988. This agrees with the basic sense that Chantraine attributes to *authentēs*, that of 'auteur responsable': P. Chantraine, *Dictionnaire Etymologique de la Langue Grèque* (Paris, 1968), *s.v. Authentēs*.

deed' (*ton authentēn . . . tēs praxeōs: History* 22.14.2.3). Diodorus Siculus (*c.* 60 BC–*c.* 20 AD) tells how Gracchus had in his followers not merely supporters but 'sponsors or perpetrators of his own daring acts' (*authentas . . . tēs idias tolmēs: Photian fragment* 35.25.1). Josephus (AD 37–*c.* 90) has the expression *tous authentas tou sphagentos*, 'perpetrators of the slaughter' (*Jewish War* 2.240.5). The word clearly signifies a person who is actively or directly responsible for an action. When a personal noun in the genitive case is attached, *authentēs* means 'murderer': so, for example, Euripides, *Hercules* 1359: 'You see in me the murderer of my children' (*paidōn . . . authentēn emōn*). But this is uncommon and it is not a usage attested for the verb *authenteō*. Generally speaking, the verb does not appear to have the same negative connotations that *authentēs* has (*e.g.* perpetration of a crime or murder), though it is perhaps not impossible that in Paul's time the verb had assimilated overtones of this sort from a natural association with the noun.

The question now needs to be asked, of course: what relevance does this have to the argument in 1 Timothy 2:12? Why did Paul at this point use an uncommon word which strongly suggested a particular situation and purpose in connection with which a woman might exercise authority or exert influence over a man? What situation and what purpose might he have had in mind? In order to answer these questions we must consider first the general rhetorical structure of the passage, and then the story of Adam and Eve.

The argumentative structure of 1 Timothy 2:11–15

The development of Paul's argument in verses 11–15 is not at all easy to determine. There are, however, certain observations to be made regarding the structure of the passage that will help us to follow the movement of thought.

1. There are good reasons for thinking that verse 12 intrudes into the passage as something of a parenthesis – or at least as a dislocation of the train of thought. This may initially seem a rather arbitrary literary judgment, but it is not without textual basis. The verse is grammatically clumsy: *ouk epitrepō* ('I do not permit') is not the proper governing antecedent for *einai en hēsychia* ('to be in silence'), which requires a word such as *parakalō* or *boulomai* (*cf.* vv. 1, 8: 'I urge . . . I desire').[47] The connection with verse 11 is abrupt, with the change from an imperative ('let a woman learn') to a first person indicative ('I do not permit') and the emphatic position of *didaskein* at the beginning of the sentence.[48] The repetition of *en hēsychia* would also be more easily explained if

[47] *Cf.* Dibelius & Conzelmann 1972: 47. Technically this is an instance of zeugma (*cf.* 1 Tim. 4:3); curiously, the same construction with *epitrepō* appears in 1 Cor. 14:34 if *hypotassesthai* is read rather than *hypotassesthōsan*; see Blass-Debrunner-Funk §479(2).

[48] The point of this, in response to Schreiner's (1995: 125 n. 90) objection, is not that the indicative has no imperative force but only that there is a change in grammatical form.

the verse were regarded as a rather hurriedly constructed afterthought. It is as though, having begun to speak of the need for women to learn in all submission, Paul interrupts himself: 'Incidentally, I do not permit a woman to teach . . .'

More significant, however, is the fact that the discussion of Adam and Eve in verses 13–14 relates not to the woman teaching but to the woman *learning*. The emphasis is not on what Eve said or did but on the fact that she was deceived; she is depicted not as an active propagator of ideas, or as a teacher – Paul does not tell us what she said to Adam – but as a *recipient* of (false) ideas. Although Eve knew of the command not to eat of the fruit of the tree, the serpent persuaded her that the command was mistaken and, indeed, repressive. And so she came into transgression. Paul requires that women by contrast, should learn in such a way that they are *not* deceived. Thus the *gar* ('for') that introduces verse 13 refers back quite naturally to verse 11, supporting not the injunction against teaching but the exhortation to 'learn in all submission'. The repetition of 'to be in quietness' at the end of verse 12 also serves to reinforce the connection with verse 11.

This is important, for under such an interpretation it can no longer be maintained that Paul adduces direct scriptural support for the restrictions imposed on women in verse 12. However they are to be understood exactly, verses 13–14 are an explanation of why women should learn, not of why they should not teach.

2. Although verse 12 is badly constructed, the basic argument seems reasonably clear. Both *didaskein* and *authentein* are dependent on 'I do not permit'. There has been some debate over the grammatical and logical relationship between the two infinitives. It has been suggested that the conjunction *oude* connects them in such a way that *authentein* defines either the manner or the content of the teaching.[49] But this seems unlikely. On the one hand, although *oude* may connect two closely related ideas, it has not been shown that the second term may qualify the first in the way that has been claimed.[50] On the other, *authentein* does not exhibit the degree of semantic proximity to *didaskein* that would allow it to serve as an intensification of the first prohibition. *Oude authentein* must refer to a separate action; it does not simply modify or reinforce the meaning of *didaskein*. Moreover, the construction of the sentence, with *didaskein* placed emphatically apart at the beginning, does not suggest a close logical connection between the two ideas.

There is, however, some force to the view that *oude authentein andros* is itself parenthetic or secondary: 'I do not permit a woman to teach – *oude authentein andros* as – but to be in quietness' (*cf.* Fung 1987: 199). In this case the

---

[49] Kroeger & Kroeger 1992: 83–84, discussing an unpublished argument of P. B. Payne.

[50] See the arguments in Moo 1991: 187; Köstenberger 1995: 81–103.

prohibition against teaching should perhaps be understood absolutely, with *andros* as the object of *authentein* only. The genitive *andros* is in any case an improper object for *didaskein*, which normally takes either the accusative or the dative of the person taught (*cf.* Fung 1987: 198–199).[51] The significance of this is that we may discern a certain rhetorical differentiation between the two terms. While *didaskein* refers quite straightforwardly to a familiar activity within the church, the unusual word *authentein* has a different literary character, drawing its significance not from ordinary church practice but from the account of Eve's deception in verses 13–14. But here we are running ahead of ourselves.

3. Once verse 12 has been marked as parenthetic, a typically Pauline chiastic arrangement emerges:

A   [11]Let a woman learn in quietness in all submission . . .

B   [13]For Adam was formed first,

C   then Eve,

B'   [14]and Adam was not deceived.

A'   And the woman, having been deceived, has come into transgression.

The correspondence between lines A and A' is evident, first, in the return to 'the woman' as the subject in A' despite the fact that Eve is named in line C; secondly, in the contrast between the woman learning in quietness and the woman being deceived; and thirdly, in the antithetical relationship between 'in all submission' and 'has come into transgression'. The outer parallelism of the chiasmus may also be taken to account for the perfect tense of *gegonen* ('has come') in line A', inasmuch as the statement about Eve is at the same time a return to the situation of women in the contemporary church. The inner parallelism is quite clear: 'Adam was formed / Adam was not deceived' (*Adam . . . eplasthē / Adam ouk ēpatēthē*). Verse 15, with its assurance of salvation through the bearing of children, should be regarded as an addendum to the chiasmus intended to compensate for the negative impression left by line A'.

The correspondence between 'in all submission' and 'has come into transgression' is of some importance. Elsewhere in Paul *parabasis* refers invariably and explicitly to transgression against the law, not against any human authority.[52] Eve's transgression was not that she disobeyed Adam or usurped his authority but that, misled by the serpent's guile, she disregarded what she had been taught. This point deserves emphasis. The assumption that Paul is speaking specifically of submission to *men* in this passage has arisen only

---

[51] There would be no conflict here with the assumption, if it is correct (see above, chapter 3), that women taught other women and children in the home. But *oude authentein andros* would still in practice restrict the frame of reference to men in the congregation. See also Moo 1991: 186 and n. 16.

[52] Rom. 2:23; 4:15; 5:14; Gal. 3:19 (*cf.* also Heb. 2:2; 9:15).

from a misleading interpretation of *authentein*.[53] Apart from this word, nothing in the passage indicates that this was Paul's intention. The priority of Adam in creation is clearly important for the argument, but it is unnecessary to infer from this the subordination of the woman.[54] We have also seen (in chapter 5) that the thought of submission to an abstract idea is not foreign to Paul and that there are grounds for believing that it is the order of worship, rather than the patriarchal family, that provides the context for the submission of women in 1 Corinthians 14:34. There is some weight, therefore, to the argument that Paul is thinking here of submission not to male authority but to the teaching or, more probably, to the teaching authority within the church.[55]

One further observation may be added. In Titus 1:10 Paul describes as 'insubordinate' (*anypotaktoi*) certain false teachers, especially 'those of the circumcision', who 'give heed to Jewish myths and the commands of men who turn from the truth'. It would be natural to assume that the submission required of women at Ephesus was of much the same kind as that expected of these men in Crete: what defines the authority is not gender but the soundness of the teaching, embodied principally in the oversight of the church (Tit. 1:9). It is only of incidental significance, as far as this passage is concerned, that the teaching authority was male.

The most significant objection to the argument that verse 12 is parenthetic is probably that verses 11–12 exhibit their own rhetorical structure and that this precludes both the larger chiasmus and the parenthetical character of verse 12.[56] Certainly there is a close connection between these two verses, felt most notably in the deliberate contrast between learning and teaching. But this does not in itself vitiate the argument that verse 12 is parenthetic or secondary; the fact that the verse intrudes into the passage as an afterthought does not mean that it does not to some extent reflect the language and structure of its context. Moreover, whatever linguistic affinity verse 12 might have with the surrounding passage does not alter the fact that it exhibits signs of grammatical awkwardness; nor does it nullify the observation that verses 13–14 are not essentially about the woman teaching. We should also point out that the parallelism between verses 11 and 12 is not as tidy or as consistent as has sometimes been claimed. The phrase *en hēsychia* constitutes at best only an

---

[53] Moo's argument that since verses 12–14 bring into view the relationship between men and women, it must be the submission of women to male authority that is spoken of in verse 11 (Moo 1991: 183; *cf.* 190), entirely misses the point of the allusion to the Genesis story.

[54] Against Moo 1991: 190. See below, chapter 7.

[55] *Cf.* Dibelius & Conzelmann 1972: 47; Gritz 1991: 130, though the reason Gritz supplies (use of the noun rather than the verb) is irrelevant. For the general interpretation *cf.* Padgett 1987: 24; Barnett 1989: 230; Bowman 1992: 199.

[56] *Cf.* Schreiner 1995: 124–125. Others have found a chiastic structure in verses 11–12: Barnett 1989: 228–229; Harris 1990: 340.

imperfect *inclusio* since it does not, in fact, introduce verse 11;[57] and it is by no means clear that Paul instructed women to learn in submission to men. I would suggest, therefore, that the correspondences between verses 11 and 12 are real but that they do not belong to the primary rhetorical structure of the passage; like verse 12 itself they are an afterthought and for that reason inconsistent.

The trouble with Eve

Although the argument of this passage appears more coherent if verse 12 is marked as a parenthesis, this does not mean that the language Paul uses in this verse is unaffected by the rhetorical context. I shall argue, in fact, that the use of the curious word *authentein* here presupposes in a quite specific way the story of Adam and Eve as it is told in verses 13–14. This story, however, is tersely narrated and poses interpretive difficulties of its own. What, in particular, is the connection between the order in which Adam and Eve were 'formed' and the fact that Eve, rather than Adam, was deceived?

The deception of Eve

Paul makes use of the Genesis story principally in order to support the requirement that women should learn in quietness and in all submission. The injunction against teaching is secondary and not directly supported by the allusion to Scripture. The emphasis on the woman's 'submission', on the one hand, and on Eve's 'transgression' against the word of God, on the other, makes it clear that Paul's concern is not simply that women should learn, but that they should learn in such a way that they remain obedient to the 'sound teaching'. This is the thrust both of the explicit command in verse 11 and of the Old Testament story – as is apparent from Paul's lack of interest in how Eve came to know the command of God in the first place.

Still, the force of the argument in verses 13–14 is not primarily that Eve transgressed, since Adam also was a transgressor (*cf.* Rom. 5:14), but that unlike Adam she was deceived. Now a further distinction needs to be made: it is not the subjective aspect of the deception that interests Paul (he is not imputing an inherent gullibility to women)[58] but the objective activity of the serpent in deceiving Eve. This is evident from the statement that 'Adam was not deceived' – not because he was able to see through the deception but because the serpent did not attempt to deceive him.[59] The point, therefore, is that transgression came about *through deception*, through the activity of the

[57] Against Schreiner 1995: 124–125.

[58] As assumed, for example, by Kelly 1963: 68. See also Scholer's (1986: 211–212) discussion of the issue.

[59] *Cf. 2 Enoch* 31:6 (trans. by F. I. Andersen, in Charlesworth 1983: 91–213): 'In such a form he (the devil) entered paradise, and corrupted Eve. But Adam he did not contact.'

serpent in persuading Eve to believe something that was not true. So Paul appeals to the creation story for a specific reason; he fears that through the fallacious arguments of heretical teachers women will again be deceived and fall into transgression.

This emphasis on the active role of Satan already places a considerable restriction on how we understand Paul's use of the Genesis story, because it shifts attention away from that which is intrinsic to created human nature. But the point can be taken further. The chiastic structure of verses 11, 13–14, as we have seen, has produced a rather exact and marked parallel between 'Adam was formed first' and 'Adam was not deceived'. But what is the *logical* connection between these two statements?

The connection between formation and deception

One explanation might be that Paul attributes to the man a natural moral and intellectual advantage over the woman, and therefore a greater resistance to deception, on the grounds that Adam was created first. 'Adam's superiority', runs one interpretation, 'is established by his priority in the order of creation and by his wisdom in not being seduced by the serpent' (Wicker 1975: 144).

As noted already, however, it is not the innate foolishness or gullibility of the woman that causes the problems but the objective meddling of the deceiver. In that respect the passage gives us no reason to believe that Adam would have fared any better had the serpent chosen to entice him, rather than Eve, with the promise of wisdom. Schreiner's (1995: 145) argument that the serpent approached the woman 'because of the different inclinations present in Adam and Eve' is simply unfounded. Moreover, if verse 12 is parenthetic and verses 13–14 give primarily the grounds for a woman learning obediently, then any appeal to an order of being ordained at creation seems misplaced. It is not on account of her relationship to the man that the woman should learn in submission to the truth but because of her entanglement with the deceiver. There is something about Eve that made her a target for the serpent, but it does not have to do with her status *vis-à-vis* the man. Certainly we read too much into the passage if we think that the priority of Adam is indicative of a position of authoritative 'headship' over the woman. It forms no part of Paul's argument that Eve violated her ordained submission to Adam.[60]

In this connection it has been argued that verses 13–14 provide an answer to the question, 'Who was at fault at the fall?' Eve transgressed because she was deceived; Adam was not deceived but transgressed knowingly and deliber-

---

[60] Against Moo, who says: 'The woman's being created after man, as his helper, shows the position of submission that God intended as inherent in the woman's relation to the man, a submission that is violated if a woman teaches doctrine or exercises authority over a man' (1991: 190; *cf.* Fung 1987: 201; Bowman 1992: 206, 213).

ately. R. Fung (1987: 202) draws the inference from this exposition that Paul is appealing for a restoration of the 'position of headship and responsibility both in the home and in religious matters' that was originally given to Adam.[61] But this is to reverse the thrust of Paul's argument. The passage is not concerned with Adam's responsibility but with the situation of the woman. The underlying question is not 'Who was to blame for the fall?' but 'Why, in this situation, should women learn and not teach?' Fung's argument is a subterfuge, one more attempt to insinuate ideas of subordination into a passage that has no need of them.

In view of this, some other explanation of the connection between the creation of Eve and her deception by the serpent needs to be found. Two possibilities present themselves; but first we should give some thought to the rhetorical and logical function of the Old Testament story.

There is much to be said for Padgett's (1987: 26–27) argument that Paul makes use of the Genesis story typologically.[62] The motif of Eve's deception is certainly used figuratively in 2 Corinthians 11:3: 'I am afraid lest in some way, as the serpent seduced Eve by his cunning, your thoughts might be led astray from sincerity and purity towards Christ.' In 1 Timothy 2:13–14 the figurative character of the allusion is not made explicit, but it is strongly suggested by the fact that the point of relevance in the story is the action of the serpent, not anything in the created nature of Eve. If Eve's transgression had been attributed to some natural weakness that has since been transmitted to all women, then we should have to conclude that Paul saw in the story a fundamental and universal objection to women taking spiritual initiative. But this is not the case. The source of trouble is the serpent's deception of Eve, which, as an event, has no essential or determinative continuity with the subsequent history of womankind; Paul does not make the sort of extrapolation from Eve's deception that he does from Adam's sin (Rom. 5:12–21).[63] The action of the serpent is not transmitted to all women, but it does naturally stand as a figure or type for the deception of women at other times.

The typological explanation also accounts both for the trouble taken over

[61] *Cf.* Hurley 1981: 214–216.

[62] *Cf.* Redekop 1990: 243; Harris 1990: 349–350; Keener 1992: 117. 'Typology' is a difficult category to deal with in Paul's letters (see Perriman 1987), and its use here misleading if taken to suggest a prefigurative or normative relationship. To speak, as Padgett does, of a 'cautionary typology' is more accurate, but in some respects it may be better simply to describe the application of the Genesis story as 'figurative'.

[63] Womankind suffers from the consequences of the fall (*cf.* 1 Tim. 2:15), but not because women are implicated specifically in the transgression of Eve; it is through the trespass of one man that all humankind has sinned, and it is through the righteousness of one man that all humankind is justified (Rom. 5:12–21).

the chiastic structure and for the confusion or intermingling of the two 'narratives'. On the one hand, because Paul is thinking of Adam, 'man' is spoken of in the singular when one would expect the sort of authority at issue to be one over 'men'.[64] On the other, the contemporary situation shows through the Old Testament narrative in places: the reversion to 'the woman', for example, in verse 14; the use of the perfect ('has come into transgression') rather than the aorist.[65] The Old Testament narrative has been subtly reshaped precisely to encompass the figurative function.

We could, in fact, push the point further and suggest that verses 13–14 are statements not so much about a state of affairs established at creation that has prevailed to the time of writing as statements about the situation in Ephesus – in language *borrowed* from the Genesis story. Verse 14 is certainly ambiguous in this respect. It would then be a small step to take to argue that the appropriateness of this type or 'model' is determined not by some absolute principle embedded in the story of Eve's deception but by the actual situation faced in the church. The type is relevant because – perhaps only because – an analogous situation has emerged in Ephesus; we cannot legitimately infer from it a pattern for the whole experience of womankind. The type, as such, is descriptive rather than prescriptive. This being the case, in a situation in which women are no more likely than men to be seduced into moral or spiritual error, a model derived from Genesis 2:21–23 may be less appropriate than, say, the egalitarian model of Genesis 1:26–27.[66]

Now, however, we are in a position to consider the likely rationale connecting the ideas of formation and deception. One explanation that has sometimes been put forward interprets the prior formation of Adam as a figure for the greater educational or spiritual maturity of the men in the church of Ephesus.[67] Eve, formed after Adam, knew of the commandment not to eat of

---

[64] Schreiner (1995: 128) says that *andros* is used generically, as *gynē* is. This is possible in principle, but a strong impression still remains that in changing from the plural in verses 8–10 to the singular in verses 11–12 Paul has adapted his argument to the terms of the Genesis narrative.

[65] *Cf.* Redekop 1990: 244.

[66] The debate over whether *gar* ('for') in verse 13 gives a reason for the preceding instructions or an explanation of them has been somewhat misconceived (*e.g.* Liefeld 1986b: 223; Witherington 1988: 122; Harris 1990: 349–350; Keener 1992: 115; Pierce 1993: 350). The story of Adam and Eve cannot be understood as an *explanation* of Paul's instructions; it provides a reason. The question is what kind of reason.

[67] The word *plassō*, which is taken directly from the Old Testament narrative (Gn. 2:7, 8, 15), is not clearly used in this figurative sense in the LXX or NT (though note Ps. 32:15, LXX; Is. 53:11). There are, however, instances in classical usage where the verb is used in this way, perhaps most strikingly in Plato, *Republic* 377C, where both a physical and an intellectual shaping is denoted: '. . . to form [*plattein*] their souls by myths much more than their bodies by hands'.

the tree of knowledge only at second hand. In the same way, the women of Ephesus, being socially and educationally retarded, were less well equipped than the men to resist the charms and sophistries of the false teachers.[68] An intriguing extension of this interpretation is found in an article by R. W. Pierce. He suggests that, in Paul's view, Eve's secondary place in the order of creation represents not an immutable hierarchal distinction between the man and the woman but merely a postponement of women's full self-realization (1993: 350–351). Man was formed first, historically, but women would eventually be 'formed' themselves, thus acquiring full social equality. The particular attraction of this interpretation is that it accounts, at least partly, for the 2,000-year hiatus between the granting of equality in Christ and its practical fulfilment – still incomplete – through the education and emancipation of women.

This explanation of Paul's use of the story of Adam and Eve in this context, however, is not without its problems. One is that although Eve was 'formed' after Adam, she was nevertheless formed *before* she was deceived. Eve was not ignorant of the command not to eat of the fruit of the tree (Gn. 3:3), and Paul makes nothing of the fact that she learnt of this prohibition from Adam rather than directly from God. So if 'formed' is a figure for the acquisition of knowledge, we still do not have an explanation of why Eve was deceived and not Adam.[69] Piper and Grudem (1991: 81–82) also make the point that Paul does not himself give the lack of education as the reason why women should not be allowed to teach.[70] They object further that formal training in Scripture was not required for leadership in the New Testament church and, in any case, basic literacy was to be found among both men and women. They also point out that Priscilla may well have been in Ephesus at the time Paul wrote 1 Timothy and no doubt there were other women like her who were well versed in the Scriptures. Yet no exception is made. These criticisms carry some weight.

Nevertheless, it would be a mistake to dismiss this interpretation of the typology altogether. Pierce's attempt to project the narrative on to social history is too inventive, but it is possible to understand Adam's precedence over Eve more in qualitative than in historical terms. Let us suppose Paul's assumption to be – on the basis of what he knows of things at Ephesus and elsewhere – that in a situation in which men are advantaged or privileged, whether socially or educationally, it is the women who are more likely to be fooled, just as Eve was, by misrepresentations of the word of God. This is likely to have been a commonplace judgment. It is worth recalling Plutarch's

---

[68] *Cf.* Padgett 1987: 26–27; Keener 1992: 116.

[69] This is contrary to the view expressed previously in Perriman 1993: 139.

[70] *Cf.* Baugh 1995: 45–47.

view that women, when deprived of a husband's intellectual guidance, are inclined to 'conceive many untoward ideas and low designs and emotions' (*Moralia* 145DE, Loeb).

It could be argued, then, that Paul saw in the priority of Adam's creation a prefiguring of the historical dominance of the man without thereby relegating the woman to a position of unalterable inferiority. The order of creation accounts for the relative advantage of the man, but it does not make this a matter of innate or permanent created difference – just as an elder brother may have some advantages over the younger without necessarily being superior to or having authority over him. Paul himself does not elaborate upon the point and this should warn us against seeking to interpret the typology too precisely. If the idea of 'formation' is in some way a figure for social development, then the *order* of formation may signify no more than the relative advantage of the man.

There is no need, moreover, to restrict the focus of the interpretation to the lack of formal education. The susceptibility of the women at Ephesus to deception was the result of a more comprehensive social, intellectual and spiritual immaturity than is envisioned by Piper and Grudem's objection; women lacked not only intellectual competence but also *experience* in public affairs. Whether Priscilla was present in Ephesus at the time is a matter of conjecture. But even if she was, it is still possible that Paul felt it to be a more effective and acceptable procedure to prohibit all women from teaching than to make exceptions.[71] If this is viewed as a pragmatic measure rather than the application of a theological principle, there is no real difficulty in the fact that Paul dealt with the specific issue by imposing a general ban.[72] Moreover, given the overall context of the passage, it is likely that the injunction against teaching applies specifically to the worship service, not to the sort of informal and impromptu teaching within the home that we know Priscilla engaged in. It is also worth recalling from our previous chapter the general disapproval of women voicing an opinion in public in the ancient world.

The argument remains viable, therefore, if not too much weight is placed on the chronological aspect of the typology and if the priority of Adam's formation is taken to represent something broader than just educational superiority. Women should commit themselves to learning *in submission to the teaching* because too many women, lacking spiritual and educational maturity,

[71] Keener (1992: 110) suggests alternatively that Paul intended this as 'a general statement that might admit certain obvious exceptions'.

[72] Paul does not mean, of course, that it is acceptable for women to teach false doctrine to other women (*cf.* Moo 1991: 190). The emphasis on women teaching men in 1 Tim. 2:12 owes much to the typology: *andros* connects more closely with *authentein*, a thought most clearly conditioned by the Adam and Eve typology, than with *didaskein*, which belongs to the contemporary situation.

were proving susceptible to the guile of false teachers. This is Paul's primary argument; but for the same reason, and as a natural corollary, he adds that women should not be permitted to teach in the assembly. It is not an argument against this view that it appears to be men rather than women who were responsible for promulgating false teaching (*cf.* 1 Tim. 1:20; 2 Tim. 2:17–18). Paul instructs Timothy to confront those clearly identified as false teachers directly (1 Tim. 1:3). Women posed a special problem, for the reasons already mentioned and for another reason to which we must now turn.

The second explanation for the connection between formation and deception sets out from the observation that the creation of Eve *after* Adam introduces a sexual dimension into humanity. This opens a door to temptation and seduction in general terms, but there is also perhaps the thought that the woman will be the more likely target for any seducer. While this is not explicit in verses 13–14, other considerations suggest that it provides a significant part of the underlying rationale for Paul's use of this story. The words generally translated 'to deceive' in these verses (*apataō* and *exapataō*) acquire quite pronounced sexual connotations in the Septuagint and in the Old Testament Pseudepigrapha when used in the context of relations between men and women.[73] Exodus 22:15, LXX, for example, reads: 'if anyone seduces [*apatēsēi*] a virgin who is not his betrothed and sleeps with her . . .' In the story of Judith we are told that 'Holofernes' heart was ravished with her and he was moved with great desire to possess her; for he had been waiting for an opportunity to deceive [*apatēsai*] her, ever since the day he first saw her' (Judith 12:16, RSV). No real suggestion that the deception of Eve had sexual overtones attaches to the use of *apataō* in the original account in Genesis (3:13). A strong Jewish tradition, however, regarded the deception as a matter of sexual seduction, and it seems likely that this interpretation was known to Paul; the language of 2 Corinthians 11:2–3, in particular, gives the idea of the deception of Eve by the serpent an overtly sexual connotation.[74] That Paul explicitly denies that Adam was deceived lends further weight to this view – or at least is consistent with it.[75]

In the end, it is probably unnecessary to choose between these two explanations. It is characteristic of figurative language that it draws together

---

[73] Delilah is told to 'entice [*apatēson*] your husband and have him tell you the riddle' (Jdg. 14:15; *cf.* 16:5); 'beauty deceived [*exēpatēsen*] you and lust perverted your heart' (Susanna 1:56); 'restrain me, O God, from sordid sin, and from every evil woman who seduces the foolish. And may the beauty of a criminal woman not deceive [*apatēsatō*] me . . .' (Psalms of Solomon 16:7–8, trans. by R. B. Wright, in Charlesworth 1985: 665).

[74] Urbach (1979: 169) quotes the Tosefta: 'So, too, we find in the case of the serpent, who set his mind on killing Adam and taking Eve to wife'; and R. Joshua b. Qorha: 'Because he saw them engaged in sexual intercourse and he lusted for her.' See also references in Dibelius & Conzelmann 1972: 48; Martin 1986: 333–334.

[75] *Cf.* Dibelius & Conzelmann 1972: 48.

different associations and allusions, leaving the reader some freedom – though not unlimited freedom – to determine how these things create meaning within the context of the passage. It is always important to respect the vagueness and openness of a text. Women should be encouraged to learn in submission to the teaching both on account of their relative social and intellectual immaturity and because women – young widows in particular – were especially vulnerable to seduction. Given these circumstances a woman should not teach, but this is not a direct argument from the Old Testament narratives.

Saved through the bearing of children

If there are overtones of sexual seduction in Paul's use of the Genesis story, this may provide a rather more intelligible basis for the interpretation of verse 15: women will be saved – perhaps specifically from the dangers of being deceived or seduced – by confining their sexuality within marriage, as signified by the 'child-bearing', provided that they remain faithful and chaste.[76] Here again we see the shaping effect of the typology. The 'child-bearing' (*teknogonia*) is at one level an allusion to, and has been determined by, the judgment of Genesis 3:17, LXX, that 'in pain you shall bear children' (*en lypais texē tekna*). But as a figure for the contemporary situation it is a synecdoche for a whole set of domestic activities, which are alluded to as 'good works' in verse 10 and set out in greater detail in 5:9–10 (child-rearing, hospitality to strangers, washing the feet of the saints, helping the afflicted) and 5:14 (marriage, child-bearing, household management).[77] The reason Paul chose this particular term to denote the whole gamut of domestic responsibility is simply that it makes the connection with the story of Eve.

The woman's salvation should be understood in the sense of enduring to the end, persevering in the faith, not succumbing to false teaching, not straying after Satan (5:15). Similar ideas are found in 1 Timothy 4:16, where Paul urges Timothy: 'Take heed to yourself and to the teaching, persevere in these; for by so doing you will save both yourself and your hearers.' In 2:4 salvation is directly linked to the attainment of 'knowledge of the truth'. In 2 Tim. 2:10–13 salvation is not only a matter of dying and living with Christ; it requires also endurance and faithfulness. Paul saw in the activity of the false teachers a serious threat to the salvation of believers (*cf.* 1 Tim. 1:19–20). To be saved, therefore, in this context at least, has the quite concrete sense of remaining faithful in the face of error and deception. We should probably also find in the emphasis on child-bearing a specific rebuttal to those false teachers who 'forbid marriage' (4:3).[78]

---

[76] *Cf.* Dibelius & Conzelmann 1972: 48.

[77] *Cf.* Tit. 2:3–5. See also Redekop 1990: 243–244; Bowman 1992: 210.

[78] *Cf.* Harris 1990: 350.

This does not mean that a woman's salvation is made dependent on works.[79] Rather Paul counsels an adherence to the outward order of domesticity, on the one hand, and to the inward qualities of faith, love and holiness, on the other, as a defence against error.[80] Such a lifestyle reduces the vulnerability of women to deception and gives them less opportunity to mislead others.

There is another implication, perhaps, that gives a more corporate perspective to Paul's concerns. The reason given in 1 Timothy 5:14 for insisting that younger widows should marry, bear children and manage a household is that the enemy should be given 'no occasion to revile us'. It is also likely that the phrase *meta sōphrosynēs* ('with decency or self-control') added in 2:15 has one eye on how Christian women are perceived by the pagan community in which they live. Part of the reason Paul connects the salvation of women so closely to child-bearing and domesticity is that the reputation and stability of the whole community is put in jeopardy by the reckless and profligate behaviour of some women.[81]

Eve and authentein

Finally, the typological or figurative interpretation of the relationship between Paul's reconstruction of the Genesis story and the circumstances in Ephesus best accounts for the choice of *authentein* in verse 12.

That Eve 'took the initiative' or 'exerted influence' in causing Adam also to sin is only implicit in verses 13–14, since the passage is concerned primarily with the deception of Eve through the specious insinuations of an intruder. Paul stops short of relating what Eve did to Adam because his main interest is not in women teaching but in women learning in such a way as not to be led into transgression. Nevertheless, it is probable that this thought both prompted the insertion of verse 12 and shaped its language. So when Paul wrote *oude authentein andros*, somewhat as an afterthought, he was thinking specifically of what Eve did to Adam; and Eve did not *have* authority, but *in her action became* responsible for – became the cause of – Adam's transgression. She exerted an influence over him in a particular situation and as a result he also sinned.[82] In the overlapping of the two contexts – that of the scriptural 'type' and that of

---

[79] Against Barron 1990: 457.

[80] This interpretation assumes that the woman is saved 'by means of' the child-bearing rather than 'in the circumstances of' the child-bearing. The threat to the woman's 'salvation' is not the pain and perilousness of childbirth but the activity of false teachers. Gn. 3:16 speaks of the pain of childbirth, but it does not obviously have in view the risk of dying in childbirth.

[81] *Cf.* Scholer 1986: 197–200.

[82] In this context the nuance of 'perpetrating a crime', though it belongs principally to the noun rather than the verb, may not be altogether inappropriate; and given the close connection between transgression and death in Paul's theology (*cf.* Rom. 5:12–14) the thought of 'murder' may also have some point to it. Note also Rom. 7:11: 'For sin, having

the contemporary situation at Ephesus – *authentein* refers both to what Eve once did by persuading Adam to eat and to what women now should not do by exercising a damaging teaching role.

It is very difficult, however, to capture the exact sense of this word in English; no one word or phrase provides a satisfactory semantic equivalent and Paul's argument is too condensed for the meaning to be clearly inferred from the context. Indeed, the style of Paul's argument here does not encourage us to explicate the significance of *oude authentein andros* in too much detail. We come close to the meaning with an expression like 'to exert influence over', but for the verse to be properly understood we must keep in mind the use that Paul makes of the Genesis story. Taken out of this context the word becomes almost meaningless. Like other elements in this passage *authentein* bridges the two narratives: it serves to project – far too concisely to be easily intelligible – the type of Eve's transgression upon the contemporary situation.

In the words *oude authentein andros*, therefore, we do not have simply a second prohibition alongside the one against teaching. Paul's argument at this point has taken on a rhetorical twist; the clause is an allusion – probably an *ad hoc* and improvised allusion – to the influence that Eve had over Adam. It points, in effect, to the foreseen consequences of women teaching. This causal connection, however, is to be read not so much from the *oude* construction as from the function of the clause against the background of the typological argument.

Conclusions

In this passage Paul has asked that women commit themselves to learning the word of God with a willingness to accept its authority. In order to underline the urgency of this requirement he retells the story of Eve's deception by the serpent, making of it a metaphor or type for the influence of false teachers over women in the church at Ephesus. The creational element in the story – the fact that Adam was formed first – serves to explain why it was Eve rather than Adam who was deceived. It does not directly support either the exhortation to learn or the prohibition against teaching. Paul does not explain how this connection between formation and deception is to be understood. Two distinct ideas, however, appear to lie behind his argument. At one level, the prior formation of Adam functions within the typological structure as a figure for the male's social and intellectual advantage – without necessarily endorsing that position. At another level, the creation of Eve represents the introduction of sexuality into human creation and with it a greatly increased potential for temptation and seduction.

---

found an opportunity through the commandment, deceived [*exēpatēsen*] me and through it killed me.'

This is the main argument of the passage, within which verse 12 reads as a parenthesis. The exhortation to learn elicits the related restriction: women should not regard learning as a qualification for teaching. But the typological argument has also prompted an elaboration of the prohibition against teaching that succinctly expresses the damaging impact that unqualified and immature women teachers might have on the Christian community. The unexpected verb *authentein* evokes the influence that Eve exerted over Adam and her decisive role as an instigator or perpetrator in the fall; Paul fears that her disastrous action will be re-enacted in the church in Ephesus if women are allowed to teach.

What are the implications of this interpretation for the participation of women in Christian ministry?

1. The passage does not enjoin submission to *male* authority; it is to the teaching, and to the teaching authority of the church, that women should be submitted. In the context, this submission must be understood quite specifically: it finds expression not in subordination but in holding fast to the word of God. This is the extent of the Old Testament argument. The point of the Genesis narrative is not that Eve usurped Adam's authority or sought an illegitimate equality, but that she was deceived with regard to the command of God and transgressed. The prior formation of Adam is not taken to signify any inherent superiority or authority over the woman.

2. If anything, the language of 'permission' is even more personal here than in 1 Corinthians 14:34.[83] The injunction has all the force of Paul's apostolic authority, backed up implicitly by the custom of 'all the churches of the saints'; but at the same time it shares in the contingent character of that authority. The verb *epitrepō* suggests that what Paul had in mind was not the application of a universal principle but a pragmatic response to a particular set of circumstances – even if those circumstances are reckoned to have prevailed throughout the churches of the apostolic era.

3. It is quite certain that *oude authentein andros* does not mean 'or to hold a position of authority over a man'. In all probability Paul would not at this time have allowed a woman to become an elder in the church, but this is not what he means by this expression. Verse 12 is a prohibition only against teaching; the clause 'or to exert influence over a man' draws its form and significance from the Genesis typology and has reference to the likely consequences of a woman teaching.

4. The passage does not attribute any innate moral, intellectual, or spiritual incompetence to women. Some explanation is needed of why Eve was deceived and not Adam, but this has to do, on the one hand, with the circumstantial social advantage that the male has had throughout history, and

---

[83] See chapter 5 above.

on the other, with the dimension of sexuality that entered the world with the creation of Eve. The social balance has certainly changed over the centuries. The damaging impact of sexuality on human relations and the life of faith is as significant as ever, but we should probably want to recognize that the *forms* of havoc wreaked by the winds of human sexuality do not remain constant. If Paul were writing now, he might draw attention instead to the vulnerability to sexual temptation of high-profile male leaders: 'I do not permit a man to counsel a woman alone . . .', for example. In other words, ecclesiastical regulations of this sort should address the actual problems encountered in Christian ministry, not the hypothetical and anachronistic concerns of theologians.

5. Paul, however, did not envisage any social changes of this nature. To his mind the participation of women in the public teaching ministry of the church was likely to bring both the community and the gospel into disrepute. There were fears, on the one hand, that women would become a conduit for false teaching, and on the other, no doubt, that for women to hold prominent teaching positions would invite criticism and scorn from outsiders.

The concern that Christian behaviour should be not only consistent with the gospel but also immune to public censure runs right through his teaching. Towards the end of the letter he charges Timothy to 'keep the commandment spotless and irreproachable [*anepilēmpton*] until the appearing of our Lord Jesus Christ' (6:14). This eschatological perspective is important. Paul knew that the community at Ephesus would be harried by false teachers, 'ruthless wolves' (*cf.* Acts 20:29–30). The Spirit had made it known that 'in later times some will fall away from the faith, giving heed to deceitful spirits and the teachings of demons' (1 Tim. 4:1). Paul's teaching, therefore, is aimed principally at *safeguarding the stability and eternal salvation of the community*. Too many had already wandered from the truth (1:6–7, 19–20). His instructions regarding women have nothing to do with the abstract status of women; they have to do with the survival of the church right through to the coming of Christ. Too many women had already 'strayed after Satan' (5:15).

6. The distinction between *didaskalia* and 'gospel' is not a hard and fast one, and certainly does not simply equate to a distinction between relative and absolute truth. Nevertheless, 1 Timothy demands recognition of the fact that much of Paul's teaching is pragmatically oriented. Its value derives to some extent at least from its effectiveness in supporting the fundamental truth, which is the advent of salvation in Jesus Christ (*cf.* 3:15–16). It then becomes legitimate to evaluate the usefulness of the particular injunction according to whether or not it satisfies that purpose. The prohibition against women teaching is not creationally mandated. It is not made a necessary consequence of redemption, nor is it presented as a positive aspect of the outworking of the Spirit within the community. It seems entirely appropriate, therefore, to

regard it as an attempt to regulate matters in such a way that the integrity and accessibility of the gospel and the stability of the Christian community should be most effectively safeguarded within the social and historical circumstances faced by churches such as that at Ephesus.

The objection has been put forward that it is improper simply to assume that 'if one can identify local or temporary circumstances against which the passage is written then one can conclude that the text has only limited application' (Moo 1991: 188).[84] Moo points to the fact that Paul develops his doctrine of justification by faith in Galatians in response to a particular local crisis. But is this a valid comparison? A distinction must surely be made between teaching that aims to correct a false understanding of the truth and teaching that deals with the circumstances under which error arises and is propagated. The question then is whether Paul's teaching in 1 Timothy 2:11–15 constitutes a correction of certain mistaken views about the status and role of women or an attempt to control the involvement of women in the spread of false teaching. We have argued that it is not fundamentally false teaching about the position of women that is at issue. Paul is not 'correcting the erroneous views of the place of women vis-à-vis men taught by the false teachers', as Moo (1991: 189) claims. While the opposition of the false teachers to marriage certainly has implications for the position of women in the church, the position of women does not itself form part of the content of this view. Paul's overriding concern in 1 Timothy 2:11–15 is to ensure that women in the church are not led astray by false teachers, that they learn in submission to the authority of God's Word, and, somewhat incidentally, that they should not be put in a position where they might mislead others.

There are significant differences between the sexes. Both men and women have their strengths and their weaknesses; women may fall into error one way, but men have their own peculiarly masculine temptations and misjudgments to cope with. Paul chose to deal with a particular threat to the integrity of the gospel by refusing women permission to teach. The question facing the church today is still: where does the threat to the integrity of the gospel come from? And then: what steps need to be taken in order to counter that threat? Although there is freedom in Christ, sometimes it will be necessary to impose restrictions on the exercise of ministry – but restrictions that are effective and relevant, not merely repressive.

---

[84] Keener (1992: 112) provides a clear example: 'Since this passage is related so closely to the situation Timothy was confronting in Ephesus, we should not use it in the absence of other texts to prove that Paul meant it universally.'

7. Women and men: creation and re-creation

Paul's instructions regarding the position of women in the church are almost entirely practical in their orientation, addressing such mundane issues as the wearing of head-coverings while praying and prophesying, the vocal participation of women in the assemblies, comportment and dress in worship, the special needs of widows, and so on. His teaching on the marriage relationship takes us rather closer to the essential nature of man and woman, but still the practical aims predominate: how should husbands and wives live out their new status as sons and daughters of God within the framework of an institution whose structure, customs and values were essentially pagan and from which they could only partially disengage themselves? This body of diverse parenetic material, however, is drawn around two important theological focal points: the creation of man and woman as narrated in the first chapters of the book of Genesis, and the re-creation of men and women in Christ.

So we should consider, first, how Paul's understanding of the creation narratives shaped his teaching on the position of women. To some extent this simply entails collating thoughts that have emerged already in the course of this study. But we might also attempt to read the Old Testament narratives, especially as they appear in the Septuagint, as Paul would have read them. Then, secondly, we should give careful attention to Galatians 3:28, where, in an apparent allusion to the creation story, Paul says that in Christ 'there is not "male and female"'.

The creation narratives

A number of distinct motifs emerge from Paul's use of the Old Testament creation narratives in the context of his teaching about women: the priority of the man in the order of creation; the creation of the woman 'for the sake of' the man; the union of husband and wife as 'one flesh'; and the deception of Eve by the serpent. These are no more than brief allusions: the Genesis texts are not interpreted, nor is any attempt made to justify their use.

Adam was formed first

Adam gar prōtos eplasthē, eita Heua. [14]*kai Adam ouk ēpatēthē, hē de gynē exapatētheisa en parabasei gegonen.*

For Adam was formed first, then Eve, [14]and Adam was not

deceived. But the woman having been deceived has come into transgression (1 Tim. 2:13–14).

Anēr men gar ouk opheilei katakalyptesthai tēn kephalēn eikōn kai doxa theou hyparchōn; hē gynē de doxa andros estin. [8]*ou gar estin anēr ek gynaikos alla gynē ex andros.*

For indeed a man ought not to veil the head, being the image and glory of God; but the woman is the glory of a man. [8]For man is not from woman but woman from man (1 Cor. 11:7–8).

The formation of Adam before Eve is referred to most clearly in 1 Timothy 2:13, apparently in typological fashion, to explain why the serpent chose to deceive Eve rather than Adam. In our study of this passage it appeared that the connection between formation and deception may be understood in two ways. Paul may be thinking of the man's social and educational advantage, in which case 'formed first' is, by way of a play on words, the extension of a simple temporal priority into the social realm. Or he may have in mind the potential for sexual seduction introduced into human existence with the creation of Eve. Perhaps both thoughts are relevant, and loosely related; the woman's sexual vulnerability is exacerbated by her social and intellectual naïvety.

In 1 Corinthians 11:7–8 the thought is rather different. Whereas man is the image and glory of God, the woman is the glory of the man because she was created 'from man' (1 Cor. 11:7–8). The order of creation accounts for what Paul sees as a fundamental distinction between the sexes – a distinction which in this passage at least is expressed by means of the typically Jewish category of 'glory'. The woman is created not merely after man but *from* man, and as such she embodies for Paul, in her creation if not in herself, the essential relatedness of male and female. She is not an entirely separate creature. The point of this will become clearer when we come to consider the purpose behind the creation of the woman.

The temporal priority of the man also finds expression in the metaphor of the man as 'head' of the woman (1 Cor. 11:3; Eph. 5:23), particularly in view of the analogy between the man as head and Christ as head. There is a close connection in Paul's thought, encapsulated in the figure of headship, between the prominence of the man in relation to the woman and his precedence in the order of creation – just as there is a connection between the prominence or exaltation of Christ and his precedence in the order of resurrection. The prominence of the man inevitably affects the nature and balance of the male–female relationship, and in certain circumstances may impose practical constraints on the woman. In Paul's world it meant, among other things, that a woman should cover her head when praying or prophesying – not because this was theologically necessary but because *in ancient culture* the prominence of the man exposed him to dishonour and shame. It meant, too, that a woman should submit to her husband in the marriage relationship – not because the woman was naturally subordinate to the man but because the prominence of the man had become inextricably bound up with structures of dominance and subordination.

Paul appears, therefore, to have made use of the priority of Adam in creation in two basic ways. The first has to do with the social prominence of the man, the second with the sexual relationship. But how does this motif appear in the text of the Septuagint?

There are two creation narratives in the first two chapters of Genesis. In Genesis 1:27 man and woman are created simultaneously: 'And God made the man [*ton anthrōpon*]; according to the image of God he made him; male and female [*arsen kai thēly*] he made them.' They are created with the express divine purpose of exercising shared dominion over other living creatures (v. 26), and they are instructed by God to 'increase and multiply' (v. 28). Paul makes reference to this account only in his description of the man as 'the image and glory of God' in 1 Corinthians 11:7 and, probably, in the phrase 'male and female' (*arsen kai thēly*) in Galatians 3:28.

The second creation narrative in Genesis 2 differs in a number of respects from the first. The man (*ton anthrōpon*) is formed, 'dust from the earth', as a single individual at the beginning of the process (v. 7), not as a couple at the end. Instead of the mandate to *subdue* a world already created, he is placed in a garden, planted afterwards, which he is to *cultivate* (v. 8, 15). This arrangement is reinforced by the statement in verse 5 that the plants and grass of the field had not yet sprung up, 'for God had not sent rain upon the earth and there was no man to work it'.

So the man is in the first place a cultivator. But two other things are also established before the creation of the woman: Adam is forbidden to eat of the 'tree of knowing good and evil' (v. 17); and he is found to be in need of a 'helper according to him' (v. 18). No direct connection between these two ideas is apparent, but they are closely juxtaposed in the narrative and an inevitable tension arises between the man's need for a helper and the potential for moral and spiritual disaster. The man's existence, therefore, before the arrival of the woman is both unsatisfactory and unstable. But what sort of 'man' is this?

It has sometimes been pointed out that in the Hebrew text it is '*āḏām* (man as a species, as distinct from animals, angels, and so on) that is created in 2:7, not '*îš* (man as distinct from woman).[1] Adam is not referred to as '*îš* until the creation of the woman (v. 23). The same linguistic distinction is found in the Septuagint. For most of Genesis 2 the Hebrew word '*āḏām* is translated in the

---

[1] *Cf.* Hayter 1987: 96–99.

Septuagint either by *Adam* as a proper name or by the usually inclusive term *anthrōpos*. The word *anēr* (corresponding to *'îš*) likewise appears first at verse 23, at the point where male and female are first differentiated: 'she shall be called woman because she was taken out of her man [*ek tou andros autēs*]'.[2] In Genesis 3 *anēr* appears twice, when the woman gives the fruit to 'her husband' (v. 6), and when she is told by God that 'your turning will be to your husband' (v. 16); otherwise the man is referred to by his name *Adam*, not as *anthrōpos*. In view of this, it might be argued that Adam was created as a sexually undifferentiated person ('proto-humanity', to use Trible's phrase)[3] and became distinctively male only with the creation of the woman. This, in effect, would abolish the priority of the male in creation and any advantage that the man might gain from it.

The significance of this change in terminology, however, particularly for the Greek text, should not be pressed too far. *Anthrōpos* can be used to refer exclusively to the male (*cf.* 1 Cor. 7:1; Gal. 5:3);[4] it is certainly more closely associated in general usage with the male than the female; and in verse 24 it is used for the 'man' who leaves his father and mother and clings to his wife, even though the Hebrew text has *'îš*.[5] Generally speaking, we would expect *anēr* to be used where it is necessary to differentiate between man and woman. It seems unlikely, therefore, that Paul would have understood *ton anthrōpon* in verse 7 to signify an asexual human person. In any case, to say that God created a 'person' does not mean that that person cannot be either male or female; one could say that Adam's maleness was simply irrelevant or unrealized prior to the creation of the woman. Adam, moreover, does not appear to be changed in any way by the creation of Eve and the differentiation of gender. Most importantly for our study, such an interpretation is probably incompatible with the use that Paul makes of the Genesis text. The argument of 1 Corinthians 11:7–8 has no place for such an undifferentiated Adam; and the Adam who was 'not deceived' cannot be any different from the Adam who was 'formed first' (1 Tim. 2:13–14).

We should also take note of the fact that the man retains both precedence and prominence throughout the creation narrative. It is Adam to whom God calls in the garden (3:9). The pair are repeatedly referred to as 'Adam and his wife' (2:25; 3:8; 3:21). Adam names his wife (3:20; *cf.* 2:23). It is Adam who is expressly said by God to have 'become as one of us, to know good and evil',

[2] *Cf.* Jeremias 1964: 364; Hayter 1987: 96–99. In the Hebrew text the inclusive term *'āḏām* is used to refer to 'man' except at 2:23 ('she shall be called woman [*'iššâ*] because she has been taken out of man [*'îš*]'); 2:24; 3:6, 16.

[3] Quoted in Hayter 1987: 97.

[4] This is perhaps less true for *'āḏām*; but note Sirach 7:28.

[5] When Eve says at the birth of Cain, 'I have gained a man [*anthrōpos*]' (4:1), the point is not that Cain is male but that she has produced another person.

and who is cast out of the garden 'lest he stretch out his hand and take from the tree of life and eat and shall live forever' (3:22–24). Possibly this prominence already reflects the postlapsarian perspective that is expressed most acutely in the judgment pronounced on the woman in 3:16, LXX: 'your turning will be to your husband, and he will rule over [*kyrieusei*] you'.[6] Nevertheless, it appears in the text as a natural continuation of the prior creation of Adam. The theoretical equality of the man and the woman that appears in 2:24, therefore, is somewhat belied by the Adam-centred focus of the narrative as a whole.

On the other hand, the creational priority of the man is nowhere made an argument for the subordination of the woman.[7] A. L. Bowman has argued that 'Adam's chronological primacy in creation carried with it some degree of authority', suggesting that the Old Testament concept of primogeniture, the right of the firstborn, provides an appropriate rationale for the idea.[8] The chief objection to this argument is that the creation story is couched in quite different terms: Adam and Eve were 'formed', not born; Adam is not described as a 'son', nor Eve as a 'daughter'; and in any case, primogeniture was operative only in relation to other sons. The primary significance of the concept is not that the firstborn has authority over subsequent offspring but that he inherits a double portion – for he is the 'first of his father's strength' (Dt. 21:17). This again is not an idea that is reflected either in the creation narratives or in the use that Paul makes of them. There is no suggestion that the man has inherited more than the woman; on the contrary, they are equally heirs of the Spirit.

Eve was created 'for the sake of' Adam

> . . . *kai gar ouk ektisthē anēr dia tēn gynaika alla gynē dia ton andra.*
> . . . for in fact man was not created for the sake of the woman but woman for the sake of the man (1 Cor. 11:9).

The assertion that Eve was created 'for the sake of the man' (1 Cor. 11:9) has reference to the purpose given for the creation of the woman in the account of Genesis 2. 'It is not good,' the Lord God says, 'for the man to be alone; let us make for him a helper according to him' (2:18, LXX).

The word *boēthos*, which translates the Hebrew word *'ēzer*, is applied

---

[6] In 4:7 God says to Cain, apparently with reference to his brother Abel rather than to sin as in the Hebrew text, 'to you [shall be] his turning, and you shall rule over [*arxeis*] him'. In the Hebrew text it is not clear that sin's 'desire' for Cain is specifically a desire to rule over or control (against Hurley 1981: 219; Ortlund 1991: 108–109). The image of sin 'lying at the door' may rather suggest seduction: sin, therefore, is like a seductive woman who leads a man into error. The same idea, therefore, may lie behind the Hebrew text of Gn. 3:16.

[7] *Cf.* Hayter 1987: 97–98.

[8] Bowman 1992: 205, taking up a proposal made by Hurley 1981: 207–208.

frequently in the Septuagint, and especially in the Psalms, to God with the sense of 'one who rescues, saves, delivers from danger'. 'But I am poor and needy, O God, help me,' David cries; 'you are my helper and my deliverer, O Lord; do not delay' (Ps. 69:6, LXX = Ps. 70:5).[9] In these passages, moreover, there is a strong echo of the underlying meaning of 'running to answer a call for help': in 1 Chronicles 12:19, for example, *boēthos* is used of the sons of Benjamin and Judah who 'came to the help [*ēlthon . . . eis boētheian*] of David' (v. 17).[10] In more general terms this suggests that *boēthos* means 'helper' not in the sense of a subordinate 'assistant' but as an independent person who makes up a significant deficiency or helplessness in the other.[11] What the word defines essentially is not the status of the helper (the helper may be either superior or inferior) but the condition of the one in need of help. This is of considerable importance. We cannot conclude from the description of Eve as 'helper' that she was placed under the authority of the man.

In the context of the Genesis story the man's deficiency is identified by the words 'it is not good for the man to be alone'. In the first place, this has to do with the work of cultivating the garden in which the man has been placed (2:15; *cf.* 2:5). But verse 24 makes it clear that the story of the creation of the woman is also, and perhaps primarily, an explanation of the institution of marriage.

The helper must be 'according or corresponding to him' (*kat' auton*) or 'like him' (*homoios autō*, v. 20). The animals of the field and the birds of the sky, which were also created from the earth (v. 19), proved inadequate in this respect: they were not 'like him', but were of a different nature. So God fashioned the woman from the man's rib (literally, 'built the rib into a woman'), and Adam declared (one imagines with some relief), 'This now is bone from my bones and flesh from my flesh; she will be called woman [*'iššâ*], because she was taken from her man [*'îš*]' (v. 23).

The creation of the woman from the man's rib contrasts with the creation of the other living creatures, in the manner of Adam's creation, 'from the earth'.[12] The implication is quite clear: if Eve had been created from the earth, she too would have been a different creature, not *like* Adam; as it is, she shares the same biological nature as the man and is sexually compatible

---

[9] *Cf.* Ex. 15:2; 18:4; Dt. 33:7, 26, 29; 1 Kingdoms 7:12; 2 Sa. 22:42; Pss. 9:10 (= 10:14); *et al.*; Judith 9:11; 2 Macc. 3:39; Sirach 51:2.

[10] *Cf.* Acts 21:28; see Büchsel 1964: 628–629.

[11] *Cf.* Hurley 1981: 209. The meaning of *'ēzer* is essentially the same. Note Wenham 1987: 68: 'To help someone does not imply that the helper is stronger than the helped; simply that the latter's strength is inadequate by itself.'

[12] Note Hayter (1987: 99): "*'iššâ* is "taken out of" *'îš*, but so is *'ādām* "taken out of" *'ªdāmāh*, "earth", and *'ādām* is not portrayed as a supernumerary addition to the earth nor as subordinate to it.'

with him.[13] The significance of the prepositional phrase *kat' auton* is that, while being of the same nature, the woman makes up the deficiency of the solitary Adam through her differentness (*cf.* Fee 1987:517). The same thought is found in the Hebrew text: the word $k^e neğdô$, which occurs only in this passage in the Hebrew Old Testament, has the literal sense 'like opposite him', suggesting both likeness and difference or complementarity.

The search for an adequate helper also provides the background against which the act of naming the woman should be interpreted. That Adam names the woman has often been understood as an assertion of authority over her.[14] But the context does not support this. In Genesis 1 God 'names' the various elements as they are created (vv. 5, 8, 10), and in so doing establishes their identity and differentiates between them (*cf.* Bechtel 1993:86). In each case the naming accompanies an explicit *separation* of one element from another. Likewise, by naming the animals (2:19–20) Adam does not demonstrate his rule over them, but rather differentiates and identifies each creature in hope of finding one suitable to be a 'helper'. It is in the process of naming that they are found to be inadequate. The woman, however, is recognized as corresponding to the man and is named accordingly: 'this one shall be called woman, because this one was taken out of the man'. By naming her, Adam marks her out as being fundamentally both different from the animals and related to himself. This is an act of recognition, not of rule; the only advantage he has is that he preceded her.

Essentially the complementarity of man and woman is sexual, not hierarchal: the woman was taken out of her husband, and 'for this reason a man shall leave his father and his mother and shall cling to his wife, and the two shall be as one flesh' (2:24).[15] That Paul understood this principally in terms of sexual union is evident from 1 Corinthians 6:16: 'Do you not know that he who joins himself to a prostitute is one body? For it is said, "The two shall become one flesh." ' There are rhetorical factors at work here which should warn us against the assumption that Paul regarded this as a straightforward and literal application of the Genesis text. Nevertheless, it is striking that he could speak of the occasional and uncommitted union of a man with a prostitute in such terms.

---

[13] The same distinction between the human couple and the animals is found in Gn. 1. Man is created 'according to our image and likeness' in contrast to the other living creatures which the earth brings forth 'according to their kind' (*kata genos:* Gn. 1:22–24, LXX). Being in the image and likeness of God man has dominion over all living creatures (1:26, 28). *Cf.* also Hayter 1987: 100: 'Woman alone amongst all living creatures is *homoousious* with man; man and woman are of the same nature and substance.'

[14] See, for example, Hurley 1981: 210–212.

[15] In agreement with 1:26–27 it is the creation of man *as male and female* that is the climax of creation. *Cf.* Hayter 1987: 96, 100.

Paul makes more conventional use of the text in Ephesians 5:28–31, in support of his argument that 'the men should also love their own wives as being their own bodies' (v. 28). He quotes Genesis 2:24 in full: 'For this reason a man shall leave his father and mother and be joined to his wife, and the two shall become as one flesh.' If husband and wife are one flesh, then the woman is as much part of the man as his own body.[16] Paul's teaching here presupposes a certain social inequality between the man and the woman; the love of the wife for her husband must take into account the submission that society expected of her; the love of the husband for his wife, conversely, is in tension with the position of superiority and dominance that society bestowed on him. Otherwise, 1 Corinthians 7:4 suggests that the argument could just as well have been directed to the woman; the wife should love her husband as being her own body, for 'the man does not have authority over his own body, but the woman does'.

So when Paul speaks of the woman as having been created 'for the sake of the man', it is likely that he is thinking fundamentally of the creation of the woman as the sexual counterpart to the man. In so far as the relationship is defined sexually, it is asymmetrical: the woman is 'for the sake of the man'; she is the 'glory' of the man. This has to do partly with the nature of sexual attraction (though it might be unwise to suppose that the woman is more naturally an object of desire than the man); and partly, no doubt, with functions closely connected with the central purpose of marriage: procreation and the upbringing of children. Beyond this it is for anthropologists, psychologists, sociologists, and such like, to decide what attitudes, roles, patterns of behaviour, and so on, if any, are naturally or typically either male or female. The manner in which the original asymmetry established at creation is extended into the public or social sphere is to a large extent culturally determined. It may take the form of patriarchy and the subordination of the woman, but this is not a scriptural requirement. The asymmetry that emerges with the introduction of sexuality may be expressed just as well, if not better, within an egalitarian culture in which the man is afforded no intrinsic social advantage or authority over the woman.

Mutual dependence in 1 Corinthians 11:11–12

Plēn oute gynē chōris andros oute anēr chōris gynaikos en kyriō; [12]*hōsper gar hē gynē ek tou andros, houtōs kai ho anēr dia tēs gynaikos; ta de panta ek tou theou.*

Nevertheless, neither woman without man, nor man without

---

[16] Behind this statement is no doubt also the commandment of Lv. 19:18: 'you shall love your neighbour as yourself' (*cf.* Bruce 1984: 391; Lincoln 1990: 378).

woman in the Lord; [12]for as the woman from the man, so also the man through the woman; and all things from God (1 Cor. 11:11–12).

But how is this original asymmetry, linked to the prior creation of the man, to be reconciled with Paul's assertion in 1 Corinthians 11:11–12 that in the Lord there is in fact symmetry and mutuality?

Despite its careful organization, the argument of this passage is ambiguous. At first glance verse 11 appears to describe a specifically Christian or eschatological conception of the interdependence of men and women – *in the Lord*. Verse 12, however, explains this in terms of the natural realities of creation ('the woman from the man') and reproduction ('the man through the woman'). So the question arises: is Paul talking about a special interdependence that is found in Christ, or is he saying that this is the natural condition of humankind? Probably the point here is not that in the kingdom of God a new state of affairs between the sexes prevails, but that believers should recognize the implications of the *natural* interdependence of men and women. In any case, both men and women owe their existence equally to God.[17] Or perhaps more accurately: it is specifically *in Christ* that it becomes possible to acknowledge and respect this natural interdependence. In the context of the passage these verses serve to forestall any potential misunderstanding of the differentiation between men and women marked by the woman's head-covering when she is praying and prophesying. Although men and women are set apart by the manner in which they pray and prophesy, this does not signify the one-sided dependence of the woman on the man or spiritual inferiority on the part of the woman.[18]

So whereas the order of creation gives priority to the man, the order of nature offsets this with a reciprocal arrangement. The implication of the phrase 'in the Lord' may be quite remarkable. In the world – for most of its history at least – it is overwhelmingly the prominence given to man in the order of creation that has determined relations between men and women. In Christ, however, Paul says, it is possible for social relations to be shaped not only by the woman's creational dependence on the man but also by the man's reproductive dependence on the woman.[19] There is an inevitable tension here,

[17] Against Fee (1987: 523 n. 41), who thinks that 'in the Lord' refers to the ' "sphere" of their existence in the new age' (see also Fiorenza 1983: 229).

[18] Fiorenza's (1983: 229) argument that *chōris* in 1 Cor. 11:11 means 'different from' rather than 'without' or 'apart from' cannot be sustained. It lacks any lexical basis, and it renders the verse tautological: 'woman is not different from man, nor is man different from woman'. Paul is not saying here that there is no difference between men and women but that they are naturally interdependent.

[19] Does Paul mean by this that in some sense – perhaps not in the same sense – the man also brings glory to the woman?

but one which precisely reflects the ambiguous situation of a Christian community which must live in two worlds. It is a tension which Murphy-O'Connor (1996:290) overlooks when he acclaims these verses as 'the first and only explicit defence of the complete equality of women in the New Testament', and then maintains, on the basis of this insight, that 'the directive that women must keep silent in church . . . cannot come from the pen of Paul'.

The deception of Eve

The creation of the woman also introduces the possibility of deception and sin. At the moment when the man and the woman are presented naked and unashamed in a tableau that concludes the process of creation, the serpent sneaks into the picture (2:25 – 3:1). The juxtaposition may hint at a sexual undercurrent to the story of the deception,[20] but otherwise no indication is given as to why the serpent approached Eve rather than Adam. Did this wiliest of creatures regard her as more gullible or vulnerable to deception than Adam? Philo was of the opinion that the serpent spoke to the woman because she 'is more accustomed to be deceived than man . . . she easily gives way and is taken in by plausible falsehoods which resemble the truth' (*Quaestiones in Genesin* 33, Loeb). But the text gives us no reason to believe that this was the case.[21] The emphasis is on the character and role (though not the motives) of the serpent, who creates in Eve's mind enough uncertainty about the purpose of God's Word for her to be enticed by the appearance of the fruit and the prospect of becoming like gods. It is not the stupidity of Eve but the cleverness of the serpent, who so plausibly distorts what God had said, that is the cause of the problem. Nor is there any suggestion that Eve's sin was worse than Adam's. Indeed, 3:17 seems to imply that Eve repeated the serpent's arguments to Adam; he knew what he was eating.

In the course of the Lord God's judgment on the three miscreants, however, a certain disparity emerges. The woman is simply told that she will endure pain in childbirth, her 'turning' will be towards her husband, and he will rule over her (3:16). God does not say to Eve, as he does to the serpent and to Adam, 'Because you did this . . .' (vv. 14, 17). Upon Adam a more

[20] Perhaps this is reinforced in the Hebrew text by a play on words: the word for 'shrewd' in 3:1 is '*ārûm*, whereas the word for 'naked' in the preceding verse is '*ārôm* (*cf.* Wenham 1987: 72; Hamilton 1990: 187). Also, although the knowledge of 'good and evil' must presumably be understood in general moral terms, the immediate consequence of eating the fruit is an awareness of nakedness.

[21] Hess argues that as caretaker of the garden and namer of the animals Adam would have recognized the character of the serpent (Hess 1993: 16). But the salient characteristic of the snake is that it was shrewd, not deceptive or wicked. Nor do we have any reason for thinking that Eve could not equally have recognized the nature of the snake.

comprehensive judgment is pronounced. Not only is the pain of working the ground directly attributed to his action ('Because you listened to the voice of your wife . . .'), but also it is Adam who receives the sentence of death: 'In the sweat of your face you will eat your bread until you return to the earth from which you were taken, for you are earth and to earth you shall return' (v. 19). Adam, in other words, is made responsible for the catastrophe in a way in which Eve is not. She is cast less in the role of a protagonist than as a victim – the serpent's dupe and an instrument in Adam's fall. This is consistent with the prominence that Adam has generally in the narrative.

Paul makes use of the motif of Eve's deception in two places. In 1 Timothy 2:14 it is used in support of the instruction that women should learn submissively and not engage in public teaching. On the one hand, the woman generally speaking was disadvantaged educationally and socially and therefore more likely to become a conduit for false teaching. On the other, the woman was regarded as susceptible to the improper enticements of false teachers. The second passage, however, makes it clear that Paul did not regard women alone as capable of being deceived:

> I am jealous for you with the jealousy of God, for I betrothed you to one husband, to present you a pure virgin to Christ. But I am afraid lest somehow, as the serpent deceived Eve by his cunning, your thoughts may be seduced from sincerity and purity towards Christ (2 Cor. 11:2–3).

Here Eve's deception is a figure for the deception of the whole church: Paul understood that men no less than women could be seduced by falsehood.

New creation

> *Pantes gar hyioi theou este dia tēs pisteōs en Christō Iēsou;* [27]*hosoi gar eis Christon ebaptisthēte, Christon enedysasthe.* [28]*ouk eni Ioudaios oude Hellēn, ouk eni doulos oude eleutheros, ouk eni arsen kai thēly; pantes gar hymeis heis este en Christō Iēsou.* [29]*ei de hymeis Christou, ara tou Abraam sperma este, kat' epangelian klēronomoi.*

> For you all are sons of God through faith, in Christ Jesus; [27]for as many of you as were baptized into Christ put on Christ. [28]There is neither Jew nor Greek, there is neither slave nor free, there is not 'male and female'; for you all are one in Christ Jesus. [29]And if you are of Christ, then you are seed of Abraham, according to the promise heirs (Gal. 3:26–29).

Paul's statement in Galatians 3:28 is remarkable. The rhetorical structure and comprehensive embrace of the verse give it a strongly programmatic and axiomatic resonance – all the more so if the Galatians heard in it an allusion to words pronounced at their baptism, as has often been argued. But this prominence creates a difficulty, because it raises more acutely the question of to what extent this statement goes beyond the terms and conditions of Paul's argument in Galatians 3 – 4. Does this proclamation of 'oneness' have relevance only in so far as it fits the discussion about justification and inheritance? Or does it have an independent status as some sort of charter for redeemed humanity – 'The Magna Carta of Humanity', as P. K. Jewett famously called it?[22] The implications of these questions will become clearer as we examine Paul's argument in this complex passage.

The first two chapters of Galatians locate the main point of contention within the historical context of Paul's calling and ministry. It is the account of how he received the gospel of Jesus Christ, which is a gospel of grace and freedom, and defended it – to the point of opposing Peter himself at Antioch – against subversion by Jewish Christians who wished to impose the law, and especially circumcision, upon Gentile believers. Paul is quite adamant: none of the benefits of the gospel – not 'freedom' (2:4), or 'justification' (2:16, 21), or 'life' (2:19–20) – is to be found through the law, but only through faith in Christ.

In chapter 3 Paul addresses the argument directly to the Galatians. How did they account for what they themselves had seen and felt? Was it by 'works of the law' that they received the Holy Spirit and experienced his miraculous power (3:1–5)? Or by the 'hearing of faith'? This appeal to the Galatians' own experience is supported by the long argument about sonship in 3:6 – 4:7, because reception of the Spirit is essentially a consequence of being adopted as sons: 'because you are sons, God sent out the Spirit of his Son into our hearts' (4:6). In many of its details, and especially in its relation to the arguments of Paul's opponents, this passage is extremely problematic; but the central line of thought is not too difficult to follow.

According to the Scriptures the nations will be blessed in Abraham; and since Abraham was justified by faith, it is those who have faith who are 'sons of Abraham' and who will be blessed with him (vv. 6–9). Those under the law, however, are under a curse because no-one is justified before God by the law (vv. 10–12). The solution to this predicament lies in the fact that through his death Christ bought us back from the curse of the law (v. 13). The consequences of this are twofold (v. 14): on the one hand, the Gentiles receive the 'blessing of Abraham'; on the other, the Spirit is received through faith. The question then arises whether the law does not invalidate the promise made earlier to Abraham. Has not the law superseded anything that might have gone before? Paul's response is that the law was given as a means of dealing with sin only until the 'seed' should come to whom, along

---

[22] Jewett 1975: 142 (cited in Johnson 1991: 154).

with Abraham, the promise was made. Thus the law served as a 'guardian until Christ' (v. 24). But with the coming of faith this guardian has been made redundant and, under the new conditions of faith, all are 'sons of God' (v. 26), all have 'put on Christ' (v. 27), all are 'one in Christ Jesus' (v. 28), all are 'seed of Abraham', and therefore 'according to the promise heirs' (v. 29).

What still needs to be clarified is the logical progression that defines the changing status of the believer. Before the coming of Christ a person is in the position of a child under the tutelage and discipline of a guardian (3:24), or under 'foremen and stewards' (4:2). As such he is enslaved, either to the law or to the elements of the world (4:3; *cf.* 4:9). Through Christ's death, however, he is redeemed from this slavery, and is adopted instead as a son (4:5). Thus he becomes a 'son of Abraham' (3:7), he receives the 'blessing of Abraham' (3:14a), he becomes 'seed of Abraham' (3:29). Finally, he receives the promised Spirit (3:14b; *cf.* 3:22), he becomes an inheritor of the Spirit (3:29; 4:7), which is the point at which Paul began his exposition in 3:2–5. These three stages are clearly articulated in 4:7: 'So you are no longer a *slave* but a *son*; and if a son, also an *heir* through God.'

The passage that interests us here (3:26–28) belongs to the second stage in this progression. It speaks of the new status of believers as 'sons of God', that is, as those who have 'put on Christ' – who through adoption have acquired the same status that Christ had as God's Son (4:5–6). Just as Christ at his baptism was designated 'Son' and received the Holy Spirit (Mt. 3:16–17; Mk. 1:10–11; Lk. 3:22), so believers at their baptism put on Christ, becoming 'sons' like him, and receive the Holy Spirit. But there is a particular emphasis in verses 26–27 on the *inclusiveness* of this new status: *all of you* are sons of God, Paul affirms, and *as many of you as* were baptized into Christ put on Christ.[23] This inclusiveness is picked up in verse 28: no-one who has been baptized into Christ is excluded from adoption as sons (*cf. hyiothesian*, 4:5), whether Jew or Greek, slave or free, male or female. It is in this respect that they are 'all one in Christ Jesus'; they all have received exactly the same status as sons of God, seed of Abraham. They all, therefore, regardless of such distinctions, inherit the promise of the Spirit.[24]

In Christ a Gentile can become a son, a descendant of Abraham and an inheritor of the promise made to him, even though he is not born a Jew. In Christ a slave may enjoy the blessings that belong by right to the free son, even though he is not free. In Christ a woman can also become a 'son', even though she is not male. This is not a repudiation of her womanhood; if anything, it is a

---

[23] Both *pantes* and *hosoi* are placed at the beginning of the sentence.

[24] Following Dautzenburg, Snodgrass (1986: 175) argues that Joel 2:28–32 lies behind Gal. 3:28.

repudiation of the exclusive significance of sonship and, therefore, precisely an affirmation of the value of being female.[25]

It has sometimes been maintained that the slave/free and male/female antitheses are incidental to Paul's argument at this point, which has to do principally with the significance of circumcision for membership of the people of God.[26] There is some truth in this. The division between Jew and Gentile, being fundamentally a religious dichotomy, was a far more serious affront to the gospel than the other antitheses. The law constituted an alternative to salvation in Jesus Christ in a way in which slavery and patriarchalism did not. It is clear, however, that Paul would have regarded any attempt to deny the fullness of salvation to slaves and women, on whatever grounds, as a reversion to the 'elements of the world' to which humankind apart from Christ is enslaved (4:3, 9).

Even according to Jewish law, the religious status of slaves (particularly Gentile slaves) and of women was significantly inferior to that of a free Jewish male.[27] Slaves and women were not denied 'salvation' or membership of Israel under the law, but they could not *fulfil* the law in the way that a free man might hope to, and therefore they could not inherit the same blessings from the law. 'Wherewith do women acquire merit? By sending their children to learn Torah in the Synagogue and their husbands to study in the Schools of the Rabbis' (*Berakot* 17a). In Christ, however, these underprivileged groups not only belonged to God's people, they also inherited the blessings of the Spirit.[28]

Whether the formulation of verse 28 is a deliberate rejoinder to parallel assertions of privilege popular in the ancient world is difficult to say. The three 'benedictions' of Jewish morning prayers, by which a Jewish male gives thanks that God did not make him a Gentile, a 'brutish man' or slave, or a woman, can be traced back to the middle of the second century AD and may well reflect an earlier tradition.[29] An analogous saying appears in Greek writings, attributed variously to Socrates, to Plato, and to Thales (sixth century BC), who is reported to have given thanks to Fortune for three blessings: 'first, that I

[25] Paul is certainly not arguing for androgyny in Gal. 3:28 (against Meeks 1974: 165–208; Betz 1979: 195–200; Martin 1995: 229, 231–232). The distinction between male and female is annulled only with respect to adoption as 'sons' and the reception of the Spirit. Paul no more envisages a genderless form of human existence here than he envisages a state in which men and women are neither slaves nor free. The verse has nothing to do with sexual asceticism. Note Fiorenza 1983: 205–206; Snodgrass 1986: 171.

[26] *Cf.* Betz 1979: 195; Fiorenza 1983: 208.

[27] See Cohen 1949: 159–161, 201–203; Snodgrass 1986: 177–178.

[28] Snodgrass (1986: 178) argues that since slaves and women already belonged to Israel, 'one cannot speak of Galatians 3:28 as if it merely pertains to salvation'. But he misses the point about the Spirit.

[29] Cohen 1949: 157; Betz 1979: 184–185 n. 26; Bruce 1982: 187; Longenecker 1990: 157.

was born a human being and not one of the brutes; next, that I was born a man and not a woman; thirdly, a Greek and not a barbarian'.[30] At least we can say that Paul's statement stands in pointed contrast to a commonplace opinion that religious privilege was apportioned according to certain well-defined racial, social and biological categories.

Social implications

The significance of Galatians 3:28 in the context of Paul's argument in the letter, therefore, is quite clear: women, no less than men, receive adoption as 'sons' because their baptism is equally a 'putting on' of Christ; and therefore women, no less than men, inherit the promised Holy Spirit. The passage has nothing directly to do with social relations; it does not define for us 'God's ideal social order' (Keener 1992: 205). Galatians 3:28, in so far as it constitutes part of Paul's general argument in this chapter, is concerned not with the question of unity or relations within the body of Christ, but with a oneness or equality of identity and status.[31] Nevertheless, especially in view of the rhetorical character of the verse, we might ask whether it does not have wider ramifications.

In the first place, sonship and the reception of the Spirit certainly constitute the basis for a new type of community, and this provides some grounds for extending the implications of the assertion that 'there is not "male and female"'. The later chapters of the letter give some indication of how this might be developed. The freedom that believers have as sons of God, Paul says, is an opportunity to 'serve one another through love' (5:13). Surely he would have meant by this that Jews should serve Gentiles, freemen should serve slaves, men should serve women – just as, for example, the Roman Christians were encouraged to serve Phoebe (Rom. 16:1–2). The 'fruit of the Spirit' has a marked social orientation: these qualities have to do with how people treat one another within the body of Christ (5:22–23). Those who live by the Spirit should not be proud, they should not provoke one another or be envious of one another (5:25–26). Those who are 'spiritual' should restore the person who sins in a spirit of gentleness (6:1). To sow to the Spirit is to 'do good to all people, especially to those of the household of faith' (6:7–10).

These are certainly to be counted as social implications of Galatians 3:28; all those baptized into Christ are sons of God, therefore all should be loved and served in the same way. Moreover, practically speaking they are of radical and far-reaching importance for the Christian community. But this is very different from saying that this oneness in Christ in itself entails the abolition of

---

[30] Diogenes Laertius, *Vita* 1.33, Loeb.

[31] Against Snodgrass (1986: 175). Witherington (1988: 77–78) argues from the form 'male *and* female' that one social implication of this verse is that there is a place for single women in the church. But this seems somewhat remote from Paul's intentions in this passage.

relationships of authority. It may be the case that the subordination of the woman in the family and the church makes it much more difficult to accord her the respect to which she is entitled as a 'son' of God; but it is doubtful whether it can be argued on the basis of Galatians 3:28 that these two things are *in principle* incompatible.

An underlying baptismal formula?

It might be maintained that Paul is quoting a baptismal formula which, as a confessional or liturgical statement, has more extensive implications than is suggested by the context in Galatians (*cf.* Fiorenza 1983: 208–218). But on what grounds? If the same basic formula is presupposed in 1 Corinthians 12:13 (and we should not forget that Paul omits the male–female pair here) the most that may be said is that women, having drunk of the same Spirit, are not less qualified charismatically than men. This seems reasonable if Galatians 3:28 means that women inherit the *fullness* of the Spirit. Perhaps, then, women may be gifted as 'apostles' (*cf.* Rom. 16:7) or 'teachers' (1 Cor. 12:28).[32] Or if it lies behind Colossians 3:9–11, the implication is only that women, as much as men, should take off the 'old person [*anthrōpon*]' and put on the new 'which is being renewed towards knowledge according to the image of the one who created it'. Still, nothing is found in this to suggest that Paul imagined that within the new community of the church the patriarchal order, or more generally the social advantage of the man, would be suspended or abolished.

Fiorenza (1983:210) argues that the 'baptismal pronunciation' of freedom and equality would have been heard 'as a ritual, "performative utterance," which not only had the power to shape the "symbolic universe" of the Christian community but also determined the social interrelationships and structures of the church'. In other words, the theological ideals represented by the baptism of the believer were meant to have a profound impact at the practical level on relationships; and in general terms this is correct. But, basing her case to a large degree on the finding of 'feminist studies' that 'most perceived sex differences or gender roles' are the product of culture rather than biology, she goes on to draw rather more radical conclusions:

> Gal. 3:28 not only advocates the abolition of religious–cultural divisions and of the domination and exploitation wrought by institutional slavery but also of domination based on sexual divisions. It repeats with different categories and words that within the Christian community no structures of dominance can be tolerated (Fiorenza 1983:213).

[32] Note Dunn (1993: 207): 'it is highly unlikely that [Paul] would have allowed gender or social status as such, any more than race, to constitute a barrier against any service of the gospel'.

Now the argument that, beyond certain minimal functions related to sex and procreation, it is culture that largely determines what type of behaviour is considered appropriate for men and women may have some validity; biological differences do not have to be translated into hierarchy, for example. But the inferences with regard to Galatians 3:28 are not valid. The passage does not *advocate* the abolition of domination, either of the master over the slave or of the man over the woman.[33] Our previous exegesis made this clear, but it is also evident from Paul's terminology. He does not say, 'there is neither slave nor master', but, 'there is neither slave nor *free*'. It is the condition or status of each, not the relationship between them, that is at issue. Likewise, it is not the patriarchal relationship between husband and wife, or between man and woman, that is annulled in Christ but the significance, from the point of view of salvation, of being either male or female. The Christian community *can* accommodate 'structures of dominance'. What cannot be tolerated is any religiously or socially sanctioned behaviour that hinders a person's access to grace and the fullness of the Spirit, that reimposes enslavement to the 'elements of the world', or that impairs fellowship in Christ.

The same basic mistake is repeated by Fiorenza in a later statement: 'Just as born Jews had to abandon the privileged notion that they alone were the chosen people of God, so masters had to relinquish their power over slaves, and husbands that over wives and children' (1983:218). This is logically inconsistent. What those born free must renounce is not their power over slaves but, like the Jews, any notions of religious advantage; likewise, it is the sense of *religious privilege* that men must give up, not their power over women. Conversely, slaves and women were to give up any notions of religious inferiority.

Far from proclaiming the abolition of these distinctions, Galatians 3:28 presupposes their continued existence. In 1 Corinthians 7:20 Paul says quite clearly, 'Each in the calling by which he was called, in that let him remain' (*cf.* vv. 17, 24). Those who are circumcised should not attempt to remove the marks of their circumcision; nor should those who are uncircumcised seek circumcision (7:18). Similarly, the slave should be content with his position (7:21). While Paul almost certainly here encourages a slave to gain his freedom if the opportunity arises, he does not appear to envisage the possibility that slavery as an institution might disappear.[34] Elsewhere the wife is instructed to remain submitted to her husband (Eph. 5:22). Within the church slaves and

---

[33] Fiorenza appears to mean by 'domination' or 'dominance' not the abuse of authority but the basic hierarchal structures of a slave-owning and patriarchal society.

[34] For the exegetical difficulties presented by the verse and the arguments for this interpretation see Fee 1987: 317. Fiorenza (1983: 220–222), however, pushes the argument too far when she denies that Paul exhorted believers to remain in the condition in which they first came to faith. First, the point of verses 18–19 is not that people should remain in a

masters for the most part remained in the relationship to one another that ancient Mediterranean society had determined for them. Similarly, men and women remained in the patriarchal relationship that society had determined for them, except that within that structure they treated each other differently.

Of course, things have changed. While the church has not yet run out of things to quarrel about, circumcision at least is no longer the divisive issue it was in Paul's time; slavery as a legitimate institution is a thing of the past; and women generally, though not universally, enjoy much greater freedom and opportunity than their foremothers. Yet we should not attempt to read these developments back into Galatians 3:28. As it stands, the verse is not incompatible with the view that God gave man some sort of sovereignty over the woman and, correspondingly, denied women access to certain levels of leadership in the church.

Freedom from the law of patriarchy?

Would Paul have classified slavery and patriarchy as 'elements of the world'? Possibly. It may be significant that in Ephesians 5:23 he instructs wives to be submissive to their husbands but does not urge husbands to exercise authority over their wives. He accepts the fact of patriarchy but does not go out of his way to promote it. On the other hand, this does not seem to be the point at issue in Galatians. His preoccupation is with religious rather than social structures, as is clear from Galatians 4:8–10, where it is the observance of 'days and months and seasons and years' that exemplifies the form of enslavement he has in mind. The emancipation that he has in mind is sudden and complete, not the (at best) gradual and difficult emancipation that he might have envisaged for slaves and women.

Could the scope of this argument be widened? It is tempting to suppose that Paul regarded the subordination of the woman as an aspect of the law that is specifically abolished in Christ. The law, Paul writes in Galatians, was added 'because of transgressions' (*tōn parabaseōn charin*, 3:19). The subordination of the woman to the man was ordained as a consequence of Eve's transgression: 'he will rule over [*kyrieusei*] you' (Gn. 3:16, LXX). Paul writes in 1 Timothy

---

state either of Jewishness or of non-Jewishness but that they should not seek either to be circumcised or to remove the marks of circumcision. Secondly, Paul's advice to slaves is principally to accept their condition and to attain their freedom only if, exceptionally, the opportunity presents itself. Fiorenza's paraphrase of verse 24 is highly improper: 'the decisive thing is to continue in the calling to freedom which one has heard and entered into in baptism'. Thirdly, if Paul allows a woman who has separated from her husband to remain unmarried (v. 11), the purpose is certainly not that she should free herself 'from the bondage of patriarchal marriage'. The bondage of marriage, as far as this chapter is concerned, is to the 'things of the world' and the need to please one's spouse, whether male or female (vv. 32–34).

2:14 that the woman was deceived and 'has come into transgression [*parabasei*]'. The judgment upon the woman does not belong to the Mosaic legal code as such, but it is part of the Torah, and it would be a reasonable theological assumption that the various laws regulating the position of women in ancient Jewish society presupposed just this primal definition of the relationship between the man and the woman. Moreover, the description of the law as 'our custodian until Christ' (Gal. 3:24) is strongly reminiscent of the position of women under male guardianship in ancient society; indeed, their status was much like that of children or slaves. Does this then allow the inference that the liberation of the believer from the custodianship of the law under Christ (Gal. 3:25) also entails the liberation of the woman from the tutelage and authority of the man? M. Hayter (1987:137) argues that it is 'the condition of male and female *as they existed under the law* which is abrogated in Christ, not the original "order of creation" ' (her italics). In being set free from the guardianship of the law women were also set free from the concrete embodiment of that guardianship in the authority that the man had over them.

On the face of it this is plausible, but there are difficulties. First, there is no literary basis for putting Eve's judgment on the same level as the law of Moses. The promise to Abraham was made after the subordination of the woman at the fall, and nothing suggests that it is incompatible with that subordination in the way that it conflicts with the custodianship of the law. Secondly, the fact that the custodianship of the law is analogous to the guardianship of the man with respect to the woman is not enough to establish a proper logical connection between them. Thirdly, if Paul saw in the abolition of the law the concomitant abrogation of patriarchy, why did he make no more explicit attempt to implement it? Instead, we have the insistence in 1 Corinthians 14:34 that women should be submissive and silent in church 'as even the law says'. At best, then, we should consider this a latent possibility, but one which is very difficult to defend in terms of Paul's expressed views on the significance of the law.

Other passages dealing with equality

Is there any evidence from other passages that Paul understood the equality of men and women in Christ to entail the abolition of patriarchy?

Earlier in this chapter we touched on the significance of 1 Corinthians 11:11–12, but these verses argue only for a recognition by believers that men and women are mutually dependent. Given the overall context of the passage, which has to do with 'glory' rather than with authority, it would be difficult to infer from this that the man has no authority over the woman.

The closest parallel in Paul's writings to this assertion of equality between men and women in Christ is 2 Corinthians 6:16–18. In this passage he speaks of believers as a 'temple of the living God', which recalls the thought of 1

Corinthians 3:16 that 'you are a temple of God and God's Spirit dwells in you'. He then quotes a number of passages from the Old Testament which, on the one hand, foretell the presence of God among his people, and on the other, warn them to separate themselves from idolatry and unrighteousness. Finally, he quotes from the promise made to David in 2 Samuel 7:14 (= 2 Kingdoms 7:14), but with important modifications: instead of 'I will be to him a father, and he will be to me a son', Paul writes, 'I will be to you a father, and you will be to me sons *and daughters*'. The implication is clear, and does not go beyond the thought of Galatians 3:26–29: women, no less than men, belong to God's people and receive the Holy Spirit.[35]

There is no mention of the male–female antithesis either in 1 Corinthians 12:13 or in Colossians 3:9–11, though both these passages are in many ways parallel to Galatians 3:28. The omission in 1 Corinthians 12:13 may have less to do with problems regarding sexual differentiation at Corinth[36] than with the fact that Paul simply did not consider gender to be as divisive as race and social status when it came to ministry within the body. The reason for this may have been that there was already a natural division of labour between men and women; or it may have been that the divisions between Jewish and Gentile households, or between the free-born and slaves, predominated over divisions within these groups between men and women. Probably this also accounts for the omission in Colossians 3:9–11. Whereas the issue in Galatians 3:28 is status and identity, in these parallel passages the underlying concern is with the unity of the body; and the distinction between male and female was not seen as a threat to that unity. The church was cracking not along the boundary between men and women, but along religious and social lines – 'Greek and Jew, circumcision and uncircumcision, barbarian, Scythian, slave, free' (Col. 3:11; *cf.* 1 Cor. 12:13).

1 Corinthians 7

In two respects 1 Corinthians 7 may be regarded as a practical extension of the principle of male–female equality established in Galatians 3:28.[37] First, the passage presents a quite remarkable pattern of parallel and equal teaching for men and women. There is to be equality with regard to sexual relations; the

---

[35] *Cf.* Tomson 1990: 134–135. Note also Is. 43:6: 'Bring my sons from a land far off and my daughters from the ends of the earth.'

[36] Against Snodgrass 1986: 173.

[37] Witherington (1988: 26) argues, following Bartchy, that 'Paul's discussion in 1 Corinthians 7 is structured along the lines of his thinking about the unity and equality of male and female in Christ'. Paul's unexpected departure from the topic of marriage and singleness in 1 Cor. 7:17–24 to discuss circumcision and slavery is explained by the fact that he has in mind the three distinctions of Gal. 3:28 (*cf.* Snodgrass 1986: 173–174; Fiorenza 1983: 220–221).

wife has authority over her husband's body just as he has authority over hers (vv. 3–4). Although Paul is talking about sexual relations here, the 'body' cannot be separated from the whole person; in some sense, in having authority over his body the woman must have authority over her husband. The unbelieving man may be sanctified in the believing woman no less than the unbelieving woman is sanctified in the believing man (v. 14).[38] Both the man and the woman are free to be separated from an unbelieving spouse; they have not been 'enslaved in these things' (v. 15). There is still a certain male bias: not everything that is said to the man is repeated for the woman (*e.g.* vv. 27–29, 36–38). It is also important to realize that the text prescribes equality only in the area of sexual and personal relations; nothing is said about economic relations, for example (*cf.* Fiorenza 1983: 224). Nevertheless, this chapter appears to represent a quite deliberate attempt to work out some of the implications of the sort of equality that is expressed in Galatians 3:28 and 1 Corinthians 11:11–12. If anything, the latter passage may be the more important cross-reference because it expresses equality in relational terms. Secondly, in its affirmation of the value of singleness and celibacy the chapter allows for a woman to be defined apart from her relation to a man (vv. 7, 8, 25–26, 32). A woman's status and role are more appropriately defined in relation to the Lord than to a husband (v. 34); such a woman is 'happier' in Paul's view (v. 40).

Conclusions

At the heart of Paul's teaching are the basic creational data: man was created first, woman was created from the man and for the sake of the man. This knot of ideas must be understood partly in terms of the natural prominence of the man (*e.g.* size, strength, aggressiveness). But more importantly they constitute a basic condition for human sexuality and the differing roles that this confers on men and women.

The woman came to be deceived by the serpent, but neither in the Genesis narrative nor in Paul is this attributed to inferiority or insubordination on the part of the woman. Paul gives little indication as to how he understood the fall to have affected the condition of women. The statement in 1 Timothy 2:15 that women will be saved through the bearing of children is too closely bound up with the particular historical circumstances that the church faced to draw from it any reliable conclusions regarding the natural state of womanhood. Nevertheless, that some connection existed in Paul's mind between the woman's domestic role and the judgment pronounced in Genesis 3:16 seems

---

[38] *Cf.* Fiorenza 1983: 222–223, quoting Daube: 'in Judaism it is invariably the woman who is consecrated as spouse by the man'. But this is a reference to the act of taking a wife rather than to consecration within marriage.

quite clear. It is also likely that he saw in the socially mandated subordination of the woman to the man a concrete expression of the pronouncement in the same verse that 'he will rule over you'. Otherwise, we must assume that he saw no difference between men and women as regards sin and salvation.

That men and women have equal access to salvation and receive equally the gift of the Holy Spirit is a cardinal Pauline doctrine. Less clear is how he viewed the practical domestic and ecclesiastical implications of this. While egalitarians have tended to claim too much for Galatians 3:28, the significance of passages such as 1 Corinthians 7 and 11:11–12 for male–female relations at least within the framework of the family has generally been overlooked by traditionalists. In the end, however, the potential for equality that is certainly latent in Paul's teaching remains largely undeveloped. The church could not entirely disengage itself from a world in which power and opportunity were assigned almost exclusively to the man, where roles were defined largely according to the division between the public and private spheres, and where women were for the most part judged to be intellectually and emotionally unstable.

8. Conclusions: Interpreting Paul

Paul's teaching on women is fragmentary. Any attempt to organize these scattered and allusive comments into a coherent picture draws attention not only to the high degree of arbitrariness inherent in the process, but also to the fact that a large number of pieces are missing. It is like trying to reconstruct a prehistoric skull: how do you infer the shape of the original from the few scraps of bone and teeth that have survived the depredations of time? Still, it is very unsatisfying not to have some sense of the whole. We should at least gather together the pieces that we do have and try to place them in proper relation to one another.

In all likelihood Paul's thinking on these matters was stimulated not by theological reflection principally but by his experience of the ministry and misdemeanours of women in the church; one imagines that he was deeply impressed by the potential women had both for strengthening and for destabilizing the community. Logically, though, we may begin with the creation narratives, for in his attempts to deal with the various practical issues raised by the participation of women in the life of the community of believers he consistently turned to these texts in order to provide clarity and underpinning for his teaching.

The creation narratives

Paul discerns in the original creation of the man and the woman two basic conditions which give definition to the contemporary relation between the sexes. The first is the creation of Adam *before* Eve, which he connects with the prominence and social advantage of the man and with the idea that the woman is 'the glory of the man' (1 Cor. 11:7). This condition has to do essentially with the man's participation and visibility in the public realm, and is encapsulated in the figure of headship. The second is the fact that with the creation of Eve, forces of sexuality burst upon the newly made and unsuspecting world. This is made the fundamental explanation for the special intimacy of the marriage relationship, for the particular character of the glory that a man receives from his wife, for the natural differentiation of personhood and roles that sexuality entails, and for the potential for deception in spiritual matters. Let us elaborate upon these two points.

The priority of Adam: the prominence of the man

Headship, for Paul, is an observable phenomenon. To describe the man as head of the woman is, in the first place, a statement about his perceived prominence in relation to her. Just as the head occupies a position of prominence at the top or front of the body, so the man occupies a position of prominence in relation to the woman – though Paul does not think of the woman as the 'body' of the man. And just as the 'head' may stand by synecdoche for the whole person, so the 'head' of the tribe or family stands for the whole group; in a sense, he sums up or represents that tribe or family among other similar groups. The unusual description of the man as head of the woman could be understood partly as a narrowing of this usage, a special application of the more common pattern.

The man has this prominence largely on account of his role in the public sphere, which gives him greater visibility and significance than a woman can have when confined to the sphere of the home. In the simplest and most general terms, the man is larger, stronger, louder, more assertive, more aggressive; it is the man who mostly takes the initiative, who takes precedence, who goes first. Generally this meant that the man was in a position of considerable social and economic advantage; the woman was variously regarded as his possession, his slave, his ward, his housekeeper, or as a device for the generation of sons. Of course, these categories do not do justice to the numerous instances of genuine love and affection between husband and wife that can be found in the writings and inscriptions of the ancients. Nevertheless, they reflect quite fairly the general framework of subordination within which women related to men: the man is above, the woman is below; the man is ahead, the woman trails behind. Inevitably, therefore, the prominence of the man, and with it the figure of headship, cannot be dissociated from other aspects of the patriarchal model that has predominated throughout history, such as authority, accountability, dependency, control and segregation. But these things should not be confused with the figure itself, which in Greek says only that a person is prominent or pre-eminent. A person may be head (of state, for example) and yet have no authority to rule. In fact, we may not be too far removed here from the idea of 'figurehead'.

In 1 Corinthians 11:3–16 the figure of male headship becomes, in effect, an expression of the sensitivity of ancient society to the honour or disgrace that a woman might bring upon a man as a result of her behaviour. Paul's basic argument is that in view of this state of affairs, and of the particular connotations connected with the exposing of a woman's head in public, a woman should not pray or prophesy with her head uncovered. If she disregards this custom, she brings disgrace upon herself – upon her own head – but she also brings disgrace upon her husband, who therefore may also be described as her 'head'. Here, in this ingenious play on words, we see the convergence of the basic metaphorical sense of *kephalē* and the Jewish idiom that views the 'head' as the point of attraction for all manner of moral and spiritual qualities, both good and bad.

Glory and shame, however, are public qualities; they draw upon what is generally accepted to be right and wrong. While they cannot be fully relativized – righteousness is a source of glory, unrighteousness of shame – neither can they be entirely separated from the prevailing ethos. What brings shame in one culture may be a matter of indifference in another. Relations between believers are unavoidably and necessarily immersed in and shaped by, and sometimes distorted by, the powerful currents of the sea of secular life, and to this extent Christian instruction must adapt itself to a set of changeable and not always congenial values – just as Paul accommodated Christian marriage to the values and constraints of ancient Mediterranean culture.

Although the description of man as head of the woman in this passage is linked to the creation story, little attempt is made generally in the letters to dictate what form the prominence of the man should take. Paul does not explicitly infer from the prior creation of Adam that it is the man and not the woman who should provide for the family's material needs, or that it is the man who should have the more public role, or that it is the man who should drive the car. Quite possibly he regarded as perfectly natural the particular tokens by which the prominence of the man was manifested in the ancient world – the general seclusion of the woman, for example – just as he considered it natural for men to have short hair and women long hair. But, as far as we can tell from the letters that have come down to us, he had no interest in defending the prevailing social order on the grounds that the man was created before the woman. The sexual dynamic certainly must be taken into consideration here: the fact that the woman was created from the man and for the sake of the man establishes a real imbalance in the relationship. But, strikingly, it is at this point that his argument is most clearly culturally conditioned; a woman's hair is no longer so potent and pre-eminent a symbol of her sexuality, and in most churches it is considered unnecessary for a woman to cover her head when praying or prophesying.

Most importantly, the order of creation is not presented as an argument for placing the woman under a man's authority. The priority of Adam is reflected in the image of headship, but the metaphor stands only as a description of the man's greater prominence. In view of the legal and social dimensions this prominence had acquired in the ancient world, it was entirely appropriate that even within the church a woman should be submissive towards her husband. The natural prominence of the man had been exploited in such a way that for a woman to disdain this arrangement would bring disgrace upon her own head and upon her husband. But the definition of this prominence that emerges from Paul's argument does not entail the necessary subordination of the woman. When he says that 'a man is head of the woman' (Eph. 5:23), he is not, in the first place, invoking some scriptural or theological norm but making an observation about how things are. The prominence of the man has its origin in creation, but the creation story is not used to validate the particular form that it had taken in the social matrix in which the early churches were embedded.

Perhaps the implications can be expressed in this way: whatever prominence or natural advantage the man appears to have is a consequence of his creation before the woman; but this does not mean that the greater prominence of the man is permanently fixed in creation. If two people are running along the road one *ahead* of the other, the relation between them could be a consequence of the fact that the one in front started first. But this does not mean that one must always be in front of the other. The one behind may catch up, or the one ahead may slow down, with the result that they run side by side. Paul does not make the *right relationship* between husband and wife dependent upon the greater prominence, and certainly not on the authority, of the man. If anything, the prominence of the man is found to be an obstacle to a right relationship that must be overcome – not, unrealistically, by attempting to overturn the social order but by the sacrificial love of the husband. Ephesians 5:22–33 is corrective teaching; it provides a counter-balance to a given situation; and while it may be necessary to lean into a strong wind in order to stay upright, if the wind drops and you continue to lean, you will fall over. It is surely not without significance that the passage begins with the image of the man as head but ends with the image of man and woman as one flesh.

The creation of Eve: the introduction of sexuality

The creation of Eve leads, first, to the idea that the man and woman are 'one flesh'. The essence of this union is the sexual relationship; but in Ephesians 5:22–33 the image of 'one flesh' is used more broadly to underpin the teaching that a man should love his wife as he loves his own body. If husband and wife are one flesh, then, Paul says, a man should not treat his wife with contempt but should nourish and care for her. Implicit in this already is a quite radical revision of the superiority and advantage that the ancient world attributed to the man.

Secondly, the woman is created 'for the sake of the man', which appears to be a restatement in more general terms of the idea that the woman was created as a 'helper according to him'. The thought is used in 1 Corinthians 11:7–9 in support of the assertion that the woman is 'the glory of the man'. This indicates an asymmetry in the relationship between the man and the woman which has to do with the nature of human sexuality. It finds concrete expression in the woman's beauty and attractiveness; a woman's hair is her 'glory' and this distinguishes her from the man, whose glory is represented visibly not by his hair but by his cloak. But more significant in the context of this passage is the fact that by praying or prophesying with her head uncovered a woman brings disgrace upon her husband. The argument is not reversible; a man praying or prophesying with his head covered dishonours not his wife but Christ. The point here appears to be that the woman, by virtue of her creation 'for the sake of the man', is an object of attraction or desire in a way that the man is not.

How much this understanding of the asymmetry is tied up with culturally determined expressions of sexuality is difficult to say; and the task of explaining what it means for the woman to be the glory of the man in a culture that is disinclined to subordinate the being of the woman to male self-interest takes us beyond the scope of this study. But it seems reasonable to assume that men and women will – and should – remain sexually distinct, and that this created differentness will continue to express itself in different forms of behaviour, particularly as regards those activities, such as mating and child-bearing, that are most closely associated with the sexual dynamic. If this is the case, then in this area of male–female relations the imbalance probably can never be fully corrected, and the church must continue to wrestle with the implications of this text. As long as there remains a tension between the forces of human sexuality – beauty, desire, lust, jealousy – and the purity and devotion demanded by worship, then the fundamental insight articulated here retains its validity.

This brings us to the third connecting line that Paul draws between the contemporary situation and the original creation of the woman. The introduction of sexuality naturally ordains a child-bearing role for the woman. The connection is not made explicitly by Paul, but it is implicit in 1 Timothy 2:13–15. It is this role that places the woman in the home and makes her the focus for a variety of domestic activities: the raising of children, management of the household, the provision of hospitality, washing the feet of the saints, the training of younger women to love their husbands, and so on (1 Tim. 5:9–10, 14; Tit. 2:3–5). But in the same way that patriarchy is a culturally rather than theologically determined development of the original prominence of Adam, so too the confinement of the woman to the home is a culturally determined extension of the woman's natural child-bearing role.

Finally, the creation of the woman after Adam is understood by Paul to provide an explanation for the fact that Eve rather than Adam was deceived by the serpent. Two basic thoughts appear to flow together here. On the one hand, the woman is perceived to be socially and intellectually disadvantaged, and therefore less competent than the man to discern sound teaching from the numerous counterfeit doctrines in circulation on the spiritual black market.

Undoubtedly Paul recognized that there could be exceptions, but in dealing with a remote situation in local churches beyond his direct sphere of influence it appeared better to impose a general ban. On the other hand, the woman, as an object of sexual attraction, or distraction, presents a more alluring and vulnerable target for the false teacher. Paul's thinking here is shaped partly by his understanding of the Genesis texts, but also by his awareness of what was happening in Ephesus (*cf.* 2 Tim. 3:6–8); the story of Eve's deception and the disruptive activities of false teachers are mutually interpretive.

Equality in Christ and in the Spirit

If the creation narratives bring into view the prominence of the man and the asymmetry of the sexual relationship, what emerges from the perspective of the *new creation* is the equality of men and women in Christ. When Paul says that in Christ Jesus there is not 'male and female' (Gal. 3:28), his words must be taken in some sense as an abrogation of a distinction that was established in creation. But in what sense? He certainly does not mean that the distinction is abolished. His point is rather that the creational differentiation of male and female cannot be used to determine the measure of a person's acceptability before God or to restrict the extent to which a person may experience the blessings of eschatological life in the Spirit.

This is not merely an ideal or spiritual equality; rather, it has profound practical implications for the whole of life. On the one hand, the believer has been set free from the tyranny of the law and the 'elements of the world'. Although a direct exegetical connection between patriarchy and these enslaving powers probably cannot be made, the more general question remains: is the idea of an *involuntary* authority from which women may not be liberated even within the kingdom of God consistent with the gospel as Paul expounds it in Galatians? There has to be authority within the church, but there is an important difference between an authority (such as that of an elder) that is appointed and which may be revoked and an authority that supposedly is fixed in human biology. On the other hand, to be baptized is to take on in a quite public way the identity of Christ and to receive the Spirit. This also has direct consequences for social relations.

First, there are implications with regard to how men and women view and treat each other. Not only are women equal with regard to salvation, but their experience of the power of the Spirit is not in any way inferior to that of men. There is no place for the pervasive, if not always acknowledged, male presumption that women's ministry, women's activities and women's spiritual experience are somehow of less value than those of men.

Secondly, the equality of men and women in Christ has a bearing on the marital relationship. 'In the Lord' the relationship between a man and a woman may be shaped not only by the priority of the man in creation but also by the reproductive dependence of the man on the woman (1 Cor. 11:8–9, 11–12). Paul's attention in this passage is centred upon a set of circumstances in which the prominence of the man is the determinative factor, but we may assume that the converse principle ('the man through the woman') may have equally concrete and practical significance. It seems likely, however, that this equality belonged to the private rather than the public sphere, a supposition that is supported by Paul's argument for equal rights in 1 Corinthians 7:3–4. In the public sphere it is the prominence of the man as signified by the figure of headship and the argument about glory and shame that is determinative. At the heart of the personal relationship, however, in the intimacy of sexual relations, where social convention has least influence, and where glory and shame are least relevant, there may be equality, the one yielding the body – and yielding herself or himself – to the other.

Thirdly, if there is no discrimination with regard to the giving of the Spirit, then in the end it may be possible to argue that there should be no discrimination in ministry. The purview of Paul's argument in Galatians 3 is too narrow to make this a proper inference from his assertion that in Christ there is not 'male and female'. But it raises in more general terms the question of the relation between ministry and authority. Is the authority of a woman to minister limited in some way? Or, if a woman receives the fullness of the Spirit, what basis is there for saying that she may exercise the gifts of the Spirit only in certain contexts, or only certain gifts of the Spirit?

Ministry and authority

It is important not to confuse the question of authority either with the ethical problem or with the question of competence. If the sexual dynamic presents an obstacle to the work of the Holy Spirit, then it may be appropriate to restrict the scope or the manner of a woman's ministry – as, for example, Paul required women to pray and prophesy with their heads covered. Similarly, if a woman is insufficiently grounded in Scripture or in any significant way doctrinally inconsistent, she should not exercise a preaching ministry – as Paul did not allow women to teach in the church. But these are criteria that should be applied equally to the ministry of men. What concerns us here is whether women may participate in the ministry of the Holy Spirit only within a framework of subordination established in creation. In practice there are two questions. First, does a woman require male authority over her in order to minister? Secondly, is it permissible for a woman to have authority over men?

The central finding of this study has been that there is no basis for the view that Paul regarded the subordination of the woman to the man as a matter of theological necessity, and that there is no objection to the egalitarian position provided (1) that the integrity and accessibility of the gospel are not compromised, and (2) that men and women are free to act in accordance with their respective creationally determined natures. But it is important nevertheless to understand how far the argument from equality in the Spirit can be taken.

There appear to be two basic types of role in the New Testament church. The first is defined according to charisma: it represents the outworking of the presence of the Spirit in the church, and Galatians 3:28 makes it clear that with regard to the giving of the Spirit there is no discrimination. Ideally at least, the authority to exercise a gift of the Spirit derives from the gift itself, or from the anointing of the Spirit that accompanies the gift; ministry does not proceed from any predetermined authority. This does not mean that the exercise of a gift may not be overruled for practical reasons – just as Paul did not *permit* women to teach. But it is difficult to see on what theological basis the gifts might be assigned, or their use regulated, according to gender.

The second type of role is that of the 'elder' or 'overseer'; for our present purposes we may treat these two terms as roughly synonymous (*cf.* Acts 20:28; Phil. 1:1; Tit. 1:5, 7). Eldership is not itself a charismatic ministry, though elders are appointed by the Holy Spirit and with the laying on of hands (Acts 20:28; 1 Tim. 5:22), and no doubt manifested appropriate charismata, such as pastoring and teaching. It is the eldership that is explicitly assigned a governing and disciplining authority in the local congregation (1 Tim. 5:17; *cf.* 1 Pet. 5:5), and which is ultimately responsible for safeguarding both the congregation and the gospel.

Eldership in the New Testament, however, unlike charismatic ministry, is not a uniquely Christian function but a development of pre-existing authority structures, notably the pattern of eldership in the Sanhedrin and the synagogue. There is little to suggest that eldership as it appears in the New Testament is understood as a divinely ordained form of church leadership. The impression given is that it was taken over from Judaism by Jewish Christianity without much reflection (the elders were those who already had a natural authority within the community) and then transmitted in a more deliberate manner by Paul to the churches of the Gentile mission (Acts 14:23; Tit. 1:5). None of the various images by which the church is described in the New Testament explicitly includes elders. Paul speaks frequently of the church as a body, but elders are not represented in this central defining metaphor; nor are they 'given' to the church in the way that apostles, prophets, evangelists, and others are (Eph. 4:11). In fact, elders appear almost incidental to Paul's understanding of the nature of the Christian community.

Given this, it is questionable whether we find in Paul a binding endorsement of the patriarchal structure of New Testament eldership. Just as plausibly we might argue that the church simply adopted as a matter of practical expediency the most appropriate model of leadership available. New Testament eldership was male, therefore, because leadership within comparable Jewish and pagan institutions was male; the model was perfectly suited to the cultural environment and, therefore, likely to be the most effective. An analogy could be drawn between authority within the church and authority within the family, particularly since the 'household' provides a natural model for the organization of the Christian community (*cf.* Eph. 2:19; 1 Tim. 3:4, 15; Tit. 2:5). If, then, Paul regards the authority of the man over the woman not as a theological absolute but as a given cultural reality, should not the pattern of leadership within the church be viewed in the same light? While charismatic ministry is in a real sense eschatological – the incursion of the powers of the age to come into the present age – ecclesiastical organization is an aspect of the social condition of the church, in which case it is unsurprising if the structures of authority are adapted to the circumstances of the world. The responsibilities of eldership and the manner in which leadership is undertaken (to act with integrity and humility, provide pastoral oversight, preach, teach and defend the word of God, pray for the sick, and so on) belong to the kingdom of God; but the *form* of authority may be socially determined. If, therefore, it has proved acceptable for women to hold positions of leadership in secular organizations, there is no reason why they should not do the same within the church. This inference cannot, of course, be made uncritically, and requires far more careful definition that we can afford it here. But the general principle seems unobjectionable: that leadership within the church should at least reflect, if not anticipate, such a significant social change as the widespread participation of women in secular leadership.

It could be argued, therefore, that there is no need to isolate Christian leadership from the breakdown of patriarchalism in the West. If society has become accustomed to the idea that the exercise of authority should not be a male prerogative, then it is likely in the long run that authority will be exercised more effectively in the church if it shares the same presuppositions.

Are we thereby merely pandering to secular interests? Not if Paul regards hierarchy as a social phenomenon, a distortion of the creational prominence of the man. Not if we recognize that forms of leadership within the church inevitably bear the impression of prevailing cultural–historical models of authority. Although the historical implications are more far-reaching, such a change does not differ in principle from the adoption of contemporary forms of music in worship or the abandonment of traditional ecclesiastical architecture. The issue then is basically pragmatic. If leadership is respected, if it mediates the authority of Christ and of the Scriptures, if it is committed to the basic tasks that we have just outlined, then there appears to be nothing intrinsic to the nature of eldership that precludes the participation of women. Indeed, the sharing of leadership in the church will inevitably be seen as a fuller realization of the equality of men and women described in Galatians 3:28. Paul may not have had this development in mind, but it is not inconsistent with the position articulated in this passage.

If the form of church government should properly take into account prevailing cultural expectations regarding the exercise of authority, then we have to ask ourselves whether it is really consistent with Scripture to preserve an outmoded pattern of leadership. The form of church government is not an end in itself, and therefore not a matter of ultimate truth. It is a means to an end, just as the driver on a bus is a means to an end. What passengers expect of a bus is that it will get them safely and efficiently from A to B; it hardly matters whether the driver is a man or a woman as long as he or she is competent. As a definition of church leadership this may seem too functional and reductive, but in the end, the eldership of a church has no intrinsic authority of its own: its authority is derived from Christ and from the word of God (*cf.* 2 Cor. 10:8; 13:10). In the West today the more appropriate model for eldership is probably not the synagogue or the civic institutions of the Hellenistic cities but the company board or the cabinet of ministers or the town council in which the presence of women is accepted (if not always enthusiastically encouraged).

The question of competence, of course, is a difficult one and cannot be properly considered here. We might, however, take issue with one argument that is sometimes put forward in support of the traditional restrictions on women's ministry. Schreiner, for example, believes that women are by nature ill-equipped for the task of teaching Christian doctrine:

> Generally speaking, women are more relational and nurturing and men are more given to rational analysis and objectivity. Women are less prone than men to see the importance of doctrinal formulations, especially when it comes to the issue of identifying heresy and making a stand for truth. Appointing women to the teaching office is prohibited because they are less likely to draw a line on doctrinal non-negotiables, and thus deception and false teaching will more easily enter the church (1995:145).

The observations about men and women may be broadly correct, but the practical conclusions drawn from them are not at all persuasive. First, the qualification 'generally speaking' is an admission that the stereotypes do not always apply: some women have powerfully analytical minds, some men are intensely relational. Why should not both men and women be allowed to function within the church according to their individual character and gifting? Secondly, if it is true that women are less prone to see the importance of doctrinal formulations, it is equally true that men are more prone to neglect the relational dimension of truth and, for that matter, to retreat from grace into doctrinal rigidity and bigotry. The fact that women are, to whatever degree, more relational is as good an argument as any, if they are otherwise qualified, for their participation in the teaching office. Thirdly, the situation has changed somewhat since Paul wrote his letter to Timothy. On the one hand, teaching no longer requires the same *personal* authority that was necessary in the apostolic era; we now have both the authoritative canon of Scripture and a long history of reflection upon God's Word. On the other, women are much better equipped than in Paul's time to deal with objective truth. Women operate no less effectively than men in other areas of public life where truth is at issue – politics, human rights, scientific research, journalism, law, and so on. What is so different about Christian truth that women cannot be trusted to distinguish it from error and defend it in the church?

Of course, in this discussion we have moved away from exegesis into the realms of generalization and inference. In the end we know too little about how Christian eldership developed and how it was understood in the New Testament to be able to pronounce final judgment. Eldership is not defined, but merely presupposed; and whether or not we regard the particular form that eldership took in the New Testament as normative for the church throughout history may have to remain a matter of hermeneutical choice. But by recognizing that women have inherited the fullness of the Spirit, that leadership patterns in the New Testament were in certain respects culturally determined, and that Paul's understanding of the relationship between men and women does not entail the permanent subordination of the woman, we at least have a coherent theoretical basis for the view that women may minister and exercise authority in the church on fundamentally the same terms as men.

Two spheres of ministry

Women were largely excluded from patriarchal leadership structures, but were visibly active in other ways in two rather distinct spheres.

First, within the local Christian community some probably functioned as deacons, either in their own right or in conjunction with their husband's ministry. They were certainly expected to perform many of the tasks of a 'servant', such as providing hospitality, washing the feet of the saints, and alleviating suffering. Older women had a responsibility to train younger women in wifely duties; and no doubt women taught the rudiments of the Christian faith to their children and quite possibly to others within the household, such as female relatives and slaves. They participated in charismatic activities, notably prayer and prophecy, perhaps also informal and impromptu instruction. One imagines too, though there is little direct evidence for it, that in so far as domestic and social circumstances allowed, women proclaimed the word of God to those who did not know Christ.

In the context of a patriarchal culture, of course, women did not have the same freedom as men to participate in the life of the church. Various factors – modesty, a sense of the imbalance of the sexual dynamic, custom – dictated that a woman should not, or should not be expected to, pray or prophesy with her head uncovered. Concern for how the novel and highly suspect Christian movement was perceived by outsiders readily accounts for the instruction that women should not speak in the assembly except to contribute something – prayer, prophecy, perhaps a hymn or teaching or tongue or interpretation – in modest and orderly fashion for the edification of the body (1 Cor. 14:26). On the one hand, there appears to have been a widespread prejudice against the participation of women in public meetings; on the other, there may have been a particular desire not to offend Jewish, and indeed Jewish Christian, sensibilities. 'Be unoffending', Paul says, 'to the Jews and to the Greeks and to the church of God' (1 Cor. 10:32). This is fully in keeping with a central principle of Paul's ministry: that it may sometimes be necessary to forgo certain aspects of one's freedom in Christ for the sake of the faith of others (*cf.* 1 Cor. 8:9; 10:23–33; Gal. 5:13).

Similar anxieties motivated Paul's injunction against women teaching in his letter to Timothy at Ephesus. Again, the dangers inherent in human sexuality, exacerbated by a woman's general intellectual disadvantage and lack of credibility and authority, persuaded Paul that it was better for women to be excluded from the process by which apostolic tradition was transmitted within the church. The typological character of the allusion in 1 Timothy 2:13–14 suggests that the story of Eve and the serpent prefigures rather than predetermines subsequent possible scenarios. The argument is only that given certain circumstances, this is likely to be the outcome, and these are the measures that should be taken to remedy the situation.

Secondly, within the loosely defined ambit of Paul's apostolic ministry women appear to have had greater freedom and certainly greater influence. Generally speaking, Paul's attitude with respect to the ministry of women in the local congregation appears to have been more conservative and more restrictive than it was towards their involvement in the independent and itinerant work of church-planting. There is a marked and rather disconcerting contrast between Paul's enthusiastic endorsement of the ministry of individual women, especially those who had worked alongside him, and the tone of those passages in which he imposes a comprehensive ban on women speaking or teaching. Partly this must be indicative of the relative lack of confidence that Paul had in the ability of these recently established churches to maintain the integrity of their life and witness. In view of the various forces, from both within and without, that threatened to corrupt or dismember the body of Christ and wreck all that he had worked for (*cf.* Phil. 2:16; 1 Thes. 3:5), it is hardly surprising that he sometimes erred on the side of caution. But it also probably reflects the extent to which the local church was subject to prevailing social custom and such circumstances as the tension between Jewish and Gentile believers. To some degree at least, Paul and the fluid coterie of men and women who worked with him operated within a more cosmopolitan sphere and, one imagines, found themselves less constrained by the parochial traditions and prejudices of local communities.

Headship today

Given what the prominence of the man meant in practice in ancient Mediterranean society, the relationship between Christ and the church provided an ideal model for Christian marriage. If Paul could have foreseen the changes that would take place in the world nearly 2,000 years later, he might have approached the subject differently. But he sought or expected the transformation of patriarchy no more than he did the abolition of slavery. His concern was to instruct people how to live Christlike lives within a context of entrenched social inequality in an age that would probably not last much longer anyway (1 Cor. 7:29–31). Given that one man was master of another, he should treat his slave justly and fairly, recognizing that he also has a master in heaven (Col. 4:1). Likewise, given that a man was head of the woman, he should love her in the same way that Christ loved the church; and given that the woman was placed in a position of subordination, she should 'fear' her husband (Eph. 5:33). *Recovering Biblical Manhood and Womanhood* is an eloquent and impressive exposition of this ideal. Whatever reservations one may have regarding its exegetical and theological foundations and its marked cultural bias, it articulates very well the biblical principles that should govern relationships between men and women *where there is unavoidable social and marital inequality*.

But today, in the West at least, the prominence of the man has greatly diminished and, more importantly, is no longer widely assumed to entail the subordination of the woman. Society has come to accept that women in principle have the same right as men to hold positions of prominence and authority without incurring disgrace and without doing damage either to their own femininity or to the masculinity of the men who find themselves governed or directed by them. Various areas of life will remain typically either male or female, but we no longer live in a world in which everything is organized with a view to asserting and maintaining the priority of the man. There does not have to be a place at the head of the table, or a comfy chair in front of the television, reserved for the dominant male.

I have suggested that Paul's approach to the question of the relationship between the man and the woman was conditioned to a large degree by the dichotomy between the private and public spheres. In the public sphere, where the man was dominant, he advocated behaviour on the part of the woman that would not compromise the standing of the man: the covering of the head when praying or prophesying, an attitude of submission, the silence of women in the congregation. In the private sphere, however, and particularly in the area of sexual relations, he believed there should be equality. We should not try to make this a sharp or entirely consistent distinction, but it helps to explain in general terms the tension that appears in Paul's thought, illustrated most clearly by the insertion of an argument for equality ('as the woman from the man, so also the man through the woman; and all things from God'; 1 Cor. 11:12) into a passage that speaks of a marked imbalance between the man and the woman with respect to 'glory'.

As the public dominance of the man is progressively eroded, however, the restrictions lose their relevance. The glory of God in a woman no longer appears to be eclipsed by the glory of the man, which is why women now rarely cover their heads when praying or prophesying. Society no longer imposes a strictly defined hierarchal order upon male–female relations. There is not the same offence when women participate in public assemblies. As a result, the potential for equality, hitherto confined to the more intimate and personal areas of married life, now has freedom to expand and embrace the public dimension of male–female relations too.

Alternative conceptions of 'headship' within the Christian family

The prominence of the man that Paul described by the 'head' metaphor has changed considerably. Some would prefer to dispense with the idea of headship altogether. But if, as I have argued, the figure is essentially descriptive rather than prescriptive, this is probably unwise. One may even hope that a revised understanding of the notion of 'headship' will have a mediatory role between the traditionalist or complementarian and the egalitarian position.

On the one hand, man is still, in many respects, 'head' of the woman; and there remains a significant discrepancy between the public and private spheres. This is especially true, of course, for the developing world. Paul's teaching in Ephesians 5:22–33, therefore, retains its fundamental, practical validity. Whatever natural or social advantage the man continues to have over his wife should be made subservient to the interests of the woman and of the family as a whole. A man should not use his superior strength to intimidate or abuse a woman, but with his strength should serve her, as Christ served the church. A man should not use his greater earning power to satisfy his own whims and ambitions at the expense of his wife's personal development and happiness, but should seek to enrich her life, as Christ enriches the life of the church. A man should not use his public or professional status to assert his independence, but should bind himself to his wife, as one flesh, as Christ has committed himself to the church which is his body. A man should not use his greater emotional strength – or callousness – to bully and manipulate his wife, but should love her and support her.

On the other hand, men and women in practice now frequently *share* the prominence that the figure signifies; both may now play a significant and visible role outside the home. One might justly speak, therefore, either of a joint headship or of a division of headship, depending on how responsibilities are apportioned within the marriage. In this case, it is not so much the specific content of Paul's teaching on headship and submission that becomes important, as the underlying principle, which is that Christian couples must seek to express the redeeming love of Christ and the reality of being one flesh within the various socio-economic parameters that define marriage today. Paul could say, in effect: 'Given the prominence of the man and the way it is interpreted in a patriarchal society, husband and wife should relate to each other thus . . .' Now, however, the right counsel might be: 'Given the general fluidity of marital role definitions and the particular character, qualifications, and so on, of the couple, they should relate to each other thus . . .'

Will such an arrangement contribute to the further undermining of the family, as many fear? It is undoubtedly true that there has been a widespread abdication of moral and spiritual responsibility towards the family on the part of men. But a man does not need to assert authority over his wife in order to take responsibility for the family; nor does he have to feel that he must take *ultimate* responsibility. The instability of family life in modern society is not an argument for male supremacy. The point is that the responsibilities traditionally associated with an exclusive male headship have not been abandoned but reassigned.

The prospect of further social change

The world is changing inexorably – a truism, but true nevertheless – and it would be unwise to assume that the seismic upheavals that have wrought such an extensive realignment of social relations are about to subside. Technology continues to advance and the social and working environment to evolve, making it increasingly possible for women to participate more or less on equal terms with men in every area of public life.

This does not mean that the traditional model of the male breadwinner and the female cake-maker is destined for the scrap heap; it has become one option among many, but certainly not an obsolescent option. If, for example, a woman chooses to commit herself to the raising of children and the maintenance of the home as a place of Christian hospitality, it can hardly be said that she has opted for second best. There is evidence, moreover, that many women are abandoning the attempt to drag their children with them up the mountain of a conventional career and are heading back to base camp.

But generally speaking there is bound to be much greater fluidity in the assignment of roles within the family, and, correspondingly, in our under-standing of how various tasks are to be accomplished. This does not mean that everything is up for grabs: perhaps the man will remain the most effective source of discipline within the family; probably women will always be better than men at nurturing infants. But it is a common mistake to assume that a task that has traditionally been performed by men can only be done in a masculine way; or that women are naturally incompetent in certain areas when in fact they have simply not had the chance to develop their own way of doing things. These changes will inevitably create problems as people and institutions adapt, often reluctantly and painfully, to new circumstances, new expectations, new opportunities. But if enough couples want to share responsibility for raising and providing for a family, then the world is likely to reorganize itself to accommodate them. And who can say where it will end?

The church faces a dilemma. The church is interpenetrated by the world; it is woven through the warp of the world and cannot help but be stretched and torn with the rest of the fabric. What this study has shown, I think, is that at the back of Paul's mind was the understanding that the patriarchal order belonged not to the kingdom of God but to the 'form of this world'. How families and societies define and ordain authority belongs to the warp, which runs through the threads that make up the church as much as through the rest of society. To some extent the church can compensate for the various obligations and inequalities and abuses that accompany whatever social order exists by adopting the attitude of Christ. But the threads cannot be torn from the cloth; the church cannot be removed from the world.

Many questions remain. By revoking the final authority of the man, do we open the floodgates to every progressive notion that the world in its infinite capacity for folly gets into its head? One of the concerns that motivated those who formulated the Danvers Statement was a recognition of 'the growing claims of legitimacy for sexual relationships which have Biblically and historically been considered illicit or perverse, and the increase in porno-graphic portrayal of human sexuality'.[1] The scope of the egalitarian argument, therefore, needs precise definition. If Paul has left the door unlocked to a properly defined egalitarianism, this does not mean that all manner of other experiments in social or moral reorganization should be allowed to slip in. The biblical ideal remains the life-long, faithful union of man and woman as the foundation for family; and as long as men and women remain sexually distinct, there will always be some differentiation of roles both in the public and in the private domains; indeed, there will always be 'complementarity' between men and women. This ideal is not in any way jeopardized, however, by an adjustment of authority structures. It is not immoral for men and women to treat each other as equals.

Is the church losing its identity? Is this still the church of Jesus Christ, who chose twelve men as the foundation for this new household of God? Inevitably, the church will look different, it will function differently, as the

---

[1] See J. Piper and W. Grudem (eds.), *Recovering Biblical Manhood and Womanhood* (Wheaton: Crossway, 1991): 469.

patriarchal colouring is washed out of it; but it will be no less the people of God, no less the body of Christ, no less the 'pillar and support of the truth' (1 Tim. 3:15). In all likelihood it will be found to represent more fully the equality of status and blessing that men and women have in Christ. The colouring, in other words, is not natural; it is a stain unavoidably absorbed from the ancient world. Moreover, in time these changes are likely to appear no more radical than many other changes (vernacular translations of the Scripture, the rise of independent churches) that have taken place in the history of the church.

Has the church simply been wrong for the last 2,000 years? No. At least, not entirely. The underlying thrust of this study has been that this is one area in which the church *should* be responsive to prevailing social conditions. The very conception of headship in Paul, in its practical implications, is essentially a recognition of *how things are*. His teaching on the role and status of women is an accommodation (in the best sense of the word) of the gospel to these conditions. We should not attempt to excuse the prolongation of abuse or overlook the extent to which the church has become trapped in an unjust worldview; nor should we regard these arguments as a licence for immorality. But it seems on the whole right that the 'emancipation' of women within the church should follow on the emancipation of women within society at large. Otherwise, there is a real danger that the church will find itself perpetuating a social order that no longer has any relevance to the modern world. Once the subordination of the woman was considered perfectly natural; now it is increasingly regarded as unnatural and unfair. By recognizing the potential for equality latent in Paul's writings we make it possible for the church to take a more positive, less isolationist, stance towards this new order of things without in any way compromising the gospel or the standards of the kingdom of God.

Finally . . .

There is a need for reconciliation. The church is being torn apart and something needs to be done about it. Perhaps exegesis can help, if it is candid, critical and constructive. But as we struggle towards scholarly consensus, something more fundamental is also required, and that is for people – pastors, theologians, teachers, believers – to stretch themselves across the divide, to love one another, and to serve one another. For we are all one in Christ Jesus.

Appendix
Inclusive-language translation of Scripture

As this book was being prepared for press, the controversy in the US surrounding the inclusive-language edition of the New International Version (NIVI) brought to prominence an aspect of the debate over the position of women in the church that has otherwise not received much attention.[1]

The NIVI has been available in the UK since 1995. The changes made mostly relate to the replacement of generic masculine forms of expression by a variety of inclusive forms. Language referring to God is unchanged and only in a few instances has it been claimed that the personhood of Christ has been compromised by a shift of emphasis from his *male* to his *human* nature. Those passages that directly describe gender roles or list the requirements for overseers and deacons remain untouched.[2] No attempt has been made to enhance the position of women or mitigate the demand for subordination. 1 Timothy 2:12 still reads, quite bluntly: 'I do not permit a woman to teach or to have authority over a man; she must be silent.'

The arguments on both sides have so far been presented mainly through Christian magazines and on the internet, and the focus in the media has been much more on the politics of the affray than on the linguistic and theological issues. It will be a while before the slow-moving tortoise of biblical scholarship catches up with the hyperactive hare of popular polemics. All we can put forward at this point, therefore, is an incomplete and provisional assessment of the arguments for and against the inclusive-language edition.

Objections to inclusive-language translations

The NIVI has caused alarm on two fronts. In the first place, there is the suspicion that the demand for an inclusive-language Bible has been driven largely by feminist ideology. J. I. Packer is quoted as saying that 'adjustments made by what I call the feminist edition are not made in the interests of legitimate translation procedure. These changes have been made to pander to a cultural prejudice that I hope will be short-lived.'[3] Certainly, the dilemma of

---

[1] An article in *World* magazine, 29 March 1997, alerted readers to the imminent arrival of a gender-neutral 'Stealth Bible'. Among other translations that use inclusive language are the New Revised Standard Version and the New Living Translation.

[2] The NRSV, by contrast, has made the 'husband of one wife' clause inclusive (1 Tim. 3:2, 12; Tit. 1:6).

[3] *World* magazine, 19 April 1997, pp. 14–15.

representing eternal truth in a changeable and pluralistic society has been sharply illustrated. There is also the more specific objection that the adoption of inclusive language will obscure distinctions between male and female roles in family and church. Since the texts that deal directly with these issues have not been changed, what the critics presumably have in mind is the reduction of the general patriarchal, male-oriented character of Scripture – and the fear that any concession to the egalitarian instinct will encourage a slide into the abyss of feminism and sexual perversion.

The second area of concern has to do with translational method. The argument is that the sort of hermeneutical bias that underlies the revisions to the NIV inevitably leads to distortion and error. No matter how trivial the implications may appear to be in any particular instance – or even how well-intentioned – there is no justification for tampering with the Word of God. More specific allegations have also been made: for example, that certain revisions are likely to add support to false doctrines associated, supposedly, with the charismatic movement, neo-orthodoxy, and Arminianism.

The argument for inclusive language

The central contention of those who favour an inclusive-language translation is that it constitutes a more accurate rendering both of the *meaning* and of the *intention* of the text. Admittedly, other factors have played a part: it can hardly be denied that the impetus to produce a new translation comes partly from cultural and commercial pressures, and there has been explicit recognition that generic masculine language may have the effect of alienating women. Nevertheless, the view is strongly maintained that both on practical-pastoral grounds and on linguistic-theological grounds the inclusive-language version is a more reliable representation of the Word of God than its predecessor. John Stott has argued:

> When *man* means human being, without any intention to exclude women, and when the use of *brothers* was never intended to exclude sisters, then to retain such gender-specific words would be offensive. Even worse, it would actually misrepresent the meaning of the biblical text.[4]

A number of arguments have been put forward. One concerns the important distinction between 'meaning' and 'intention'. A literal translation of the Hebrew text of Psalm 1:1, which has frequently been cited in the debate, would read something like: 'Blessed (is) the man ['*îš*] who has not walked in the counsel of the ungodly.' Any attempt to represent the *meaning* of this text must take account of the fact that '*îš* in Hebrew essentially signifies

[4] Quoted in *Christianity Today*, 16 June 1997, p. 53.

'man' as distinct from woman. When we come to consider the *intention* of the text, however, at least two questions must be asked. First, did the psalmist intend to exclude women or is *'iš* used inclusively? Secondly, in more general terms, is the statement equally true – within the frame of the whole Word of God – for women? The first question is difficult to answer conclusively, though elements in the psalm suggest primarily a male context: few women, for example, would have had the opportunity to meditate on the law day and night. The answer to the second, at least as I have phrased it, is surely yes – in which case the NIVI translation must be judged to represent accurately the *intention* of the text as part of the whole Word of God: 'Blessed are *those* who do not walk in the counsel of the wicked.' But we should recognize that this has involved a hermeneutical judgment inasmuch as it relies on criteria drawn from beyond the immediate literary context of the psalm.

Secondly, the revisers believe that the use of generic masculine forms is becoming increasingly unacceptable in normal English usage. In their place are substituted an assortment of more or less eccentric circumlocutions: 'he or she', for example, or the use of the indeterminate plural pronoun instead of the gender-explicit singular. How much this can be attributed to the influence of 'feminism' as an ideologically motivated social force is not clear; arguably, feminism is itself as much a symptom of deeper, less visible social changes as a cause. But in the end, regardless of the origin of these developments, we must use language as we find it, even if this results in some translational and stylistic heavy-handedness.

Thirdly, it has been argued that the inherently inclusive nature of some texts has been obscured in traditional translations by the use of generic masculine forms. The Greek word *anthrōpos*, which certainly exhibits a more inclusivist semantic profile than *anēr*, provides the clearest instance. To translate both terms by the single English word 'man' conceals an important lexical distinction. Sometimes, too, masculine forms are presupposed where the Greek text is silent or imprecise. In 2 Corinthians 5:17 the KJV reads: 'if any man be in Christ, he is a new creature', but neither 'man' nor 'he' is found in the text and the NIVI rendering ('if anyone is in Christ, there is a new creation') is perfectly legitimate.

Finally, it has been pointed out that the use of inclusive language in the Bible is not entirely a modern innovation. The KJV consistently uses 'children of Israel' rather than 'sons of Israel' for *bᵉnê yiśrā'ēl*, and occasionally has 'children' for *hyioi* ('sons') in the New Testament (*e.g.* 'children of the living God', Rom. 9:26; 'children of Abraham', Gal. 3:7; Eph. 2:2; 1 Thes. 5:5); *'iš* is sometimes translated 'person' (*e.g.* Nu. 19:18; 1 Sa. 9:2; 16:18; 2 Sa. 4:11). More significantly, Paul himself provided an inclusivist adaptation of the promise to David in 2 Samuel 7:14: 'I will be as a father to you, and you will be to me as sons *and daughters*' (2 Cor. 6:18).

Inclusivist strategies

This is not the place to embark upon a comprehensive examination of the texts that have been revised in the NIVI. We may, however, briefly outline the most prominent of the inclusivist strategies that can be exemplified from Paul's letters.

There are only a few instances in Paul where *anēr* ('man' as distinct from woman) has been rendered inclusively. When Paul quotes Psalm 32:2 in Romans 4:8, the singular masculine form [*makarios anēr*] has become 'blessed *are those* whose sin the Lord will never count against them.'[5] In 1 Corinthians 13:11 we have: 'When I became an *adult* [*anēr*], I put childish ways behind me.' The omission of *anēr* in Romans 11:4 ('I have reserved for myself seven thousand [men] who have not bowed the knee to Baal') and the translation of *eis andra teleion* as 'become mature' (Eph. 4:13) are found already in the NIV.

Where *anthrōpos* is judged to have an inclusive meaning, it is frequently translated by such expressions as 'human (being)' or 'mortal' (*e.g.* Rom. 1:23; 2:3, 9; 9:20; 14:18; 1 Cor. 1:25; 2:5, 11; 13:1), particularly if the contrast is with animals or divine figures; or more indefinitely by 'person', 'people', 'everyone', 'someone', *etc.* (*e.g.* Rom. 2:16; 3:4, 28; 7:1; 10:5; 12:17–18; 1 Cor. 6:18; Col. 1:28). Sometimes the plural is used (*e.g.* Rom. 4:6), or a paraphrase (*e.g.* 1 Cor. 11:28), or the word is not translated, as in 1 Corinthians 15:45 where 'the first man [*anthrōpos*] Adam' (NIV) becomes simply 'the first Adam' – though since in verse 47 *ho prōtos anthrōpos* is translated 'the first man' in the NIVI, it is difficult to attach much significance to this.[6]

Some other obvious lexical changes have been made in order explicitly to include women within the frame of reference. When the Greek text describes believers as *hyioi* ('sons'), the NIVI generally has 'children' (*e.g.* Rom. 8:14–17, 19; Gal. 4:1–7). 'Brethren' has mostly been expanded to include 'brothers and sisters'.[7] 'Ancestors' is substituted for 'fathers' (1 Cor. 10:1; Gal. 1:14; 2 Tim. 1:3).

Frequently, masculine singular forms are converted into plural or second-person forms in order to avoid the gender-specific pronouns ('he', 'she', 'his', 'her', *etc.*). So Romans 12:20 reads: 'If your *enemies* are hungry, feed *them*; if *they* are thirsty, give *them* something to drink. In doing this, you will heap burning coals upon *their* heads.' And Ephesians 5:29: 'After all, *people* have never hated *their* own bodies, but feed and care for *them*, just as Christ does the

---

[5] While the LXX has *anēr*, the Hebrew text has *'āḏām*.
[6] The use of 'self' or 'being' for the 'inner man' (Rom. 6:6; 7:22; Eph. 3:16; 4:22, 24; Col. 3:9) is found in the NIV.
[7] Note also 'my own race' for 'my own brethren' (Rom. 9:3); 'believer' for the sexually immoral 'brother' in 1 Cor. 5:11.

church . . .'[8] The third-person construction in 1 Corinthians 10:12 (*ho dokōn estanai blepetō mē pesē*) has been rendered: 'if *you* think *you* are standing, be careful that *you* don't fall!' In a similar way masculine participles and adjectives are given an inclusive orientation. Whereas the NIV translates *ton ponēron* in 1 Corinthians 5:13 as 'the wicked man', the NIVI has 'the wicked person'. The quotation from Leviticus 18:5 in Galatians 3:12, 'The man who does [*ho poiēsas*] these things will live by them' (NIV), has been changed to 'The one who does these things . . .' in the NIVI.

Problems

Many of the inclusivist revisions are uncontroversial. When Paul says that God our Saviour wants *pantas anthrōpous* to be saved (1 Tim. 2:4), it seems entirely reasonable to translate *pantas anthrōpous*, as the NIVI does, as 'all people'. In today's cultural and linguistic environment the decision to translate this as 'all men' would be open to interpretation as male bias and therefore contrary to Paul's meaning.

But still we need to be careful. Although the inclusive form may make good sense in the immediate context, it may introduce tensions at other points that are not apparent at first sight. The images of 'mortal *anthrōpou*' that people have substituted for the glory of the immortal God (Rom. 1:23) are images of 'human beings', in contrast to God, on the one hand, and to 'birds and animals and reptiles', on the other. Likewise, the significance of the vocative *ō anthrōpe* in Romans 2:3 is not that this figure is male but that he is a 'human being' and not God. But this does not quite mean that these passages have an inclusive orientation. There is reference to the 'godlessness and wickedness of those [*anthrōpōn*] who suppress the truth . . .' in Romans 1:18 (NIVI), but it is clear from verse 26 that Paul had men in mind: 'Even *their* women exchanged natural relations for unnatural ones . . .' Similarly, the hypothetical figure addressed in Romans 2 is a *male* Jew and what is said in this chapter is principally applicable to a male Jew, not to *people* of indeterminate sex and race. The NIVI translation of 2:28 ('A person is not a Jew who is only one outwardly, nor is circumcision merely outward and physical') is technically permissible provided that we do not understand 'person' to include both men and women, for the argument is clearly directed to men and Paul would not have addressed the situation of the Jewish woman in the same manner.

It is important to keep in mind that *anthrōpos* may have masculine overtones which are lost in an inclusive translation – indeed, in many places the NIVI retains 'man' (*e.g.* 1 Cor. 7:1, 7; Eph. 5:31; 2 Thes. 2:3; 1 Tim. 6:11). It is difficult, moreover, to find any instance in the Greek Bible where *anthrōpos* clearly refers to a woman or even to a group that *manifestly* includes women;

---

[8] Also 1 Cor. 11:29.

and the word is often used in the LXX in contexts that clearly mean 'man as opposed to woman' (*e.g.* Gn. 20:7; 26:11; Ex. 2:21; Lv. 20:10; Nu. 5:15; Is. 4:1). In this respect the word is not the simple equivalent of 'person'/'people'. We must often assume, therefore, that Paul had men in mind even though in principle women might have been included. The context of 1 Corinthians 6:18 makes it highly likely that when Paul says, 'All other sins people commit [*pan hamartēma ho ean poiēsē anthrōpos* – note the singular form] are outside their bodies', he is thinking of men, though few would claim that the verse is inapplicable to women.[9] The fact that Paul uses *anthrōpois* in 2 Timothy 2:2 ('the things you have heard me say . . . entrust to reliable *people* who will also be qualified to teach others') does not automatically mean that he included women among these potential teachers.[10]

Another passage that has received attention, and which illustrates the sort of quandary that arises when plural forms are used, is 1 Corinthians 14:28: 'If there is no interpreter, the speakers should keep quiet in the church and speak to themselves and God.' Since Paul expected women to prophesy (1 Cor. 11:5), inclusive language would appear to be appropriate here. But Wayne Grudem, fearing the use of the text to justify charismatic separationism, objects that the revision 'can easily be understood to encourage groups of tongue-speakers to go off together and speak in tongues "to themselves" '.[11] In principle this is correct: 'the speakers . . . to themselves' has connotations that are not present in the singular version. Although it seems unlikely that the verse would be misconstrued in this exact way ('in the church' still defines the context in which these people would 'speak to themselves'), the plural form certainly tends to identify tongue-speakers as a group rather than as individuals.

There are also difficulties with some of the other lexical changes. 'Brothers and sisters' for 'brethren' is relatively innocent, though it still masks the fact that Paul probably thought chiefly of the men when he addressed his congregations; women were not excluded but were, linguistically at least, subsumed within the more prominent male categories. The use of 'children' for 'sons' may be practically justified, but on closer examination some quite significant theological problems emerge. Perhaps most importantly, the connection between the status of the believer and the sonship of Christ is partly obscured: the expression 'sons of God' (Rom. 8:14, 19; 9:26; Gal. 3:26) has Christological and eschatological connotations that are lost in the inclusive rendering. The complex figure that Paul develops in Galatians 3:26 – 4:7

---

[9] 2 Tim. 3:8 appears to have men in view (*cf.* v. 6), but NIVI has 'people'; *cf.* Col. 2:8; 2 Tim. 3:17.

[10] The NIVI suggests 'men' as an alternative for 'people' in a marginal note.

[11] *World* magazine, 19 April 1997, p. 17.

depends to a large extent on the perception that believers, both men and women (3:28), have become *like* sons in that they have clothed themselves with Christ, who is God's Son; and as sons – but unlike daughters – they have *inherited* the promised Spirit.

What about the argument that inclusive language obscures gender distinctions? As we have pointed out already, the texts that deal directly with gender roles are unchanged in the NIVI. But it is likely that some more subtle amendments will cause concern. It could be argued, for example, that 'people' instead of 'sons of men' in Ephesians 3:5 favours the understanding that 'God's holy apostles and prophets' included women; or that inclusive language in 1 Corinthians 3:7–15 implies that women may potentially have apostolic status. Such objections may appear trivial, but they highlight the fact that many will regard the NIVI as a partisan translation.

On the other hand, the charge that by translating *anthrōpos* as 'human (being)' in certain texts the NIVI compromises the male character of Christ has, in my view, no real basis. In 1 Corinthians 15:21 ('since death came through a *human being*, the resurrection of the dead comes also through a *human being*') the correspondence with the *man* Adam is perhaps slightly weakened, but the fundamental point is that Christ shared the same *humanity* as Adam (not the same gender) and therefore in his resurrection stands appropriately as the 'firstfruits' of redeemed humanity. Similarly, Paul's argument in Philippians 2:7–8 is that Christ abandoned his *divine* nature and took on *human* nature; and in 1 Timothy 2:5 that the mediator between God and humankind is 'himself human'. Any suggestion that Paul saw significance in Christ's *maleness* in these texts surely risks compromising the universality of salvation.

There are also some general difficulties raised by an inclusivist translational procedure. In the first place, is it right to gloss over the intrinsically male-oriented language of the text?[12] This should be a pressing question even for those who take an egalitarian position regarding the status of women. Even if we regard the *intention* of Scripture as generally inclusive, are we justified in obscuring the *meaning* of the texts?

Secondly, has the English language really changed to such an extent that masculine forms can no longer be used inclusively? Linguistic evolution is by no means uniform or predictable. What has become unacceptable for one set of English speakers may remain perfectly normal for another. It is difficult to know how far changes of this nature will progress, particularly when they are so closely associated with highly self-conscious and possibly transient

---

[12] Note the 'Preface to Inclusive Language NIV', p. vii: 'it was recognized that it was often appropriate to mute the patriarchalism of the culture of the biblical writers through gender-inclusive language when this could be done without compromising the message of the Spirit.'

ideological movements. Feminism has gone some way towards undermining traditional usage but has found it much more difficult to develop satisfactory alternatives. As a result, there is in many cases something rather makeshift and stilted about the revisions. While it may be acceptable to use 'they' or 'them' as indeterminate singulars in common speech, the conversion of singular expressions to plural in more exact forms of discourse (*e.g.* biblical translation) is much more controversial. Nor are the attempts to substitute other expressions for 'man'/'men', *etc.* unproblematic. Words such as 'person', 'people', 'humankind', 'human beings', are not fully synonymous and there will inevitably be some loss of meaning, some shift of nuance.[13]

Inconclusive conclusions about inclusive language . . .

Inclusive-language translations such as the NIVI force us to make decisions concerning the best way to represent the meaning of particular texts; but they also pose more far-reaching questions about the nature and purpose of a translation of Scripture.

The objections of the NIVI's detractors are not without foundation. Some of the arguments undoubtedly reflect theological bias, but it has to be recognized that the revisions to the NIVI have unavoidably introduced some measure of inaccuracy and stylistic inelegance. Commenting on the numerous changes from singular to plural forms, Grudem argues that readers of the NIVI have no way of knowing whether they are reading the words of God or the words of man. 'Such revisions are not the words God originally caused to be written, and thus they are not the words of God. They are human words that men have substituted for the words of God, and they have no place in the Bible.'[14]

This is a fundamental evangelical concern, but we should also remind ourselves that any translation is a compromise between the original text and the possibilities and limitations of the language of translation. The NIV itself is an imperfect representation of the original Scriptures: at countless places strict accuracy has been sacrificed for the sake of clarity and contemporary relevance. Perhaps the NIVI takes the process a significant step further, but is there a qualitative distinction between this and normal translation procedure? Even the traditional translations conceal certain aspects of gender distinction. For example, in Greek the reflexive pronoun *seautou* ('yourself') has masculine and feminine forms which are unrecognized in English.[15]

The argument of those who favour the revisions will be that more is lost by retaining forms of language that for many readers have become tainted with

[13] For example, 'human being' depersonalizes *anthrōpos*.

[14] *World* magazine, 19 April 1997, p. 18.

[15] *E.g.* Rom. 13:9.

male prejudice than by risking new forms of expression. The church needs this freedom to communicate the Word of God in the language of its audience. What the NIVI demonstrates, to a society that has come to distrust generic masculine language, is that the Scriptures *can* be translated into inclusive forms without substantially affecting the literal meaning of the text.

We then come back to the purpose of translation. If the aim is to include women within the practical compass of grace rather than give the impression that their stake in the Word of God must be mediated through male categories, then inclusive language versions may be judged to have real value. But this may suggest that such translations pertain principally to the sphere of liturgy and to such activities as the public reading of Scripture and evangelism – situations in which the Word of God is *proclaimed*. In these contexts the translational difficulties that we have highlighted are of negligible significance, but the advantage of a direct address to women rather than the indirectness of generic language, which many consider demeaning, is great. The point of this can be demonstrated from the NIVI translation of 1 Corinthians 13:11. The use of 'adult' instead of 'man' for *anēr* ('When I became an adult . . .') makes sense only when we remember that this chapter has considerable prominence in the liturgical and devotional practice of the church: we expect it to speak for all of us, not for Paul alone.

We should not play fast and loose with the Word of God – as some have accused the revisers of the NIV of doing. But the trains of biblical scholarship are continually running up and down the track between the original texts and the multifarious expressions of God's Word through translation, preaching, writing, and so on. However strongly we may be committed to the verbal inspiration of Scripture, the fact is that no translation exists in a vacuum but forms a provisional part of the total proclamational and pedagogic ministry of the church. And there is another, equally serious risk – that we play fast and loose with the gospel, the essence of which is the incarnation of truth within the volatile circumstances of human existence and the unconditional availability of that truth to all.

Bibliography

Aalen, S. (1964), 'A Rabbinic Formula in 1 Cor. 14, 34', in F. L. Cross (ed.), *Studia Evangelica* 2:513–525. Berlin: Akademie.

Abbott, T. K. (1897), *The Epistles to the Ephesians and to the Colossians*. Reissued Edinburgh: T. and T. Clark, 1985.

Almlie, G. L. (1982), 'Women's Church and Communion Participation: Apostolic Practice or Innovative Twist?' *Christian Brethren Review* 33: 41–55.

Baldwin, H. S. (1995), 'A Difficult Word: *authenteō* in 1 Timothy 2:12', and Appendix 2, in A. J. Köstenberger, T. R. Schreiner & H. S. Baldwin (eds.), *Women in the Church: A Fresh Analysis of 1 Timothy 2:9–15*: 65–80, 269–305. Grand Rapids: Baker.

Barnett, P. W. (1989), 'Wives and Women's Ministry (1 Timothy 2:11–15)'. *Evangelical Quarterly* 61.3: 225–237.

———— (1994), '*Authentein* Once More: A Response to L. E. Wilshire'. *Evangelical Quarterly* 66.2: 159–162.

Barrett, C. K. (1971), *The Epistle to the Romans*. London: A. and C. Black.

———— (1971), *A Commentary on the First Epistle to the Corinthians*, 2nd edn. A. and C. Black.

Barron, B. (1990), 'Putting Women in their Place: 1 Timothy 2 and Evangelical Views of Women in Church Leadership'. *Journal of the Evangelical Theological Society* 33.4: 451–459.

Barth, M. (1974), *Ephesians 1 – 3, 4 – 6*. New York: Doubleday. 2 vols.

Bauer, W., Arndt, W. F., Gingrich, F. W., & Danker, F. W. (1979), *A Greek–English Lexicon of the New Testament and Other Early Christian Literature*, 2nd edn. Chicago: University of Chicago Press.

Baugh, S. M. (1995), 'A Foreign World: Ephesus in the First Century', in A. J. Köstenberger, T. R. Schreiner & H. S. Baldwin (eds.), *Women in the Church: A Fresh Analysis of 1 Timothy 2:9–15*: 13–52. Grand Rapids: Baker.

Baumert, N. (1996), *Woman and Man in Paul: Overcoming a Misunderstanding*. Collegeville: Liturgical.

Bechtel, L. M. (1993), 'Rethinking the Interpretation of Genesis 2.4B–3.24', in A. Brenner (ed.), *A Feminist Companion to Genesis*: 77–117. Sheffield: Sheffield Academic Press.

Bedale, S. (1954), 'The Meaning of *kephalē* in the Pauline Epistles'. *Journal of Theological Studies* 5: 211–215.

———— (1956), 'The Theology of the Church', in F. L. Cross (ed.), *Studies in Ephesians*: 64–75. London: Mowbray.

Bertram, G. (1965), *'theosebēs, theosebeia'*, in G. Kittel and G. Friedrich (eds.), *Theological Dictionary of the New Testament* 3: 673–682. Grand Rapids: Eerdmans.

Best, E. (1955), *One Body in Christ*. London: SPCK.

Betz, H. D. (1979), *Galatians*. Philadelphia: Fortress.

Blass, F., Debrunner, A., & Funk, R. W. (1961), *A Greek Grammar of the New Testament and Other Early Christian Literature*. Chicago: University of Chicago Press.

Bowman, A. L. (1992), 'Women in Ministry: An Exegetical Study of 1 Timothy 2:11–15'. *Bibliotheca Sacra* 149: 193–213.

Brooten, B. J. (1982), *Women Leaders in the Ancient Synagogue*. Chico: Scholars.

———— (1985), 'Early Christian Women and their Cultural Context: Issues of Method in Historical Reconstruction', in A. Y. Collins (ed.), *Feminist Perspectives on Biblical Scholarship:* 65–91. Chico: Scholars.

Brown, F., Driver, S. R., & Briggs, C. A. (1952), *A Hebrew and English Lexicon of the Old Testament*. Oxford: Clarendon. (Corrected reprint; original 1907.)

Bruce, F. F. (1982), *The Epistle to the Galatians*. Exeter: Paternoster.

———— (1984), *The Epistles to the Colossians, to Philemon and to the Ephesians*. Grand Rapids: Eerdmans.

Büchsel, F. (1964), *'boētheō, boēthos, boētheia'*, in G. Kittel & G. Friedrich (eds.), *Theological Dictionary of the New Testament* 1: 628–629. Grand Rapids: Eerdmans.

Caird, G. B. (1984), *The Revelation of St John the Divine*, 2nd edn. London: A. and C. Black.

Carson, D. A. (1991), ' "Silent in the Churches": On the Role of Women in 1 Corinthians 14:33b–36', in J. Piper & W. Grudem (eds.), *Recovering Biblical Manhood and Womanhood:* 140–153. Wheaton: Crossway.

Cervin, R. S. (1989), 'Does *Kephalē* Mean "Source" or "Authority Over" in Greek Literature? A Rebuttal'. *Trinity Journal* new series 10: 85–112.

Charlesworth, J. H. (ed.) (1983, 1985), *The Old Testament Pseudepigrapha*. London: Darton, Longman and Todd. 2 vols.

Cohen, A. (1949), *Everyman's Talmud*. New York: Schocken.

Conzelmann, H. (1975), *1 Corinthians*. Philadelphia: Fortress. (German original 1969.)

Cotter, W. (1994), 'Women's Authority Roles in Paul's Churches: Counter-cultural or Conventional?' *Novum Testamentum* 36.4: 350–372.

Delling, G. (1964), *'archō, etc.'*, in G. Kittel & G. Friedrich (eds.), *Theological Dictionary of the New Testament* 1: 478–489. Grand Rapids: Eerdmans.

———— (1972), *'tassō, etc.'*, in *ibid.* 8: 27–48.

Dibelius, M., & Conzelmann, H. (1972), *The Pastoral Epistles*. Philadelphia: Fortress. (German original 1955, 1966.)

Dunn, J. D. G. (1988), *Romans 1 – 8, 9 – 16*. Dallas: Word. 2 vols.

——————— (1993), *The Epistle to the Galatians*. London: A. and C. Black.

Ellis, E. E. (1981), 'The Silenced Wives of Corinth (1 Cor. 14:34–35)', in E. J. Epp. & G. D. Fee, *New Testament Textual Criticism: Its Significance for Exegesis:* 213–220. Oxford: Clarendon.

——————— (1989), *Pauline Theology: Ministry and Society*. Grand Rapids: Eerdmans.

Evans, M. J. (1983), *Woman in the Bible*. Carlisle: Paternoster.

Fee, G. D. (1988), *1 and 2 Timothy, Titus*. Peabody: Hendrickson; Carlisle: Paternoster. (First published New York: Harper and Row, 1984.)

——————— (1987), *The First Epistle to the Corinthians*. Grand Rapids: Eerdmans.

——————— (1994), *God's Empowering Presence: The Holy Spirit in the Letters of Paul*. Peabody: Hendrickson.

——————— (1995), *Paul's Letter to the Philippians*. Grand Rapids: Eerdmans.

Fiorenza, E. S. (1983), *In Memory of Her: A Feminist Theological Reconstruction of Christian Origins*. London: SCM.

Fitzmyer, J. A. (1957), 'A Feature of Qumrân Angelology and the Angels of I Cor XI.10'. *New Testament Studies* 4.1: 48–58.

——————— (1989), 'Another Look at *KEPHALĒ* in I Corinthians 11.3'. *New Testament Studies* 35.4: 503–511.

——————— (1992), *Romans*. London: Geoffrey Chapman.

——————— (1993), '*Kephalē* in I Corinthians 11:3'. *Interpretation* 47.1: 52–59.

Flanagan, N. M., & Snyder, E. H. (1981), 'Did Paul Put Down Women in 1 Cor 14:34–36?' *Biblical Theology Bulletin* 11.1: 10–12.

Foerster, W. (1964), '*exestin, exousia, exousiazō, katexousiazō*', in G. Kittel & G. Friedrich (eds.), *Theological Dictionary of the New Testament* 2: 560–575. Grand Rapids: Eerdmans.

Frame, J. M. (1991), 'Men and Women in the Image of God', in J. Piper & W. Gruden (eds.), *Recovering Biblical Manhood and Womanhood*: 225–232. Wheaton: Crossway.

Friedrich, G. (1968), '*prophētēs*, etc.', in G. Kittel & G. Friedrich (eds.), *Theological Dictionary of the New Testament* 6: 781–861. Grand Rapids: Eerdmans.

Fung, R. Y. K. (1981), 'Some Pauline Pictures of the Church'. *Evangelical Quarterly* 53: 89–107.

——————— (1987), 'Ministry in the New Testament', in D. A. Carson (ed.), *The Church in the Bible and the World*: 154–212. Grand Rapids: Baker; Carlisle: Paternoster.

Giles, K. (1986), 'The Ordination of Women: On Whose Side is the Bible?', in M. A. Franklin (ed.), *The Force of the Feminine*. London: Allen and Unwin.

Gill, D. W. J. (1990), 'The Importance of Roman Portraiture for Head-Coverings in 1 Corinthians 11:2–16'. *Tyndale Bulletin* 41.2: 245–260.

Gritz, S. Hodgin (1991), *Paul, Women Teachers, and the Mother Goddess at Ephesus*. Lanham: University Press of America.

Grosheide, F. W. (1953), *The First Epistle to the Corinthians*. Grand Rapids: Eerdmans.

Grudem, W. (1985), 'Does *KEPHALĒ* ("Head") Mean "Source" or "Authority Over" in Greek Literature? A Survey of 2,336 Examples', *Trinity Journal* new series 6: 38–59.

——— (1988), *The Gift of Prophecy*. Eastbourne: Kingsway.

——— (1990), 'The Meaning of *Kephalē* ("Head"): A Response to Recent Studies'. *Trinity Journal* new series 11: 3–72.

Hall, D. R. (1990), 'A Problem of Authority'. *Expository Times* 102: 39–42.

Hamilton, V. P. (1990), *The Book of Genesis: Chapters 1 – 17*. Grand Rapids: Eerdmans.

Harper, M. (1994), *Equal and Different: Male and Female in the Church and Family*. London: Hodder and Stoughton.

Harris, T. J. (1990), 'Why Did Paul Mention Eve's Deception? A Critique of P. W. Barnett's Interpretation of 1 Tim. 2'. *Evangelical Quarterly* 62.4: 335–352.

Hawthorne, G. F. (1983), *Philippians*. Waco: Word.

Hayter, M. (1987), *The New Eve in Christ: The Use and Abuse of the Bible in the Debate about Women in the Church*. London: SPCK.

Hess, R. S. (1993), 'The Roles of the Woman and the Man in Genesis 3'. *Themelios* 18.3: 15–19.

Hooker, M. D. (1964), 'Authority on her Head: An Examination of I Cor. XI.10'. *New Testament Studies* 10.3: 410–416.

Humphries, R. (1958), *The Satires of Juvenal*. Bloomington: Indiana University Press.

Hurley, J. B. (1973), 'Did Paul Require Veils or the Silence of Women? A Consideration of I Cor. 11:2–16 and I Cor. 14:33b–36'. *Westminster Journal of Theology* 35.2: 190–220.

——— (1981), *Man and Woman in Biblical Perspective*. Leicester: IVP.

Jeremias, J. (1964), '*anthrōpos, anthrōpinos*', in G. Kittel & G. Friedrich (eds.), *Theological Dictionary of the New Testament* 1: 364–367. Grand Rapids: Eerdmans.'

——— (1968), '*poimēn*, etc.', in *ibid.* 6: 485–502. Grand Rapids: Eerdmans.

——— (1969), *Jerusalem in the Time of Jesus*. London: SCM. (German original 1962, 1967.)

Jervis, L. A. (1993), ' "But I want you to know . . .": Paul's Midrashic Intertextual Response to the Corinthian Worshipers (1 Cor 11:2–16)'. *Journal of Biblical Literature* 112.2: 231–246.

——— (1995), '1 Corinthians 14.34–35: A Reconsideration of Paul's Limitation of the Free Speech of Some Christian Women'. *Journal for the*

Study of the New Testament 58: 51–74.

Jewett, P. K. (1975), *Man as Male and Female: A Study in Sexual Relationships from a Theological Point of View*. Grand Rapids: Eerdmans.

Jewett, R. (1971), *Paul's Anthropological Terms: A Study of their Use in Conflict Settings*. Leiden: Brill.

————— (1988), 'Paul, Phoebe, and the Spanish Mission', in J. Neusner *et al.* (eds.), *The Social World of Formative Christianity and Judaism*: 142–161. Philadelphia: Fortress.

Johnson, S. L. (1991), 'Role Distinctions in the Church', in J. Piper and W. Grudem (eds.), *Recovering Biblical Manhood and Womanhood*: 154–164. Wheaton: Crossway.

Käsemann, E. (1980), *Commentary on Romans*. London: SCM. (German original 1973.)

Keener, C. S. (1992), *Paul, Women and Wives: Marriage and Women's Ministry in the Letters of Paul*. Peabody: Hendrickson.

————— (1993), 'Man and Woman', in G. F. Hawthorne, R. P. Martin & D. G. Reid (eds.), *Dictionary of Paul and his Letters*: 583–592. Downers Grove and Leicester: IVP.

Kelly, J. N. D. (1963), *The Pastoral Epistles: I and II Timothy, Titus*. London: A. and C. Black.

Kimberley, D. R. (1992), '1 Tim. 2:15: A Possible Understanding of a Difficult Text'. *Journal of the Evangelical Theological Society* 35.4: 481–486.

Kittel, G. (1964), '*angelia*, etc.', in G. Kittel & G. Friedrich (eds.), *Theological Dictionary of the New Testament* 1: 56–87. Grand Rapids: Eerdmans.

Knight, G. W. (1977), *The New Testament Teaching on the Role Relationship of Men and Women*. Grand Rapids: Baker.

————— (1984), '*AUTHENTEŌ* in Reference to Women in 1 Timothy 2.12'. *New Testament Studies* 30.1: 143–157.

————— (1991), 'Husbands and Wives as Analogues of Christ and the Church', in J. Piper & W. Grudem (eds.), *Recovering Biblical Manhood and Womanhood*: 165–178. Wheaton: Crossway.

Koester, H. (1982), *Introduction to the New Testament*. New York: Walter de Gruyter. 2 vols. (German original 1980).

Köstenberger, A. J. (1995), 'A Complex Sentence Structure in 1 Timothy 2:12', in A. J. Köstenberger, T. R. Schreiner, & H. S. Baldwin (eds.), *Women in the Church: A Fresh Analysis of 1 Timothy 2:9–15*: 81–103. Grand Rapids: Baker.

Kraemer, R. S. (1992), *Her Share of the Blessings*. New York and Oxford: Oxford University Press.

Kroeger, C. C. (1986), '1 Timothy 2:12 – A Classicist's View', in A. Mickelsen (ed.), *Women, Authority and the Bible*: 225–244. Basingstoke: Marshall Pickering.

————— (1987), 'The Classical Concept of "Head" as Source', Appendix 3, in G. Gaebelein Hull (ed.), *Equal to Serve: Women and Men in the Church and Home*. Old Tappan: Revell.

————— (1993), 'Head', in G. F. Hawthorne, R. P. Martin & D. G. Reid (eds.), *Dictionary of Paul and his Letters*: 375–377. Downers Grove and Leicester: IVP.

Kroeger, R. C. & C. C. (1992), *I Suffer Not a Woman: Rethinking 1 Timothy 2:11–15 in Light of Ancient Evidence*. Grand Rapids: Baker.

Lampe, G. W. H. (1961), *A Patristic Greek Lexicon*. Oxford: Clarendon.

Lefkowitz, M. R., & Fant, M. B. (1992), *Women's Life in Greece and Rome: A Source Book in Translation*. 2nd edn. London: Duckworth.

Liddell, H. G., & Scott, R. (1940), *A Greek–English Lexicon*. Revised and augmented by H. S. Jones and R. McKenzie. Oxford: Clarendon.

Liefeld, W. L. (1986a), 'Women, Submission and Ministry in 1 Corinthians', in A. Mickelsen (ed.), *Women, Authority and the Bible*: 134–160. Basingstoke: Marshall Pickering.

————— (1986b), Response to '1 Timothy 2:9–15 and the Place of Women in the Church's Ministry', in A. Mickelsen (ed.), *ibid.*: 219–224.

Lightfoot, J. B. (1879), *Saint Paul's Epistles to the Colossians and to Philemon*. Reissued Grand Rapids: Zondervan, 1974.

Lincoln, A. T. (1990), *Ephesians*. Dallas: Word.

Lock, W. (1924), *The Pastoral Epistles*. Edinburgh: T. and T. Clark.

Longenecker, R. N. (1990), *Galatians*. Dallas: Word.

MacDonald, M. Y. (1990), 'Early Christian Women Married to Unbelievers'. *Studies in Religion / Sciences Religieuses* 19.2: 221–234.

————— (1996), *Early Christian Women and Pagan Opinion: The Power of the Hysterical Woman*. Cambridge: Cambridge University Press.

Martin, D. B. (1995), *The Corinthian Body*. New Haven: Yale University Press.

Martin, R. P. (1986), *2 Corinthians*. Waco: Word.

Martin, W. J. (1970), 'I Corinthians 11:2–16: An Interpretation', in W. W. Gasque & R. P. Martin (eds.), *Apostolic History and the Gospel*: 231–241. Grand Rapids: Eerdmans; Exeter: Paternoster.

Massey, M. (1988), *Women in Ancient Greece and Rome*. Cambridge: Cambridge University Press.

Meeks, W. A. (1974), 'The Image of the Androgyne: Some Uses of a Symbol in Earliest Christianity'. *History of Religions* 13.3: 165–208.

————— (1983), *The First Urban Christians*. New Haven: Yale University Press.

Mickelsen, B. and A. (1986), 'What does KEPHALĒ Mean in the New Testament?', in A. Mickelsen (ed.), *Women, Authority and the Bible*: 97–110. Basingstoke: Marshall Pickering.

Moo, D. (1991), 'What Does It Mean Not to Teach or Have Authority Over Men?', in J. Piper & W. Grudem (eds.), *Recovering Biblical Manhood and Womanhood*: 179–193, Wheaton: Crossway.

Morris, L. (1985), *1 Corinthians*. Rev. edn. Leicester: IVP; Grand Rapids: Eerdmans.

Moule, C. F. D. (1977), *The Origin of Christology*. Cambridge: Cambridge University Press.

Moulton, J. H., & Milligan, G. (1914–30, 1982), *The Vocabulary of the Greek Testament Illustrated from the Papyri and Other Non-Literary Sources*. Grand Rapids: Eerdmans.

Moulton, J. H., & Turner, N. (1963), *A Grammar of New Testament Greek* 3. Edinburgh: T. and T. Clark.

Moxnes, H. (1993), 'Honor and Shame'. *Biblical Theology Bulletin* 23: 167–176.

Murphy-O'Connor, J. (1980), 'Sex and Logic in 1 Corinthians 11:2–16'. *Catholic Biblical Quarterly* 42: 482–500.

———— (1986), 'Interpolations in 1 Corinthians'. *Catholic Biblical Quarterly* 48: 81–94.

———— (1988), '1 Corinthians 11:2–16 Once Again'. *Catholic Biblical Quarterly* 50: 265–274.

———— (1996), *Paul: A Critical Life*. Oxford: Clarendon.

Murray, J. (1968), *The Epistle to the Romans*. Grand Rapids: Eerdmans. (First published as 2 vols., 1959 and 1965.)

Niccum, C. (1997), 'The Voice of the Manuscripts on the Silence of Women: The External Evidence for 1 Cor. 14.34–5'. *New Testament Studies* 43.2: 242–255.

O'Brien, P. T. (1982), *Colossians, Philemon*. Waco: Word.

Odell-Scott, D. W. (1983), 'Let the Women Speak in Church: An Egalitarian Interpretation of 1 Cor. 14:33b–36'. *Biblical Theology Bulletin* 13.3: 90–93.

Oepke, A. (1964), '*gynē*', in G. Kittel & G. Friedrich (eds.), *Theological Dictionary of the New Testament* 1: 776–789. Grand Rapids: Eerdmans.

Ortlund, R. C. (1991), 'Male–Female Equality and Male Headship', in J. Piper & W. Grudem (eds.), *Recovering Biblical Manhood and Womanhood*: 95–112. Wheaton: Crossway.

Padgett, A. (1984), 'Paul on Women in the Church: The Contradictions of Coiffure in 1 Corinthians 11:2–16'. *Journal for the Study of the New Testament* 20: 69–86.

———— (1987), 'Wealthy Women at Ephesus: 1 Timothy 2:8–15 in Social Context'. *Interpretation* 41.1: 19–31.

Padgett, A. G. (1994), 'The Significance of 'ANTI in 1 Corinthians 11:15'. *Tyndale Bulletin* 45.1: 181–187.

Payne, P. B. (1986), Response to 'What Does KEPHALĒ Mean in the New Testament?', in A. Mickelsen (ed.), *Women, Authority and the Bible*: 118–132. Basingstoke: Marshall Pickering.

———— (1995), 'Fuldensis, Sigla for Variants in Vaticanus, and 1 Cor 14.34–5'. *New Testament Studies* 41.2: 240–262.

Perriman, A. C. (1987), 'Typology in Paul'. *Theology* 90: 200–206.

———— (1993), 'What Eve Did, What Women Shouldn't Do: The Meaning of *AUTHENTEŌ* in 1 Timothy 2:12'. *Tyndale Bulletin* 44.1: 129–142.

———— (1994), 'The Head of a Woman: The Meaning of *KEPHALĒ* in I Cor. 11:3'. *Journal of Theological Studies* 45.2: 602–622.

Pierce, R. W. (1993), 'Evangelicals and Gender Roles in the 1990s: 1 Tim. 2:8–15: A Test Case'. *Journal of the Evangelical Theological Society* 36.3: 343–355.

Piper, J. (1991), 'A Vision of Biblical Complementarity: Manhood and Womanhood Defined According to the Bible', in J. Piper & W. Grudem (eds.), *Recovering Biblical Manhood and Womanhood*: 31–59. Wheaton: Crossway.

Piper, J., & Grudem, W. (1991), 'An Overview of Central Concerns: Questions and Answers', in *ibid.*: 60–92.

Plisch, U.-K. (1996), 'Die Apostelin Junia: Das exegetische Problem in Röm 16.7 im Licht von Nestle-Aland[27] und der sahidischen Überlieferung'. *New Testament Studies* 42.3: 477–478.

Pomeroy, S. B. (1975), *Goddesses, Whores, Wives, and Slaves: Women in Classical Antiquity*. London: Pimlico.

Rad, G. von (1972), *Genesis*. 2nd edn. London: SCM. (From the ninth German edn, 1972.)

Redekop, G. N. (1990), 'Let the Women Learn: 1 Timothy 2:8–15 Reconsidered'. *Studies in Religion / Sciences Religieuses* 19.2: 235–245.

Reicke, B. (1968), '*proïstēmi*', in G. Kittel & G. Friedrich (eds.), *Theological Dictionary of the New Testament* 6: 700–703. Grand Rapids: Eerdmans.

Ridderbos, H. (1977), *Paul: An Outline of his Theology*. Grand Rapids: Eerdmans; London: SPCK. (Dutch original 1966.)

Robertson, A., & Plummer, A. (1914), *First Epistle to the Corinthians*. 2nd edn. Edinburgh: T. and T. Clark.

Robinson, J. A. (1922), *St Paul's Epistle to the Ephesians*. London: Macmillan.

Robinson, J. A. T. (1952), *The Body*. London: SCM.

Robinson, J. M. (1988), *The Nag Hammadi Library*. 3rd edn. Leiden: Brill.

Sanday, W., & Headlam, A. C. (n.d.), *The Epistle to the Romans*. 5th edn. Edinburgh: T. and T. Clark.

Sanders, E. P. (1983), *Paul, the Law, and the Jewish People*. Minneapolis: Fortress.

Saucy, R. L. (1994), 'Women's Prohibition to Teach Men: an Investigation into its Meaning and Contemporary Application'. *Journal of the Evangelical Theological Society* 37.1: 79–97.

Schlier, H. (1965), '*kephalē, anakephalaioomai*', in G. Kittel & G. Friedrich (eds.), *Theological Dictionary of the New Testament* 3: 673–682. Grand Rapids: Eerdmans.

Scholer, D. M. (1986), '1 Timothy 2:9–15 & the Place of Women in the Church's Ministry', in A. Mickelsen (ed.), *Women, Authority and the Bible*: 193–219. Basingstoke: Marshall Pickering.

Schreiner, T. R. (1991a), 'Head Coverings, Prophecies and the Trinity', in J. Piper & W. Grudem (eds.), *Recovering Biblical Manhood and Womanhood*: 124–139. Wheaton: Crossway.

————— (1991b), 'The Valuable Ministries of Women in the Context of Male Leadership', in *ibid.*: 209–224.

————— (1995), 'An Interpretation of 1 Timothy 2:9–15: A Dialogue with Scholarship', in A. J. Köstenberger, T. R. Schreiner & H. S. Baldwin (eds.), *Women in the Church: A Fresh Analysis of 1 Timothy 2:9–15*: 105–154. Grand Rapids: Baker.

Scroggs, R. (1972), 'Paul and the Eschatological Woman'. *Journal of the American Academy of Religion* 40: 283–303.

————— (1974), 'Paul and the Eschatological Woman: Revisited'. *Journal of the American Academy of Religion* 42: 532–537.

Sigountos, J. G., & Shank, M. (1983), 'Public Roles for Women in the Pauline Church: A Reappraisal of the Evidence'. *Journal of the Evangelical Theological Society* 26.3: 283–295.

Snodgrass, K. R. (1986), 'Galatians 3:28: Conundrum or Solution?' in A. Mickelsen (ed.), *Women, Authority and the Bible*: 161–181. Basingstoke: Marshall Pickering.

Stegemann, W. (1993), 'Paul and the Sexual Mentality of His World'. *Biblical Theology Bulletin* 23: 161–166.

Stiefel, J. H. (1995), 'Women Deacons in 1 Timothy: A Linguistic and Literary Look at "Women Likewise . . ." (1 Tim 3.11)', *New Testament Studies* 41.3: 442–457.

Strack, H. L., & Billerbeck, P. (1922–8), *Kommentar zum Neuen Testament aus Talmud und Midrasch*. Munich: Beck'sche. 4 vols.

Swidler, L. (1979), *Biblical Affirmations of Woman*. Philadelphia: Westminster.

Theissen, G. (1987), *Psychological Aspects of Pauline Theology*. Edinburgh: T. and T. Clark. (German original 1983.)

Thorley, J. (1996), 'Junia, a Woman Apostle'. *Novum Testamentum* 38.1: 18–29.

Tomson, P. J. (1990), *Paul and the Jewish Law: Halakha in the Letters of the Apostle to the Gentiles*. Assen and Maastricht: Van Gorcum; Minneapolis: Fortress.

Urbach, E. E. (1979), *The Sages: Their Concepts and Beliefs*. Cambridge, MA: Harvard University Press.

Wenham, G. J. (1987), *Genesis 1 – 15*. Waco: Word.

Whelan, C. F. (1993), 'Amica Pauli: The Role of Phoebe in the Early Church'. *Journal for the Study of the New Testament* 49: 67–85.

Wicker, K. O'Brien (1975), 'First Century Marriage Ethics: A Comparative Study of the Household Codes and Plutarch's Conjugal Precepts', in J. W. Flanagan & A. W. Robinson (eds.), *No Famine in the Land*: 141–153. Missoula: Scholars.

Wilshire, L. E. (1988), 'The TLG Computer and Further Reference to *AUTHENTEŌ* in 1 Timothy 2.12'. *New Testament Studies* 34: 120–134.

———— (1993) '1 Timothy 2:12 Revisited: A Reply to Paul W. Barnett and Timothy J. Harris'. *Evangelical Quarterly* 65.1: 43–55.

Wilson, K. T. (1991), 'Should Women Wear Headcoverings?' *Bibliotheca Sacra* 148: 442–462.

Witherington, B. (1988), *Women in the Earliest Churches*. Cambridge: Cambridge University Press.

———— (1990), *Women and the Genesis of Christianity*. Cambridge: Cambridge University Press.

———— (1995), *Conflict and Community in Corinth: A Socio-Rhetorical Commentary on 1 and 2 Corinthians*. Grand Rapids: Eerdmans; Carlisle: Paternoster.

Wolff, C. (1982), *Der erste Brief des Paulus an die Korinther*. Zweiter Teil. Berlin: Evangelische Verlagsanstalt.

Index of subjects

Index of modern authors

Plisch, U.-K., 68
Pomeroy, S. B., 52, 115, 117–118

Redekop, G. N., 126, 137, 163–164, 168
Reicke, B., 67
Ridderbos, H., 47, 56, 109, 112, 138
Robertson, A., and Plummer, A., 127
Robinson, J. A., 54, 57
Robinson, J. M., 147

Sanday, W., and Headlam, A. C., 64, 70
Sanders, E. P., 129
Saucy, R. L., 138, 143
Schlier, H., 14, 18, 25, 27, 32, 46
Scholer, D. M., 138, 144, 160, 169
Schreiner, T. R., 35, 37, 63–64, 67, 73, 78, 80, 87, 95–97,126, 156–157, 160–162, 164, 205
Scroggs, R., 25, 39, 61, 86, 101, 104, 113, 116
Sigountos, J. G., and Shank, M., 142
Snodgrass, K. R., 186–188, 193
Snyder, E. H., 108

Stegemann, W., 114, 120–121
Stiefel, J. H., 64–66, 139
Stott, J., 214
Strack, H. L., and Billerbeck, P., 116
Swidler, L., 39, 66–67, 71, 104

Theissen, G., 99
Thorley, J., 68, 72
Tomson, P. J., 89, 91, 95, 99, 118–120, 127–128, 130, 133, 193

Urbach, E., 100, 167

Wenham, G. J., 179, 183
Werner, J. R., 151, 154–155
Whelan, C. F., 52, 63–64, 68
Wicker, K. O'B., 58, 160
Wilshire, L. E., 138, 143–145, 151, 156
Wilson, K. T., 86, 88, 99, 112
Witherington, B., 25, 36, 39, 52, 56, 62–64, 67–68, 71, 79, 86–89, 94, 98, 106, 108–109, 112–113, 115–117, 122–123, 144, 164, 188, 193
Wolff, C., 40, 128